THE Ginormous
Book of Dirty
Jokes

Published in the United States by
ULYSSES PRESS
P.O. Box 3440
Berkeley, CA 94703
www.ulyssespress.com

First published as *1000 JOKES You Never Could Tell Your Mother* in
2006 in the U.K. by Facts, Figures & Fun, an imprint of AAPPL Artists'
and Photographers' Press Ltd.

Printed in the United States by Bang Printing

5 7 9 10 8 6 4

ISBN: 978-1-56975-660-7
Library of Congress Control Number: 2007907742

Acquisitions Editor: Nick Denton-Brown
Production Coordinator: Steven Schwartz
Cover design: TG Design
Cover Illustration: John M. Duggan
Editorial: Amy Hough, Lauren Harrison, Abigail Reser
Production: Lisa Kester, Tamara Kowalski

Distributed by Publishers Group West

THE Ginormous
Book of Dirty
Jokes

Over 1000 sick, filthy and x-rated jokes

Rudy A. Swale

Cartoons by

Ulysses Press

A man was wandering around a carniva' an   a
a fortuneteller's tent. Thinking it would be   od   'a 'gn   ac vent
inside and sat down.

"Ah..." said the woman as she gazed into her crystal ball. "I see you are the father of two children."

"That's what you think," said the man scornfully. "I'm the father of THREE children."

The woman grinned and said, "That's what YOU think!"

❖

Little Johnny comes in to school one morning wearing a brand new watch. His best friend, little Benny, wants to know where the watch is from, so Johnny tells his story: "I was coming from the bathroom to my bedroom when I heard a strange noise from my parent's bedroom. I walked in and saw them bouncing up and down. Dad said I could have anything I wanted as long as I didn't tell the family. I asked for a new watch and here it is."

Benny decides he wants one too, so night after night he listens outside his parents' bedroom for any strange noises and, sure enough, eventually he hears some banging and groaning from the other side of the door. He walks in and catches his parents in the act, so his dad offers him anything he wants to keep quiet about the whole affair. Benny immediately says, "I want a watch."

The dad sighs and says, "Alright, but go and stand in the corner and don't make any noise."

❖

Q. Do you know what 6.9 is?
A. A good thing fucked up by a period.

There was a guy who was struggling to decide what to wear to go to a costume party... Then he had a bright idea.

When the host answered the door, he found the guy standing there wearing only underwear.

"What the hell are you supposed to be?" asked the host.

"A premature ejaculation," said the man. "I just came in my under-pants!"

Two 90-year-olds had been dating for a while, when the man told the woman, "Well, tonight's the night we have sex!"

And so they did.

As they are lying in bed afterward, the man thinks to himself: My God, if I knew she was a virgin, I would have been much more gentle with her!

And the woman was thinking to herself: My God, if I knew the old geezer could actually get it up, I would have taken off my panty hose!

A pianist was hired to play background music for a movie. When it was completed he asked when and where he could see the picture. The producer sheepishly confessed that it was actually a porno film and it was due out in a month.

A month later, the musician went to a porno theater to see it. With his collar up and dark glasses on, he took a seat in the back row, next to a couple who also seemed to be in disguise.

The movie was even raunchier than he had feared, featuring group sex, S/M and even a dog.

After a while, the embarrassed pianist turned to the couple and said, "I'm only here to listen to the music."

"Yeah?" replied the man. "We're only here to see our dog."

It was the mailman's last day on the job after 35 years of carrying the mail through all kinds of weather to the same neighborhood.

When he arrived at the first house on his route he was greeted by the whole family there, who congratulated him and sent him on his way with a big gift envelope.

At the second house they presented him with a box of fine cigars. The folks at the third house handed him a selection of terrific fishing lures.

At the fourth house he was met at the door by a strikingly beautiful woman in a revealing negligee. She took him by the hand, gently led him through the door, and led him up the stairs to the bedroom where she blew his mind with the most passionate love he had ever experienced.

When he had had enough they went downstairs, where she made him a full breakfast with a cup of steaming coffee.

As she was pouring the coffee, he noticed a $5 bill sticking out from under the cup's bottom edge. "All this is just too wonderful for words," he said, "but what's the money for?"

"Well," she said, "last night I told my husband that today would be your last day, and that we should do something special for you. I asked him what to give you and he said, 'Fuck him, give him a fiver.'"

The lady then said, "The breakfast was my idea."

A man and his wife go to their honeymoon place for their 25th anniversary.

As the couple reflected on that magical evening 25 years ago, the wife asked the husband, "When you first saw my naked body in front of you, what was going through your mind?"

The husband replied, "All I wanted to do was to fuck your brains out, and suck your tits dry."

Then, as the wife undressed, she asked, "What are you thinking now?"

He replied, "It looks like I did a pretty good job."

A young couple on the brink of divorce visit a marriage counselor.
The counselor asks the wife, "What is the problem?"
She responds, "My husband suffers from premature ejaculation."
The counselor turns to her husband and inquires, "Is that true?"
The husband replies, "Well not exactly; it's her that suffers, not me."

It was a nice sunny day and three men were walking down a country road when they saw a bush with a pig's ass popping out.
The first man says, "I wish that was Demi Moore's ass."
The second man says, "I wish that was Pamela Anderson's ass."
Then the third man says, "I wish it was dark."

Q. Why do blondes get confused in the ladies room?
A. Because they have to pull their own pants down.

A man who just got a raise decides to buy a new scope for his rifle. He goes to a rifle shop and asks the clerk to show him a scope.

The clerk takes out a scope and says to the man, "This scope is so good, you can see my house up on that hill."

The man takes a look through the scope, and starts laughing.

"What's so funny?" asks the clerk.

"I see a naked man and a naked woman running around in the house," the man replies.

The clerk grabs the scope from the man, and looks at his house. Then he hands two bullets to the man and says, "Here are two bullets. I'll give you this scope for nothing if you take these two bullets, shoot my wife's head off and shoot the guy's dick off."

The man takes another look through the scope and says, "You know what? I think I can do that with one shot!"

What is a blonde's idea of dental floss?
Pubic hair.

Steve is shopping for a new motorcycle. He finally finds one for a great price, but it's missing a seal, so whenever it rains he has to smear Vaseline over the spot where the seal should be.

One day, his girlfriend asks him over for dinner to meet her parents. He drives his new bike to her house, where she is outside waiting for him.

"No matter what happens at dinner tonight, don't say a word." She tells him, "Our family had a fight a while ago about doing dishes. We haven't done any since, but the first person to speak at dinner has to do them."

Steve sits down for dinner and it is just how she described it. Dishes are piled up to the ceiling in the kitchen, and nobody is saying a word. So Steve decides to have a little fun. He grabs his girlfriend, throws her on the table and has sex with her in front of her parents.

His girlfriend is a little flustered, her dad is obviously livid, and her mom horrified when he sits back down, but no one says a word. A few minutes later he grabs her mom, throws her on the table and does a repeat performance. Now his girlfriend is furious, her dad is boiling, and her mother is a little happier.

But still there is complete silence at the table. All of a sudden there is a loud clap of thunder, and it starts to rain. Steve remembers his motorcycle. He jumps up and grabs his jar of Vaseline.

Upon witnessing this, his girlfriend's father backs away from the table and screams, "OKAY, ENOUGH! I'LL DO THE DISHES."

A man is in a hotel lobby. He wants to ask the clerk a question. As he turns to go to the front desk, he accidentally bumps into a woman beside him and as he does, his elbow goes into her breast.

They are both quite startled. The man turns to her and says, "Ma'am, if your heart is as soft as your breast, I know you'll forgive me."

She replies, "If your penis is as hard as your elbow, I'm in room 436."

Two young lovers go up to the mountains for a romantic winter vacation. When they get there, the guy goes out to chop some wood. When he gets back, he says, "Honey, my hands are freezing!"

She says, "Well, put them here between my thighs and that will warm them up."

After lunch he goes back out to chop some more wood and comes back and says again, "Man! My hands are really freezing!"

She says again, "Well, put them here between my thighs and warm them up." He does, and again that warms him up.

After dinner, he goes out one more time to chop some wood to get them through the night. When he returns, he says again, "Honey, my hands are really, really freezing!"

She looks at him and says, "For crying out loud, don't your ears ever get cold?"

A masked man goes into a sperm bank, points a gun at the woman behind the counter, and says, "Open the safe."

She says, "This isn't a real bank; it's a sperm bank."

He says, "Open the safe or I'll shoot."

She opens the safe, and he says, "Now take one of the bottles and drink it."

After she opens the bottle and drinks it, he takes off his mask and the woman realizes the robber is her husband.

He says, "Now you see? It's not so difficult, is it?"

A guy and his manager go down to the docks. The manager is betting every dockworker he sees that his guy can make love to 100 women in a row, without pausing, and satisfy them all.

Bets are made, and they agree that they'll meet the next day. The next day, 100 women are lined up along the dock. The guy drops his pants and starts.

True to his word, he moves from one to the next, satisfying each one without pausing: 1.. 2.. 3.. on and on he goes: 49.. 50.. 51.. He slows down somewhat: 83.... 84.... 85.... but he is still moving from one to the next, and the women are still satisfied: 97............ 98............. 99.............

...and before he can get to the last woman, he has a heart attack and dies.

The manager scratches his head in puzzlement and says, "I don't understand it! It went perfectly well at practice this morning!"

Q. What do Disney World & Viagra have in common?

A. They both make you wait an hour for a two-minute ride.

A young woman married and had 13 children. Her husband died. She soon married again and had 7 more children. Again, her husband died. But she remarried and this time had 5 more children.

Alas, she finally croaked.

Standing before her coffin, the preacher prayed to the Lord above, thanking him for this loving woman who fulfilled his commandment to "Go forth and multiply."

In his final eulogy, he noted, "Thank you, Lord, they're finally together."

Leaning over to his neighbor, one mourner asked, "Do you think he means her first, second or third husband?"

The other mourner then replied, "I think he means her legs."

Goldie was sitting on a beach in Florida, attempting to strike up a conversation with the attractive gentleman reading on the blanket beside hers.

"Hello, sir," she said. "Do you like movies?"

"Yes, I do," he responded, then returned to his book.

Goldie persisted. "Do you like gardening?"

The man again looked up from his book. "Yes, I do," he said politely before returning to his reading.

Undaunted, Goldie asked. "Do you like pussycats?"

With that, the man dropped his book and pounced on Goldie, ravaging her as she'd never been ravaged before.

As the cloud of sand began to settle, Goldie dragged herself to a sitting position and panted, "How did you know that was what I wanted?"

The man thought for a moment and replied, "How did you know my name was Katz?"

A young female teacher was giving an assignment to her class one day. It was a large assignment so she started writing high up on the chalkboard. Suddenly there was a giggle from one of the boys in the class. She quickly turned and asked, "What's so funny, Tony?"

"Well, Miss, I just saw one of your garters."

"Get out of my classroom," she yelled, "I don't want to see you for three days."

The teacher turned back to the chalkboard. Realizing she had forgotten to title the assignment, she reached to the very top of the chalkboard. Suddenly, there was an even louder giggle from another male student. She quickly turned and asked, "What's so funny, John?"

"Well, Miss, I just saw both of your garters."

Again she yelled, "Get out of my classroom!" This time the punishment was more severe, "I don't want to see you for three weeks."

Embarrassed and frustrated, she had dropped the chalk when she'd turned around again. So she bent over to pick it up. This time there was a burst of laughter from another male student. She quickly turned to see Nick leaving the classroom.

"Where do you think you are going?" she asked.

"Well, Miss, from what I just saw, my school days are over."

After some great sex, she lies there stroking his prick.

He asks, "Do you want more sex?"

"No," she replies, "I'm just admiring your cock... I really miss mine."

Q. Why do women stop bleeding when entering menopause?
A. Because they need all the blood for their varicose veins.

A man goes into a shop and starts looking around. He sees a washer and dryer but there are no prices listed on them. He asks a salesman who says, "Five dollars for both of them."

"You've got to be joking!" the man says.

"No, that's the price," the salesman says. "Do you want to buy them or not?"

"Yeah, I'll take them," the man says. He continues to look around and sees a car stereo system with a detachable face cassette player, a CD changer, amplifier, and speakers.

"How much?" he asks.

"Five dollars for the system, including installation," the salesman says.

"Is it stolen?" the man asks incredulously.

"No," says the salesman, "It's brand new. Do you want it or not?"

"Certainly," the man says. He looks around some more. As the salesman is ringing up the purchases, the man asks him, "Why are your prices so cheap?"

The salesman says, "Well, the owner of the shop is at my house right now with my wife, and what he's doing to her, I'm doing to his business!"

Q. What do a blonde and a moped have in common?
A. They are both fun to ride until a friend sees you on one.

A jumbo jet is just coming into the Toronto Airport on its final approach. The pilot comes on the intercom, "This is your captain. We're on our final descent into Toronto. I want to thank you for flying with us today and I hope you enjoy your stay in Toronto."

He forgets to switch off the intercom. Now the whole plane can hear his conversation from the cockpit. The co-pilot says to the pilot, "Well, skipper, what are you going to do in Toronto?"

"Well," says the pilot, "first I'm going to check into the hotel and have a dump, after which I'm going to take that new stewardess with the huge tits out for dinner. And then, after dinner and a few drinks, I'll take her back to my room and have sex with her all night."

Everyone on the plane hears this and immediately begins looking up and down the aisles trying to get a look at the new stewardess.

Meanwhile the new stewardess is at the very back of the plane. She's so embarrassed that she starts to run to try and get to the cockpit to turn the intercom off. Halfway down the aisle, she trips over an old lady's bag and down she goes. The old lady leans over and says, "No need to hurry, dear. He's got to take a shit first."

A guy walks into a bar with his pet monkey and orders a drink.

While he's drinking, the monkey jumps all around the place. The monkey grabs some olives off of the bar and eats them, then grabs some sliced limes and eats them. He then jumps onto the pool table, grabs one of the billiard balls, sticks it into his mouth, and to everyone's amazement, somehow swallows it whole!

The bartender screams at the guy, "Did you see what your monkey just did?"

The guy says, "No. What?"

"He just ate the cue ball off my pool table... WHOLE!"

"Yeah, that doesn't surprise me," replies the guy. "He eats everything in sight. The little bastard. Sorry, I'll pay for the cue ball and stuff." He finishes his drink, pays his bill, pays for the stuff the monkey ate, and then leaves.

Two weeks later he's in the bar again, and has his monkey with him. He orders a drink and the monkey starts running around the bar again. While the man is finishing his drink, the monkey finds a maraschino cherry on the bar, grabs it, sticks it up its ass, pulls it out, and then eats it. The bartender is disgusted.

"Did you see what your monkey did?" he asks.

"No. What?" asks the guy.

"Well, he stuck a maraschino cherry up his ass, pulled it out, and ate it!" said the bartender.

"Yeah, that doesn't surprise me," replies the guy. "He still eats everything in sight, but ever since he swallowed that cue ball, he measures things first!!"

Q. How do gays refer to hemorrhoids?
A. Speed bumps.

A paperboy is doing his monthly round of collecting money from customers. One door is opened by a fairly sexy buxom woman who is wearing a transparent lace negligee.

"Hi, Missus, I've come for the paper money. It's $5 please," says our boy, with his hand held out.

"I'm afraid I've no money in the house," the woman replies in a breathy voice, "but if you come in I'm sure I can think of something..."

So our lad goes in and the woman throws herself back on the fireside rug, pulling off the negligee, moaning, "You can have ME instead..."

The kid sighs, takes off his bag, and then produces a dick that wouldn't look out of place on a stud bull. The woman is agog. Our lad then produces a load of big rubber rings from his bag, which he proceeds to stack around his giant knob.

"What are they for?" asks the woman.

"Oh, they're just to make sure I don't go all the way in when I fuck you," replies the boy.

"To hell with them!" implores the woman. "I'll take all of you!"

Our lad replies... "Not for five fucking dollars you won't!"

In a train car there was an Englishman, a Frenchman, a spectacular-looking blonde and a frightfully awful-looking fat lady.

After several minutes the train happened to pass through a dark tunnel, and the unmistakable sound of a slap was heard. When they left the tunnel the Frenchman had a big red slap mark on his cheek.

The blonde thought—That French son-of-a-bitch wanted to touch me and must have put his hand on the fat lady by mistake, who, in turn, must have slapped his face.

The large lady thought—That dirty old Frenchman laid his hands on the blonde and she smacked him.

The Frenchman thought—That fucking Englishman put his hand on the blonde and she slapped me by mistake.

The Englishman thought—I hope there's another tunnel soon so I can smack that French twat again.

Q. Why can't blondes waterski?

A. Because when they get their crotch wet they think they have to lie down.

A new farmer buys several sheep hoping to breed them. After several weeks he notices that none of the sheep are getting pregnant and calls a vet for help. The vet tells him that he should try artificial insemination. The farmer doesn't have the slightest idea what this means but, not wanting to display his ignorance, only asks the vet how he will know when the sheep are pregnant. The vet tells him that they will stop standing around and will lie down and wallow in the grass when they are pregnant. The farmer hangs up and gives it some thought. He comes to the conclusion that artificial insemination means he has to impregnate the sheep. So he loads the sheep into his truck, drives them out into the woods, screws them all, brings them back and goes to bed.

Next morning, he wakes and looks out at the sheep. Seeing that they are all still standing around, he deduces that the first try didn't take and loads them in the truck again. He drives them out to the woods, screws each sheep twice for good measure, brings them back and goes to bed.

Next morning, he wakes to find the sheep still just standing around. One more try, he tells himself, and proceeds to load them up and drive them out to the woods. He spends all day sheep screwing, and upon returning home falls exhausted into bed.

The next morning he cannot even raise himself from the bed to look at the sheep. He asks his wife to look out and tell him if the sheep are lying in the grass.

"No," she says, "they're all in the truck and one of them is beeping the horn."

God had just about finished creating the universe, but he had a couple of left-over things in his bag of creations, so he stopped by to visit Adam and Eve in the Garden of Eden. He told the couple that one of the things he had to give away was the ability to pee standing up.

"It's a very handy thing," God told the couple, who he found hanging around under an apple tree. "I was wondering if either one of you wanted that ability."

Adam, excited by this idea, jumped up and begged, "Oh, give that to me! I'd love to be able to do that! It seems the sort of thing a man should do. Oh please, oh please, oh please, let me have that ability. It would be so great! When I'm working in the garden or naming the animals I could just let it rip. It'd be so cool. Oh please, God, let it be me who you give that gift to. Let me stand and pee, oh please..."

On and on he went like an excited little boy (who had to pee).

Eve just smiled and shook her head at the display. She told God that if Adam really wanted it so badly, and it sure seemed to be the sort of thing that would make him happy, she really wouldn't mind if Adam were the one given the ability to pee standing up. And so it was. And it was...well...good.

"Fine," God said, looking back into his bag of left-over gifts. "And what do we have left here? Oh yes, multiple orgasms..."

Q. What do you say to a virgin when she sneezes?
A. Goes-in-tight!

Little Johnny is passing his parents' bedroom in the middle of the night in search of a glass of water. Hearing a lot of moaning and thumping, he peeks in and catches his folks in the act. Before dad can even react, little Johnny exclaims, "Oh, boy! Horsie ride! Daddy, can I ride on your back?"

Daddy, relieved that Johnny's not asking more uncomfortable questions, and seeing the opportunity not to break his stride, agrees. Johnny hops on and daddy starts going to town. Pretty soon mommy starts moaning and gasping. Johnny cries out, "Hang on tight, Daddy! This is the part where me and the milkman usually get bucked off!"

A husband and wife were having difficulty surviving financially so they decided that the wife should try prostitution as an extra source of income. The husband drove her out to a popular corner and informed her he would be at the side of the building if she had any questions or problems.

A gentleman pulled up shortly after and asked her how much to go all the way. She told him to wait a minute and ran around the corner to ask her husband. The husband told her to tell the client $100.

She went back and informed the client, at which he cried, "That is too much!" He then asked, "How much for a hand job?"

She asked him to wait a minute and ran to ask her husband how much. The husband said, "Ask for $40."

The woman ran back and informed the client. He felt that this was an agreeable price and began to remove his pants and underwear. Upon the removal of his clothing the woman noticed that the man was really well hung. She asked him once more to wait a moment, then ran around the corner again.

Her husband asked, "Now what?"

The wife replied, "Can I borrow $60?"

Father, mother and son decide to go to the zoo one day. So they set off and are seeing lots of animals. Eventually they end up opposite the elephant house. The boy looks at the elephant, sees its penis, points to it and says, "Mommy, what is that long thing?"

"His mother replies, "That, son, is the elephant's trunk."

"No, at the other end."

"That, son, is the tail."

"No, mommy, the thing under the elephant."

There's a short embarrassed silence, after which she replies, "That's nothing."

The mother goes to buy some ice cream and the boy, not being satisfied with her answer, asks his father the same question. "Daddy, what is that long thing?"

"That's the trunk, son," replies the father.

"No, at the other end."

"Oh, that is the tail."

"No, no, daddy, the thing below," says the son in desperation.
"That is the elephant's penis. Why do you ask, son?"
"Well mommy said it was nothing," says the boy.
The father replies, "I tell you, I spoil that woman..."

Q. What did the blonde's mom say before the blonde's date?
A. If you're not in bed by 12, come home.

Georgie is walking down the street after a sex-change operation has transformed him into a beautiful woman. An old friend sees him and says, "Georgie, you look great...you're beautiful!"
Georgie says, "Thanks...but holy Christ, did it hurt."
His friend says, "When they cut open your chest and put in those implants?"
Georgie says, "No, that didn't really hurt."
His friend says, "When they cut off your dick and dug out a vagina?"
Georgie says, "No, that didn't really hurt."
His friend says, "Then what did hurt?"
Georgie says, "When the doctor drilled a fucking hole in my head and sucked out half my brain."

Q. Why does a penis have a hole in the end?
A. So men can be open-minded.

A young couple were invited to a swanky masked Halloween party. The wife came down with a terrible headache and told her husband to go to the party and have a good time. Being the devoted husband he protested, but she argued and said she was going to take some aspirin and go to bed. She told him there was no need for him to miss the fun. So he took his costume and away he went.

The wife, after sleeping soundly for one hour, awakened without pain, and as it was still early she decided to go to the party. Because hubby did not know what her costume was, she thought she would have some kicks watching her husband to see how he acted when she was not around. She joined the party and soon spotted her husband cavorting around on the dance floor. He was dancing with every nice chick he could, copping a feel here and taking a little kiss there. His wife sidled up to him and, being a rather seductive babe herself, he left his partner high and dry and devoted his time to the new "action."

She let him go as far as he wished, naturally, since he was her husband. Finally he whispered a little proposition in her ear and she agreed, so off they went to one of the cars and had a little bang.

Just before unmasking at midnight she slipped out, went home, put the costume away and got into bed, wondering what kind of explanation he would have for his behavior.

She was sitting up reading when he came in, and she asked him what he had done. He said, "Oh, the same old thing. You know I never have a good time when you're not there."

Then she asked, "Did you dance much?"

He replied, "I'll tell you, I never even danced one dance. When I got to the party I met Pete, Bill and some other guys, so we went into the den and played poker all evening. But I'll tell you, the guy I loaned my costume to sure had one hell of a time!"

A husband and wife are cooing over their new born baby.

"Look at the size of his penis," says the man. "It's massive!"

"Yes, dear," says the woman. "But at least he's got your ears."

Two shepherds are out rounding up sheep when all of a sudden a ewe takes off and goes wild, runs into a fence and gets her head stuck. The two shepherds run over to the fence to get her out when one says to the other, "Hey, man, this is too good an opportunity to pass up." So he unzips his fly, yanks out his cock and fucks this ewe for about ten minutes. When he's finally finished he looks back at his friend and says, "That was fantastic. Wanna try it?"

"I sure do!" grins his friend, as he drops his pants and sticks his head through the fence.

A couple gets married. Forty years later, they're in the same hotel room they spent their honeymoon in. She takes off her clothes, lies down on the bed, spreads her legs ... and he starts to cry.

She says, "What's the matter?"

He says, "Forty years ago, I couldn't wait to eat it, and now it looks like it can't wait to eat ME!"

A woman walked into the ladies' room and saw a man standing up using the toilet.

Shocked, she exclaimed, "This is just for women!"

"So is this," he replied.

Son: "Mommy, mommy, can I lick the bowl?"
Mom: "Shut up and flush."

Five men were sitting around the table at a restaurant bragging who had the largest dick. Finally one guy said, "I'll settle this; let's all put our dicks on the table; that will decide it." At about that time two gay guys walked in and were seated. The waiter asked them if they'd like to see a menu. The gay guys responded, "OH!!! NO, NO, we'll just have the buffet."

A man walks into a bar and asks for a beer. After drinking it, he looks in his shirt pocket and asks for another beer. After drinking that one, he looks in his shirt pocket again and asks for another beer.

This happens about another seven times before the bartender asks him, "Why do you keep looking in your pocket?"

The man replies, "I have a picture of my wife in there. When she looks good enough, I'll go home."

A husband tries his luck with his wife but she says, "Sorry, darling, but I have an appointment tomorrow with my gynecologist and I want to stay fresh."

The husband rolls over and thinks about this for a while, then whispers, "Do you have a dentist's appointment tomorrow?"

Q. Have you heard about the new mint-flavored birth control pill for women that they take immediately before sex?

A. They're called "Predickamints."

Q. How can you tell when an auto mechanic just had sex?

A. One of his fingers is clean.

An Englishman, a Scotsman, and an Irishman are all to give speeches to the Deaf and Dumb Society. All are intent on making an impression on their audience. The Englishman goes first, and to the surprise of his colleagues, starts by rubbing first his chest, and then his groin. When he finishes, the Scotsman and Irishman ask him what he was doing.

"Well," he explained, "by rubbing my chest I indicated breasts and thus ladies, and by rubbing my groin I indicated balls and thus gentlemen. So my speech started: 'Ladies and Gentlemen.'"

On his way up to the podium the Scotsman thought to himself I'll one-up that English bastard! He started his speech by making an antler symbol with his fingers above his head before also rubbing his chest and his groin. When he finished, his colleagues asked what he was doing.

"Well," he explained, "by imitating antlers and then rubbing my chest and groin I was starting my speech by saying, 'Dear Ladies and Gentlemen.'"

On his way up to the podium the Irishman thought to himself, I'll go even further than those bastards! He started his speech by making an antler symbol above his head, rubbing his chest, and then his groin, and then masturbating furiously. When he finished, his colleagues asked him what he was doing.

"Well," he explained," by imitating antlers, rubbing my chest and then my groin, and then masturbating, I was starting my speech by saying, 'Dear Ladies and Gentlemen, it gives me great pleasure...'"

Q. What is the difference between a golf ball and a G-spot?
A. Men will spend hours searching for a golf ball.

A married couple was lying in bed one night. The wife had curled up ready to go to sleep, and the husband put his bedside lamp on to read a book. As he was reading, he paused and reached over to his wife and started fondling her butt.

He did this for only a very short while, then he would stop and resume reading his book.

The wife eventually became aroused by this and thought that her husband was seeking some response as encouragement before going any further. She got up and started dancing naked in front of him. The husband was confused and asked, "What are you doing?"

The wife replied, "You were playing with my butt and I thought it was foreplay to initiate making love with you tonight."

The husband said, "No, not at all."

The wife then asked, "Well, what the hell were you doing then?"

"I was just wetting my fingers so I could turn the pages in my book."

Sam and Becky are celebrating their 50th wedding anniversary when Sam says to Becky, "Becky, I was wondering if you've ever cheated on me?"

Becky replies, "Oh, Sam, why would you ask such a question now? You don't want to ask that question..."

"Yes, Becky, I really want to know. Please..."

"Well, all right, three times..."

"Three, hmmm. When were they?"

"Well, Sam, remember when you were 35 years old and you really wanted to start that business on your own and no bank would give you a loan? Remember, one day the bank manager himself came over to the house and signed the loan papers, no questions asked..."

"Oh, Becky, you did that for me! I respect you even more than ever, to do such a thing for me. So when was number two?"

"Well, Sam, remember when you had that last heart attack and you needed that very tricky operation, and no surgeon would touch you? Then remember how Dr. Morris came all the way up here to do the surgery himself and then you were in good shape again..."

"I can't believe it, Becky, that you would do such a thing for me, to save my life... I couldn't have a more wonderful wife... All right then, when was the third time?"

"Well, Sam, remember a few years ago when you really wanted to be president of the fishing club and you were 97 votes short..."

A man walks into his bedroom and sees his wife packing a suitcase. He says, "What are you doing?"

She answers, "I'm moving to New York. I heard prostitutes there get paid $100 for doing what I do for you for free!"

Later that night, while on her way out, the wife walks into the bedroom and sees her husband packing his suitcase.

When she asks him where he's going, he replies, "I'm going to New York, too. I want to see you live on $200 a year!"

A recently deceased man stands at the pearly gates. St. Peter tells him that he cannot go to heaven right away because he cheated on his income taxes. The only way he might get into heaven would be to sleep with a stupid, ugly woman for the next five years and enjoy it. He decides that this is a small price to pay for an eternity in heaven. So off he goes with this woman, pretending to be happy. As he walks along, he sees his friend up ahead with an even uglier woman.

When he asks what's going on, the friend replies, "I cheated on my income taxes and scammed the government out of a lot of money." They both shake their heads in understanding and figure that they might as well hang out together to help pass the time. Now the two friends and their two ugly women are walking along minding their own business when they see someone who looks like their old friend.

This man is with an absolutely gorgeous supermodel. Stunned, they approach the man and discover that it is indeed their friend. They ask him how come he's with this unbelievable goddess, while they're stuck with these god-awful women.

He replies, "I have no idea, but I'm definitely not complaining. This has been absolutely the best time imaginable, and I have five years of the best sex any man could hope for to look forward to. There is only one thing that I can't seem to understand. Every time we finish having sex, she rolls over and murmurs to herself, 'Damn income taxes!'"

A man walks into a public bathroom and begins using one of the urinals. He looks to his left and sees a very short man also peeing. Suddenly, the short man looks up at the taller man, and the taller man is completely embarrassed about staring at the smaller man's penis.

"Sorry," says the taller man. "I'm not gay or anything, but you have the longest penis I've ever seen, especially on a man so small!"

"Well," says the little man, "that's because I'm a Leprechaun! All Leprechauns have penises this size!"

The taller man says, "Incredible! I'd give anything for mine to be that long."

"Well, what with me being a Leprechaun and all, I can give you your wish! If you let me take you into that stall over there and screw you, I'll give you your wish!"

"Gee," says the man, "I don't know about that. Oh, to hell with it. OK!"

Soon, the Leprechaun is behind the taller man, humping away. "Say," says the Leprechaun, "how old are you, son?"

Finding it difficult to turn with the Leprechaun humping him so ferociously, the tall man says over his shoulder, "Uh-uh, thirty-two..."

"Imagine that," says the little man, "thirty-two and he still believes in Leprechauns!"

Q. Why don't little girls fart?
A. Because they don't get assholes until they're married.

One rainy night a taxi driver spotted an arm waving from the shadows of an alley. Even before he rolled to a stop at the curb, a figure leaped into the cab and slammed the door. Checking his rear view mirror as he pulled away, he was startled to see a dripping wet naked woman sitting in the back seat.

"Where to?" he stammered.

"Central Station," answered the woman.

"OK," he said, taking another long glance in the mirror.

The woman caught him staring at her and asked, "Just what the hell are you looking at, driver?"

"Well, ma'am, I noticed that you're completely naked, and I was just wondering how you'll pay your fare."

The woman spread her legs, put her feet up on the front seat, smiled at the driver and said, "Does THIS answer your question?"

Still looking in the mirror, the cabbie asked, "Got anything smaller?"

A boy comes home after school one day. His mother notices that he's got a big smile on his face.

She asks, "Did anything special happen at school today?"

"Yes, Mom. I had sex with my English teacher!"

The mother is stunned. "You're going to talk about this with your father when he gets home."

Well, when dad comes home and hears the news he is pleased as punch. Beaming with pride, he walks over to his son and says, "Son, I hear you had sex with your English teacher."

"That's right, Dad."

"Well, you became a man today—this is cause for celebration. Let's head out for some ice cream, and then I'll buy that new bike you've been asking for."

"That sounds great, Dad, but can I have a football instead? My ass is killing me."

Joe rented an apartment and went to the lobby to put his name on his mailbox. While there, an attractive young lady came out of the apartment next to the mailboxes wearing a robe. Joe smiled at the young woman and she started a conversation with him. As they talked, her robe slipped open, and it was obvious that she had nothing else on. Poor Joe broke out into a sweat trying to maintain eye contact.

After a few minutes, she placed her hand on his arm and said, "Let's go to my apartment. I hear someone coming."

He followed her into her flat. She closed the door and leaned against it, allowing her robe to fall off.

Now completely naked, she purred at him, "What would you say is my best feature?"

Flustered and embarrassed, Joe finally squeaked, "It's got to be your ears!"

Astounded and a little hurt she asked, "My ears? Look at these breasts—they are full and 100% natural! I work out every day! My butt is firm and solid! Look at my skin—no blemishes anywhere! How can you feel that the best part of my body is my ears?!"

Clearing his throat, Joe stammered, "Outside, when you said you heard someone coming?"

"Yes."

"Well, that was me."

Did you hear that Rosie O'Donnell has been busted for drug smuggling at Los Angeles International Airport?

Seems she bent over and someone saw 50 lbs. of crack.

A doctor who had been seeing an 80-year-old woman for most of her life finally retired. At her next checkup, the new doctor told her to bring a list of all the medicines that had been prescribed for her. As the young doctor was looking through these, his eyes grew wide as he realized she had a prescription for birth control pills.

"Mrs. Smith, do you realize these are BIRTH CONTROL pills?"

"Yes, they help me sleep at night."

"Mrs. Smith, I assure you there is absolutely NOTHING in these that could possibly help you sleep!"

She reached out and patted the young doctor's knee. "Yes, I know that. But every morning I grind one up and mix it in the glass of orange juice that my 18-year-old granddaughter drinks... And believe me, it helps me sleep at night."

Larry is 95 and lives in an old folks' home. Every night after dinner, Larry goes to a secluded garden behind the center to sit and ponder his accomplishments and long life. One evening, Florence, age 87, wanders into the garden.

They begin to chat and, before they know it, several hours have passed. After a short lull in their conversation, Larry turns to Florence and asks, "Do you know what I miss most of all?"

She asks, "What?"

"SEX!!!"

Florence exclaims, "Why, you old fart, you couldn't get it up if I paid you!"

"I know," Larry says, "but it would be nice if a woman just held it for a while."

"Well, I can oblige," says Florence, who gently unzips his pants, removes his manhood and proceeds to hold it.

Afterward, they agree to meet secretly each night in the garden where they will sit and talk and Florence will hold Larry's manhood. Then, one night, Larry didn't show up at their usual meeting place. Alarmed, Florence decided to find Larry and make sure that he was OK. She walked around the gardens and she found him sitting by the pool with another female resident holding his manhood!

Furious, Florence yelled, "You two-timing old creep! What does she have that I don't have?"

Larry smiled happily and replied, "Parkinson's disease!!"

A kid comes home from school and says, "Mom, I've got a problem." She says, "Tell me."

He tells her that the boys at school are using two words he doesn't understand. She asks him what they are.

He says, "Well, pussy and bitch."

She says, "Oh, that's no big deal. Pussy is a cat like our little Mittens, and bitch is a female dog like our Sandy."

He thanks her and goes to visit dad in the workshop in the basement. He says to his dad, "Dad, the boys at school are using words I don't know, and I asked mom and I don't think she told me their exact meaning."

Dad says, "Son, I told you never to go to mom with these matters; she can't handle them. What are the words?"

He tells him, "Pussy and bitch."

Dad says, "OK," and pulls a *Playboy* down from the shelf. He takes a marker and circles the pubic area of the centerfold and says, "Son, everything inside this circle is pussy."

"OK, dad, so what's a bitch?"

"Son," he says, "everything outside that circle."

Mario and Marie, a nice young couple, were getting married and were planning on living with Marie's mother until they could establish a place of their own. On their wedding night, they went upstairs and were getting ready for bed. Mario started to get undressed, taking off his shirt first. He had hair all over his chest. Marie ran downstairs and told her mother.

"Mommy!! Mommy!! He's got hair all over his chest!"

Her mother replied, "Marie, you go upstairs and make your mother proud."

So Marie ran upstairs and found Mario taking off his pants. He was extremely hairy all over his legs. Marie ran down the steps to tell her mother.

"Mommy, he's got hair all over his legs."

"Marie, you go upstairs and make your mother proud."

Marie ran upstairs and found her new husband sitting on the bed taking off his socks. Unfortunately, he had lost half of his foot in the war. Marie took one look, and ran downstairs.

"Mommy, Mommy! He's only got a foot and a half!"

At this, her mother yelled, "Marie, you wait here. I'm going to go upstairs!"

Mother is in the kitchen making supper for her family when her youngest daughter walks in.

"Mom, where do babies come from?"

"Well, dear, a mommy and daddy fall in love and get married. One night, they go into their room and they kiss and hug and have sex. (The daughter looks puzzled.) That means the daddy puts his penis in the mommy's vagina. That's how you get a baby."

"Oh, I see, but the other night when I came into your room you had daddy's penis in your mouth. What do you get when you do that?"

"Jewelry, dear."

A man and a woman who have never met before find themselves in the same sleeping carriage of a train. After the initial embarrassment, they both manage to get to sleep, the woman on the top bunk and the man on the lower.

In the middle of the night the woman leans over and says, "I'm sorry to bother you, but I'm awfully cold and I was wondering if you could possibly pass me another blanket."

The man leans out and, with a glint in his eye, says, "I've got a better idea. Let's pretend we're married."

"Why not," giggles the woman.

"Right," he replies. "Get your own fucking blanket."

Q. Why is the space between a woman's breasts and her hips called a waist?

A. Because you could easily fit another pair of tits in there.

A nun gets into a cab in New York. She demurely says in a small, high voice, "Could you please take me to Times Square?"

In a thick Brooklyn accent the cab driver initiates conversation, "Hey, sista, that's kinda a long drive. You mind if we, like, chat?"

The nun says, "Why no, my son, whatever is on your mind?"

The cab driver says, "About dis celibacy thing. Are you telling me you never think about doin' it?"

The nun replies, "Why certainly, my son, the thought has crossed my mind a time or two. I am of weak human flesh, you understand."

The driver says, "Well, would ya ever consider, you know, doin' it?"

The nun replies, "Well, I suppose under certain conditions, in a very unique circumstance, I might consider it."

The cab driver says, "Well what would those conditions happen to be?"

The nun replies, "Well, he'd have to be Catholic, unmarried and could certainly have no children."

The cab driver says, "Well, sista, today is your lucky day. I am all three. Why don't youse come on up here...I won't even make you really break your vows. All you gotta do is go down on me."

The nun looks around: They are awfully far away from where anyone would recognize her. At the next light she gets into the front with the driver. By the next light, the nun is getting back into the rear of the cab, and the cab driver is smiling from ear to ear. As she settles in, the nun hears the cab driver begin to laugh.

The nun inquires, "Why, my son, what is so humorous?"

The cab driver sneers, "Sista, I got ya. I'm Protestant, I'm married, and I've got four kids."

And from the back of the cab comes the nun's low-voiced response, "Yeah, well my name's Dave and I'm on my way to a costume party."

On the farm lived a chicken and a horse who loved to play together. One day, the two were playing when the horse fell into some quicksand and began to sink. Scared for is life, the horse whinnied for the chicken to go get the farmer for help.

Off the chicken ran, back to the farm. Arriving at the farm, he searched and searched for the farmer to no avail, for he had gone to town with the only tractor. Running around, the chicken spied the farmer's new Z-3 series BMW. Finding the keys inside, the chicken sped off with a length of rope, hoping he still had time to save his friend's life.

Back in the quicksand, the horse was surprised but happy to see the chicken arrive in the shiny BMW, and he managed to get a hold of the loop of rope the chicken tossed to him. After tying the other end to the rear bumper of the farmer's car, the chicken then drove slowly forward and, with the aid of the powerful car, rescued the horse! Happy and proud, the chicken drove the BMW back to the farmhouse, and the farmer was none the wiser when he returned.

The friendship between the two animals was cemented: best buddies, best pals. A few weeks later, the chicken fell into a mud pit, and soon he too began to sink, crying out to the horse to save his life. The horse thought a moment, then walked over and straddled the large puddle. Looking underneath, he told the chicken to grab his "thing" and he would then lift him out of the pit. The chicken got a good grip and the horse pulled him up and out, saving his life.

The moral of the story?

When you're hung like a horse, you don't need a BMW to pick up chicks.

A guy was shipwrecked and ended up on an island. After wandering around for a few hours he was captured by the local tribe of cannibals and taken back to the village. After a good meal and a rest he was taken before the king and told that, as it was the king's birthday, he would get a chance to live, but only if he passed three tests in three huts.

The first had a keg of rum inside: He had to drink the keg dry.

The second had a tiger with a sore tooth: He had to remove it.

The third had a woman who had never been satisfied: He had to satisfy her.

With confidence he strode into the first, and about an hour later stumbled out plastered.

"Get me to the next hut!" he yelled.

In the second hut all was quiet, and then roars and screams were heard. This was followed by sudden quiet again.

As he stumbled out of the hut he roared, "OK, goddammit, now where's that woman with the sore tooth?"

A man returns from the tropics feeling very ill. He goes to see his doctor, who immediately rushes the man to the hospital to undergo tests. After the tests are completed, the man wakes up to the ringing of a telephone in his private room at the hospital. On the other end of the line, the doctor explains, "We've received the results back from your tests. We've found that you have an extremely nasty STD called G.A.S.H., which is a combination of gonorrhea, AIDS, syphilis, and herpes."

"Oh my god," cries the man. "Doc! What am I going to do?"

"Well, we're going to put you on a diet of pizzas, pancakes, and pita bread."

"Will that cure me?" asks the man curiously.

"Well no, but it's the only food we can get under the door."

A Priest went to the doctor in a panic and asked him, "What does it mean, Doc, if when I take a pee it burns like the fire of Satan and I have this god-awful drip?"

The doctor smiled and said, "It means the altar boy lied—he wasn't a virgin."

A bum finds a five-dollar bill in the street. He decides to go to the liquor store and buy a bottle of white wine. After knocking back the booze the bum falls into a drunken stupor and collapses in a small alleyway.

About ten minutes later, a passing gay guy happens upon the sprawled body of the bum. Not having greased the pole for a while, the queer whips down the bum's pants and gives him one up the butt. As the rear gunner is just about to leave he gets a pang of conscience and tucks five bucks into the tramp's hand.

Upon waking up the next day, the bum discovers the fiver. Hardly believing his good fortune, he rushes back to the liquor store and purchases another bottle of white wine. Yet again he downs the vino and falls into a drunken sleep in his favorite alleyway. A little later the same butt pirate passes the alleyway and sees the bum. Unable to contain himself, the butt plugger divests the tramp of his shorts and gives him another ass stretching. Again he leaves five bucks out of guilt for his actions.

Upon waking up the bum discovers another fiver in his hand and so hurries back to the liquor store. He grabs a bottle of red wine and hands it to the sales assistant. The sales assistant, by now familiar with the bum's usual habits, asks why he is buying red wine this time, to which the bum responds, "I like the white wine but it just makes my ass so fucking sore."

A woman gives birth to a baby and afterward the doctor comes in and says, "I have to tell you something about your baby."

The woman sits up in bed and says, "What's wrong with my baby, Doctor? What's wrong?"

The doctor says, "Well, now, nothing's wrong, exactly, but your baby is a little bit different. Your baby is a hermaphrodite."

The woman says, "A hermaphrodite. What's that?"

The doctor says, "Well, it means your baby has the...er... features... of a male and a female."

The woman turns pale. She says, "Oh my god! You mean it has a penis... AND a brain?"

Q. What did Adam say to Eve?
A. Stand back; I don't know how big this thing gets!

Three women were sitting around throwing back a few drinks and talking about their love lives.

One woman said, "I call my husband the dentist. Nobody can drill like he does."

The second woman giggled and confessed, "I call my husband the miner because of his incredible shaft."

The third woman quietly sipped her whiskey until her friend asked, "Say, what do you call your husband?"

She frowned and said, "The postman."

"Why the postman?"

"Because he always delivers late, and half the time it's in the wrong slot."

A businessman was getting ready to go on a long business trip. He knew his wife was a flirtatious type with an extremely healthy sex drive, so he thought he'd buy her a little something to keep her occupied while he was gone.

He went to a store that sold sex toys and started to look around. He thought about a life-sized sex doll, but that was too close to another man for him. He was browsing through the dildos, looking for something special to please his wife, when he started talking to the old man behind the counter. He explained his situation.

"Well, I don't really know of anything that will do the trick. We have vibrating dildos, special attachments and so on, but I don't know of anything that will keep her occupied for weeks, except..." and he stopped.

"Except what?" the man asked.

"Nothing, nothing."

"C'mon, tell me! I need something!"

"Well, sir, I don't usually mention this, but there is The Voodoo Penis."

"So what's up with this Voodoo Penis?" he asked.

The old man reached under the counter and pulled out a very old wooden box carved with strange symbols and erotic images. He opened it, and there lay a very ordinary-looking dildo. The businessman laughed and said, "Big deal. It looks like every other dildo in this shop!"

The old man replied, "But you haven't seen what it'll do yet." He pointed to a door and said, "Voodoo Penis, the door."

The Voodoo Penis miraculously rose out of its box, shot over to the door and started pounding the keyhole. The whole door shook with the vibrations, so much so that a crack began to form. Before the door split, the old man said, "Voodoo Penis, return to box!" The Voodoo Penis stopped, levitated back to the box and lay there quiet once more.

"I'll take it!" said the businessman.

The old man resisted, saying it wasn't for sale, but finally surrendered to $500.

The guy took it home to his wife, told her it was a special dildo and that to use it all she had to do was say "Voodoo Penis, my crotch."

He left for his trip satisfied that things would be fine while he was gone. After he'd been gone a few days, his wife was getting unbearably horny. She thought of several people who would willingly satisfy her, but then she remembered the Voodoo Penis. She stripped off, opened the box and said, "Voodoo Penis, my crotch!"

The Voodoo Penis shot into her and started pumping. It was absolutely incredible, like nothing she'd ever experienced before. After three mind-shattering orgasms she became very exhausted and decided she'd had enough. She tried to pull it out but it was stuck in her, still thrusting. She tried and tried to get it out but nothing worked. Her husband had forgotten to tell her how to shut it off.

Worried, she decided to go to the hospital to see if they could help. She put her clothes on, got in the car and started to drive, quivering with every thrust of the dildo. On the way, another incredibly intense orgasm made her swerve all over the road. A traffic policeman saw this and immediately pulled her over.

He asked for her license, and then asked how much she'd had to drink. Gasping and twitching, she explained, "I haven't had anything to drink, officer. You see, I've got this Voodoo Penis thing stuck in my crotch and it won't stop screwing me!"

The officer looked at her for a second, shook his head and said, "Voodoo Penis? Voodoo Penis, my ass..."

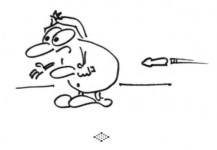

Q. Did you hear about the new paint called "Blonde" paint?
A. It's not very bright, but it spreads easy.

Little Johnny woke up in the middle of the night and went to the bathroom. On the way back to bed, he passed his parents' room.

When he looked in, he noticed the covers bouncing. He called to his dad, "Hey, Dad, what are you doing?"

The dad answered, "Playing Cards."

Little Johnny asked, "Who's your partner?"

The dad answered, " Your mom."

Little Johnny then passed by his older sister's room. Again, he noticed the covers bouncing. He called to his sister, "Hey, Sis, what are you doing?"

The sister answered, "Playing Cards."

Little Johnny asked, "Who's your partner?"

She answered, "My boyfriend."

A little later, dad got up and went to the bathroom. As he passed Little Johnny's room, he noticed the covers bouncing. He called to his son, "What are you doing?"

Little Johnny answered, "Playing Cards."

Dad asked, "Really? Who's your partner?"

Little Johnny answered, "You don't need a partner if you have a good hand!"

There was a married couple who were in a terrible accident. The woman's face was burned severely. The doctor told the husband they couldn't graft any skin from her body because she was so skinny. The husband then donated some of his skin. However, the only place suitable to the doctor was from his buttocks.

The husband requested that no one be told of this, because after all this was a very delicate matter!

After the surgery was completed, everyone was astounded at the woman's new beauty. She looked more beautiful than she ever did before! All her friends and relatives just raved about her youthful beauty!

She was alone with her husband one day and she wanted to thank him for what he had done. She said, "Dear, I just want to thank you for everything you did for me! There is no way I could ever repay you!"

He replied, "Oh don't worry, Honey, I get plenty of thanks every time your mother comes over and kisses you on your cheek!"

Q. What is the difference between erotic and kinky?
A. Erotic is using a feather. Kinky is using the whole chicken.

A guy takes his wife to the Doctor. The Doc says, "Well, it's either Alzheimer's disease or AIDS."

"What do you mean?" the guy says. "You can't tell the difference?"

"Yeah, the two look a lot alike in the early stages. Tell you what, drive her way out into the country, kick her out of the car, and if she finds her way back, don't fuck her."

A penguin takes his car to a mechanic because there is a funny noise coming from under the hood.

"Leave it with me," says the mechanic. "Come back in 20 minutes."

So, off goes the penguin. It's a pretty hot day and he's a cool weather kind of guy so on spotting an ice cream van he goes and buys himself a 99. Now, penguins aren't very good at eating ice creams—the lack of opposable thumbs makes it tricky. So by the time the penguin has finished his 99, he is completely covered in ice cream. It is all over his beak and all over his flippers. Feeling a little sticky, he goes back to the garage.

"Oh, hello," says the mechanic, wiping his hands on a cloth.

"Hello," replies the penguin. "Was it anything serious?"

"Not really, but it looks like you've blown a seal."

"Oh no, no, no!" says the penguin, wiping his mouth. "It's just ice cream."

A little boy gets up to go to the bathroom in the middle of the night. As he passes his parents' bedroom he peeks in through the keyhole. He watches for a moment, then continues on down the hallway muttering to himself, "And she gets mad at me for sucking my thumb."

Two cows are standing next to each other in a field.
Daisy says to Dolly, "I was artificially inseminated this morning."
"I don't believe you," replies Dolly.
"It's true, no bull!"

Q. What's the difference between a Catholic wife and a Jewish wife?
A. A Catholic wife has real orgasms and fake jewelry.

A man wakes up one morning with the worst hangover and no recollection of the night before. Slowly opening his eyes, he sees a bottle of aspirin and a glass of water on the bedside table.

He looks around the room to find his clothes are neatly folded on the dresser with a clean shirt on top. The bedroom is immaculate. On the bedside table is a note that says, "Darling, your breakfast is in the kitchen. I love you."

Downstairs, he finds his favorite cereal, croissants, fresh OJ and freshly brewed coffee waiting for him, along with the morning paper and his 15-year-old son who is finishing his own breakfast.

"Tell me, son," he asks, "what happened last night?"'

"Well," says the boy, "you came home so drunk you didn't even know your own name. You nearly broke the door down, then you were sick in the hallway, then you knocked the furniture over and when mom tried to calm you down, you thought she was the police, so you gave her a black eye."

"Christ!" says the man. "Then how come my clothes are all folded, the house is tidy and my breakfast is ready?"

"When mom dragged you into the bedroom and tried to get your pants off to put you into bed, you shouted at her, 'Get your filthy hands off me, you whore, I'm married!'"

Q. When is a pixie not a pixie?

A. When he's got his head up a fairy's skirt, then he's a goblin.

A man came home from work sporting two black eyes.

"What happened to you?" asked his wife.

"I'll never understand women," he replied. "I was riding up an escalator behind this pretty young girl, and I noticed that her skirt was stuck in the crack of her ass. So I pulled it out, and she turned around and punched me in the eye!"

"I can certainly appreciate that," said the wife. "But how did you get the second black eye?"

"Well, I figured she liked it that way," said the husband, "so I pushed it back in."

It's a beautiful warm spring day and a man and his wife are at the zoo. She's wearing a cute, loose-fitting, sleeveless pink spring dress with straps. As they walk through the ape exhibit and pass in front of a very large gorilla, the gorilla goes ape. He jumps up on the bars, holding on with one hand (and 2 feet), grunting and pounding his chest with the free hand. He is obviously excited at the pretty lady in the wavy dress. The husband notices his excitement and suggests that his wife tease the poor fellow. The husband suggests she pucker her lips, wiggle her bottom and play along. She does, and Mr. Gorilla gets even more excited, making noises that would wake the dead. Then the husband suggests that she let one of her straps fall. She does, and Mr. Gorilla is just about to tear the bars down.

"Now try lifting your dress up your thighs," the husband says. This drives the gorilla absolutely crazy. Suddenly the husband grabs his wife by the hair, rips open the door to the cage, slings her in with the gorilla and says, "Now, tell HIM you have a headache."

A young couple are on their way to Vegas to get married. Before getting there, the girl says to the guy that she has a confession to make: The reason that they have not been too intimate is because she is very flat-chested. If he wishes to cancel the wedding, it's okay with her. The guy thinks about it for a while, and says he does not mind that she is flat, and sex is not the most important thing in a marriage. Several miles down the road, the guy turns to the girl and says that he also wants to make a confession: He says that below his waist he is just like a baby. If the girl wants to cancel the marriage, it's okay with him. The girl thinks about it for a while and says that she does not mind, and that she also believes there are other things far more important than sex in a marriage. They are happy that they are honest with each other and go on to Vegas and get married. On their wedding night, the girl takes off her clothes; she is as flat as a washboard. Finally, the guy takes off his clothes. One glance at the guy's naked body and the girl faints and falls to the floor. After she regains consciousness the guy says, "I told you before we got married. Why did you still faint?"

The girl says, "You told me it was just like a baby."

The guy replies, "Yes, 8 pounds and 21 inches.

Q. What are the three words men hate to hear during sex?
A. "Are you done?"
Q. What are the three words women hate to hear during sex?
A. "Honey, I'm home!"

Q. Why is it called a Wonder Bra?
A. When she takes it off, you wonder where her tits went.

A couple were having trouble conceiving a child, so they went to a doctor.

He examined them and concluded that the problem was one of insufficient penetration. He suggested to the man that they try the rear-entry position.

The man said, "What is that?"

The doctor replied, "Just watch the dogs and do like they do."

The man said, "My wife is very shy and she won't do that."

The doctor replied, "Try giving her a glass of wine or two and she will lose all inhibition."

Some while later, the doctor met the man, pushing a stroller.

"I see it worked!" the doctor said.

"Yes it did, Doc, but now the problem is my wife is an alcoholic!"

"How did that happen?" the doctor asked.

"Well, every time we did it, it took seven or eight drinks just to get her out into the front garden!"

Q. Why don't women blink during foreplay?

A. They don't have time.

A man met a beautiful girl and he decided he wanted to marry her right away. She protested, "But we don't know anything about each other."

He replied, "That's all right; we'll learn about each other as we go along."

So she consented and they were married, and they went on honeymoon to a very nice resort.

One morning, they were lying by the pool when he got up off his towel, climbed up to the 30-foot high board and did a two-and-a-half-tuck gainer, entering the water perfectly, almost without a ripple. This was followed by three rotations in jack-knife position before he again straightened out and cut the water like a knife. After a few more demonstrations, he came back and lay down on his towel.

She said, "That was incredible!"

He said, "I used to be an Olympic diving champion. You see, I told you we'd learn more about ourselves as we went along."

So she got up, jumped in the pool and started doing laps. She was moving so fast that the ripples from her pushing off at one end of the pool would hardly be gone before she was already touching the other end of the pool. After about thirty laps, completed in mere minutes, she climbed back out and lay down on her towel, barely breathing hard.

He said, "That was incredible! Were you an Olympic endurance swimmer?"

"No," she said, "I was a prostitute in Venice and I worked both sides of the canal."

Q. What's the difference between a bitch and a whore?

A. A whore blows everybody at the party, and a bitch blows everybody at the party except you.

A man calls in to work and says, "Sorry, I can't come in today, I'm sick."

The boss says, "How sick are you?"

"Well," the man replies, "you judge—I'm in bed with my sister."

On their way to get married a couple gets into a fatal car accident. They are sitting outside the Pearly Gates waiting for St. Peter to turn up and register them. While they're waiting, they wonder if they could possibly get married in heaven. St. Peter finally shows up and they ask him.

St. Peter says, "I don't know, this is the first time anyone's ever asked. Let me go and find out," and he leaves.

The couple sits around for a couple of months and begins to wonder if they really should get married in heaven, what with the eternal aspect of it all.

What if it doesn't work out, they wonder. Are we stuck together forever?

St. Peter returns after another month looking somewhat worn out. "Yes," he informs the couple, "you can get married in heaven."

"Great," says the couple, "but what if things don't work out? Could we also get a divorce in heaven?"

St. Peter, red-faced, slams his clipboard onto the ground.

"What's wrong?" exclaims the frightened couple.

"Christ!" St. Peter exclaims. "It took me three months to find a priest up here! Do you have any idea how long it's going to take me to find a lawyer?"

Bob goes into the public bathroom and sees this guy standing next to the urinal. The guy has no arms. As Bob's standing there, taking care of business, he wonders to himself how the poor guy is going to take a leak.

Bob finishes and starts to leave when the man asks Bob to help him out. Being a kind soul, Bob says, "Errr, OK, I'll help you."

The man asks, "Can you unzip my zipper?"

Bob says, "OK."

Then the man says, "Can you pull it out for me?"

Bob replies, "Uh, yeah, OK."

Bob pulls it out and it has all kinds of mold, red rashes and scabs all over it, and it smells dreadful. Then the guy asks Bob to point it for him, which Bob does. Bob then shakes it, puts it back in and zips it up.

The guy tells Bob, "Thanks, I really appreciate it."

Bob says, "No problem, but what the hell's wrong with your prick?"

The guy pulls his arms out of his shirt and says, "I don't know, but I'm not touching it."

A man walking along a California beach was deep in prayer. All of a sudden, he said out loud, "Lord, grant me one wish." Suddenly the sky clouded above his head and in a booming voice, the Lord said,

"Because you have TRIED to be faithful to me in all ways, I will grant you one wish."

The man said, "Please, Lord, build a bridge to Hawaii so I can drive over anytime I wish."

The Lord said, "Your request is very materialistic. Think of the enormous challenges for that kind of undertaking, the supports required to reach the bottom of the Pacific, the concrete and steel it would take! I can do it, but it is hard for me to justify your desire for worldly things. Take a little more time and think of another wish, a wish you think would honor and glorify me."

The man thought about it for a long time. Finally he said, "Lord, I wish that I could understand women. I want to know how they feel inside, what they are thinking when they give me the silent treatment, why they cry, what they mean when they say 'nothing', and how I can make a woman truly happy."

The Lord said, "Do you want two or four lanes on that bridge?"

A man, a sheep and a dog were survivors of a terrible shipwreck. They found themselves stranded on an island.

After being there a while, they got into the habit of going to the beach every evening to watch the sun go down. One particular evening, the sky was red with beautiful cirrus clouds, the breeze warm and gentle—a perfect night for romance.

As they sat there, the sheep started looking better and better to the man. Soon, he leaned over to the sheep and put his arm around it. But the dog got jealous, growling fiercely until the man took his arm from around the sheep. After that, the three of them continued to enjoy the sunsets together, but there was no more cuddling.

A few weeks passed by and lo and behold, there was another shipwreck. The only survivor was a beautiful young woman, the most beautiful woman the man had ever seen. She was badly injured when they rescued her, and they slowly nursed her back to health. When the young maiden was well enough, they introduced her to their evening beach ritual. It was another beautiful evening: red sky, cirrus clouds, a warm and gentle breeze—perfect for a night of romance.

Pretty soon the man started to get "those feelings" again. He fought them as long as he could, but he finally gave in, leaned over to the young woman and cautiously whispered in her ear, "Would you mind taking the dog for a walk?"

An old couple had been married for 50 years. They were sitting at the breakfast table one morning when the old gentleman said to his wife, "Just think, we've been married for 50 years."

"Yeah," she replied. "Just think, fifty years ago we were sitting here at this breakfast table together."

"I know," the old man said, "but we were probably sitting here stark naked fifty years ago."

"Well," Granny snickered, "what do you say, should we strip?"

So the two stripped to the buff and sat down at the table.

"You know, honey," the little old lady said, "my nipples are as hot for you today as they were fifty years ago."

"I wouldn't be surprised," replied Gramps. "One's in your coffee and the other is in your porridge."

There once was a fellow named Dave
Who dug up a whore from her grave
She was moldy as shit
And missing a tit
But think of the money he saved!

Tony had been feeling guilty all day long. No matter how much he tried to forget about it, he couldn't. The guilt and sense of shame was overwhelming. But every once in a while he'd hear that soothing voice trying to reassure him: "Tony, don't worry about it. You're not the first surgeon to sleep with one of your patients and you won't be the last. And, you're single. So just let it go."

But invariably the other voice would bring him back to reality: "Tony, you're a veterinary surgeon..."

A cowboy is walking in the woods one day when he comes to a clearing. There on a blanket is a naked Indian with a hard on.

"What are you doing?" the cowboy asks.

The Indian answers, "Me tell time."

"OK. If you are so good, what time is it?"

The Indian looks down at his prick and the shadow it's casting and says, "It's 2 o'clock."

The cowboy looks at his watch and says, "By golly, you are right!"

The cowboy starts walking again and comes upon another naked Indian lying on a blanket. "Don't tell me... You're telling time too?"

The Indian looks up at him and says, "Yes, me telling time."

"Okay, smart ass, what time is it?"

The Indian looks up at the sun, then down and says, "It's 4 o'clock."

The cowboy is amazed at the Indian. He keeps walking and hours later he comes upon an Indian on a blanket, masturbating. "Don't tell me you're telling time!"

The Indian looks up at him and says, "No, me winding watch!"

Q. What's the difference between a toad and a horny toad?
A. One goes "ribbit" the other goes "rub it."

Two men were having lunch at their favorite restaurant when they noticed a young woman at the next table having trouble breathing.

One of the men got up, walked over to her table, took her face in his hands and said, "Can you swallow?"

She shook her head. "No."

"Can you breathe?"

Again she shakes her head. "No."

The man grabs her around the waist with one of his hands, turns her over, pulls up her skirt, pulls down her panties and licks her ass! Of course the young woman was so shocked that she coughed causing the food to dislodge. The man pulls up her panties, pulls down her skirt, turns her right side up, and returns to his seat.

His companion is sitting there stunned. "I have never seen anything like that in my whole life!" he says to his friend.

"Well, I'll tell you, that hind lick maneuver works every time!"

Putting up a tent is very much like making love to a beautiful woman: You rent her, unzip the door, put up your pole and… slip in to the old bag.

A successful businessman flew to Vegas for the weekend to gamble. He lost the shirt off his back and had nothing left but a quarter and the second half of his round trip ticket. If he could just get to the airport he could get himself home. So he went out to the front of the casino where there was a cab waiting.

He got in and explained his situation to the cab driver. He promised to send the driver money from home; he offered him his credit card numbers, his driver's license number, his address, etc., but to no avail.

The cab driver said, "If you don't have fifteen dollars, get the hell out of my cab!"

So the businessman was forced to hitchhike to the airport and was barely in time to catch his flight.

One year later the businessman, having worked long and hard to regain his financial success, returned to Vegas and this time he won big. Feeling pretty good about himself, he went out to the front of the casino to get a cab ride back to the airport. Well, who should he see out there at the end of a long line of cabs but his old buddy who had refused to give him a ride when he was down on his luck.

The businessman thought for a moment about how he could make the guy pay for his lack of charity and he hit on a plan. The businessman got in the first cab in the line,

"How much for a ride to the airport?" he asked.

"Fifteen bucks," came the reply.

"And how much for you to give me head on the way?"

"What?! Get the hell out of my cab."

The businessman got into the back of each cab in the long line and asked the same questions, with the same results.

When he got to his old friend at the back of the line, he got in and asked, "How much for a ride to the airport?"

The cab driver replied, "Fifteen bucks."

The businessman said, "OK," and off they went.

Then, as they drove slowly past the long line of cabs the businessman gave a big smile and thumbs up sign to each of the other cab drivers.

A little girl came running into the house bawling her eyes out and cradling her hand, "Mommy, quick! Get me a glass of cider!" she wailed.

"Why do you want a glass of cider?" asked her mom.

"I cut my hand on a thorn and I want the pain to go away!"

Confused but weary of the child's whining, the mother obliged and poured her a glass of cider. The little girl immediately dunked her hand in it.

"Ouch! It still hurts! This cider doesn't work!" she whined.

"What are you talking about?" asked mom. "What ever made you think that cider would ease the pain?"

"Well, I overheard my big sister say that whenever she gets a prick in her hand, she can't wait to get it in cider."

Two young boys, both from well-to-do families, were talking.

1st Boy: "Our new French maid is a robot."

2nd Boy: "A Robot? Maids aren't robots."

1st Boy: "But ours is... I overheard my dad telling one of his golf buddies that he screws her ass off every Saturday!!"

A flight attendant was stationed at the departure gate to check tickets. As a man approached, she extended her hand for the ticket and he opened his trench coat and flashed her.

Without missing a beat, she said, "Sir, I need to see your ticket, not your stub."

One morning, the members of a farm family were coming to the kitchen for breakfast. Just as Junior seated himself, his mother told him he was not going to get anything to eat until he went to the barn and fed the animals.

Irritated at this, he stomped out the door and headed for the barn. As he fed the chickens, he kicked each one in the head. As the cow bent down to start in on the fresh hay he had just put in the stall, he kicked it in the head. He poured food into the trough for the pigs, and as they started eating, he kicked them in the head. He went back to the kitchen and sat down again.

His mother was furious. "I saw what you did and as you kicked the chickens you'll get no eggs for breakfast. And since you kicked the cow, you'll get no milk. And no bacon or sausage because you kicked the pigs."

Just then, the father came down the stairs and nearly tripped on the family cat. On impulse, he kicked the cat off the stairs. The boy looked at his mother and asked, "Are you going to tell him or should I?"

A salesman is going door to door. At one house, a snotty little brat answers the door.

"Tell you what," he says to the salesman, "I can persuade my parents to buy pretty much anything. If you can do everything I can do, I'll talk them into buying something. If you lose, then you give $10."

Figuring that there's no way a nine-year-old brat could outsmart him, the salesman agrees to the deal. Immediately, the kid climbs up the drainpipe and hops onto the flat roof. The salesman does exactly the same.

The kid then runs across the roof, does a triple cartwheel and lands in the back garden, with the salesman following suit.

Then the kid runs to where his teenage sister is sunbathing topless. He rushes over to her and kisses her on the left breast. Not to be outdone, the salesman leaps over and does the same.

The kid then gropes both his sister's tits. So does the salesman. Then the kid pulls down her bikini bottoms and licks her pussy, the salesman does likewise.

Then the brat pulls out his dick, wraps it round his little finger and says, "Where's my $10?"

A 75-year-old man went to his doctor's office to get a sperm count. The doctor gave the man a jar and said, "Take this jar home and bring me back a sample tomorrow."

The next day, the 75-year-old man reappeared at the doctor's office and gave him the jar, which was as clean and empty as on the previous day.

The doctor asked what had happened and the man explained: "Well, Doc, it's like this. First I tried with my right hand, but nothing happened. Then I tried with my left hand, but still got nothing. Then I asked my wife for help. She tried with her right hand, but nothing happened, then she tried with her left, but still nothing happened. She even tried with her mouth, first with the teeth in, then with the teeth out, and still nothing happened. We even called up the lady next door and she tried with both hands and her mouth too, but there was nothing doing."

The doctor was shocked. "You asked your neighbor?"

The old man replied, "Yep, but no matter what we tried we couldn't get the stupid jar open!"

A woman tells her friend that Interflora just delivered a bunch of flowers from her husband. "Now I guess he'll want me to spend the entire weekend on my back with my legs in the air."

"Why?" asks her friend. "Don't you have a vase?"

Did you hear about the heavyset guy who had tried every diet in the world in an attempt to lose weight? He tried the Scarsdale diet, the Navy diet, Weight Watchers, and many more. None worked. Then, one day, he was reading the Washington Post when he noticed a small ad that read:

Lose weight. Only $5.00 a pound. Call (202) 555-0238.

The man decided to give it a try and called the number. A voice on the other end asked, "How much weight do you want to lose?"

The man responded, "Ten pounds."

The voice replied, "Very well, give me your credit card number and we'll have a representative over to your house in the morning."

At about 9:00 a.m. the next morning the man got a knock on the door. There stood a beautiful redhead, completely naked except for a sign around her neck stating, "If you catch me, you can have me."

Well, the hefty fellow chased her upstairs, downstairs, over sofas, through the kitchen, all around the house. Finally, panting and wheezing like a dog, he did catch her. When he was through enjoying himself, she said, "Quick, go into the bathroom and weigh yourself."

He did just that and was amazed to find that he had lost ten pounds, right to the ounce!

That evening he called the number again. The voice on the other end asked, "How much weight do you want to lose?"

The somewhat-less-overweight man replied, "Twenty pounds."

"Very well," the voice on the phone told him. "Give me your credit card number and we'll have a representative over to your house in the morning."

At about 8:00 a.m. the next morning, the man receives a knock on the door. When he opens the door he sees a beautiful blonde dressed only in track shoes and a sign around her neck stating, "If you catch me, you can have me." The chase took a good while longer this time and the man nearly passed out, but he finally did catch her. When he was through she told him, "Quick, run into the bathroom and weigh yourself." He ran to the bathroom and found he had lost another 20 pounds!

This is fantastic! he thought to himself. Later that evening he called the number again and the voice at the other end asked, "How much weight do you want to lose?"

"Fifty pounds!" the man exclaimed.

"Fifty pounds?" the voice asked. "That's an awful lot of weight to lose at one time."

The man replied, "Listen, here's my credit card number. You just have your representative over here in the morning!" and he hung up the phone.

About 6:00 a.m. the next morning the man got out of bed, splashed on some cologne and got ready for the next representative.

At about 7:00 a.m. he heard a knock on the door. When he opened the door, he saw this large gorilla with a sign around his neck stating: "If I can catch you, I can have you!"

Q. What's the difference between Mad Cow disease and PMS?
A. Nothing.

An old man was on the beach and he walked up to a beautiful girl in a bikini.

"I want to feel your breasts," he said.

"Get away from me, you dirty old man," she replied.

"I want to feel your breasts. I will give you $5," he said.

"$5!! Get away from me!"

"I want to feel your breasts. I will give you $10," he said.

"NO! Get away from me!"

"$50," he said.

She paused to think about it, but then came to her senses and said, "I said NO!"

"$100 if you let me feel your breasts," he said.

She thought, well he is old and $100 would be very handy. "Well, OK, but only for a minute," she said.

She loosened her bikini top and while they're both standing there on the beach, he slid his hands underneath and began to feel...and then he started saying, "OH MY GOD...OH MY GOD," while he was caressing them.

So, out of curiosity, she asked him, "Why do you keep saying 'Oh my god?'"

While continuing to fondle her tits he answered, "OH MY GOD... OH MY GOD... Where am I ever going to get $100?"

A week after arriving back home from Mongolia, a guy wakes one morning to find his dick covered with bright green and purple bumps. Horrified, he immediately goes to see a doctor.

The doctor, never having seen anything like it, orders some tests and tells the man to return in two days.

The man returns in a couple of days and the doctor says: "I've got bad news for you. You've contracted Mongolian VD. It's very rare and almost unheard of here. We know very little about it."

The man looks a little perplexed and says: "Well, give me a shot or something and fix me up, Doc."

The doctor answers: "I'm sorry, there's no known cure. We're going to have to amputate your penis."

The man screams in horror, "Absolutely not! I want a second opinion."

The doctor replies: "Well, it's your choice. Go ahead if you want, but surgery is your only choice."

The next day the man seeks out a Chinese doctor, figuring that he'll know more about the disease. The Chinese doctor examines his penis and proclaims: "Ah, yes, Mongolian VD. Velly lare disease."

The guy says to the doctor: "Yeah, yeah, I already know that, but what can you do? My doctor wants to operate and amputate my penis."

The Chinese doctor shakes his head and laughs: "Stupid Engrish doctah, always want to opelate. Make more money, that way. No need to opelate!"

"Oh, thank goodness!" the man replies.

"Yes," says the Chinese doctor. "You no worry! Wait two weeks, fall off by itself... You save money."

A guy walks into the psychiatrist wearing only plastic wrap for shorts. The shrink says, "Well, I can clearly see you're nuts."

A man walks into a sex shop and tells the woman behind the counter he's looking for a blow up doll.

The woman asks, "Would you like a Christian or Muslim doll?"

Confused the man says, "What's the difference?"

"Well," replies the woman, "the Muslim one blows herself up!"

The whales were fed up with ships crossing their feeding grounds, migration paths, and breeding areas, not to mention years of being hunted and killed, so they got together to decide what to do. Discussion continued until a plan of attack was proposed by their leader.

"What we will do, is gather in two groups, one behind the other. The first group will swim under each ship and blow together. This will create a huge bubble of air under the ship, which will capsize it, dropping the sailors into the water. The following group of whales will then gobble them up."

After the cheering died down, one whale, towards the outside of the meeting slapped his tail on the water for attention.

The leader said, "Yes, Mervin? Do you have something to say?"

Mervin replied, "Well, I can go along with the blow job, but I won't swallow any seamen."

A man is having marital problems. He and the wife are not communicating at all and he's lonely, so he goes to a pet store thinking a pet might help. The store he happens into specializes in parrots. As he wanders down the rows of parrots he notices one with no feet. Surprised, he mutters, "I wonder how he hangs onto the perch?"

The parrot says, "With my penis, you dummy."

The man is startled and says, "You certainly talk well for a parrot."

The parrot says, "Of course, I'm a very well-educated parrot. I can discuss politics, sports, religion, almost any subject you wish."

The man says, "You sound like just what I am looking for."

The parrot says, "There's not much of a market for maimed parrots. If you offer the proprietor $20 for me I bet he'll sell."

The man buys the parrot and for three months things go very well. When he comes home from work the parrot tells him about the latest sports results and what happened in politics that day.

One day the man comes home from work and the parrot waves a wing at him and says, "Come in and shut the door."

The man says, "What's up?"

The parrot says, "I don't know how to tell you this, but the postman came today. Your wife answered the door in her negligee and he kissed her right on the lips."

The man says, "Oh, a momentary flight of passion."

The parrot says, "Well, maybe, but then he fondled her breasts."

The man says, "He did?"

The parrot says, "Yes. Then he pulled her negligee down and started sucking on her breasts."

The man says, "My God, what happened next?!"

The parrot says, "I don't know. I got a hard-on and fell off my perch!"

Man: My wife's kinky. She likes sex in her ear.

Friend: Why's that?

Man: Well every time I try to put it in her mouth she turns her head.

A nude woman looks in the bedroom mirror and says to her husband, "I look horrible, fat and ugly. Can you please pay me a compliment?"

The husband replies, "Well, your eyesight's excellent."

An Indian chief decided it was time to give his three sons their adult names as they had reached manhood. So he gathered them in to his tent together with the elders of the tribe.

He turns to the first son, "Son, you will be called Eagle."

The third son interrupts, "Father, father, what will I be called?"

"All in good time, my son," replied the Chief.

He continued, "You will be called Eagle because you are strong and wise."

The Elders agreed.

He then turned to the second son, but the third son said, "Father, father, what will I be called?"

"All in good time, my son," he replied.

He then continued to the second son, "Son, you will be called Swallow."

The third son said again, "Father, father, what will I be called?"

"All in good time, my son," he replied.

He then continued, "You will be named Swallow because you are quick and cunning."

The Elders agreed.

He then turned to the third son who was asking, "Father, father, what will I be called?"

"Son, you will be called Thrush."

"Why is that father?" he asked excitedly.

"Because you are an irritating little c**t."

A guy walks into a bar and sees a sign that reads ...

HAMBURGER: $1

CHEESEBURGER: $2

HAND JOB: $3

He calls to the attractive blonde behind the counter.

"Can I help you?" she asks with a smile.

"I was wondering," whispers the man. "Are you the one who gives the hand jobs?"

"Yes," she purrs, "I am."

"Well wash your hands," he says. "I want a cheeseburger."

A man went into a tattoo parlor and asked to have a fifty dollar bill tattooed on his dick.

The tattoo artist said, "I've had some strange requests but this one tops the lot. Why in the hell would you want me to tattoo your prick with a picture of a banknote?"

The man replied, "There are three reasons.

One, I love to play with my money.

Two, when I play with my money, I love to see it grow.

Three, and this is the most important of all, the next time my wife wants to blow fifty bucks, she won't have to leave the house!"

Q. What's the difference between a fridge and a blonde?
A. A fridge doesn't fart when you take your meat out.

A guy is in the bar's restroom taking a piss when the door opens. In walks a very large, very muscular guy. This guy proceeds to pull down his pants, revealing a monster prick.

To the man's amazement, the muscular guy growls and slams his dick into the sink attached to the wall. It shatters, spraying pieces and water everywhere. Next, the muscular man growls louder and slams it into one of the stalls, making the entire thing collapse. Then he slams it into the wall of the room, knocking a very large hole into it.

The giant approaches the scared guy taking a piss.

"Hey, buddy, do you see this very large, very strong cock?" he asks.

"Yes," replies the guy taking a leak.

"Do you know what I am going to do with this very large, very strong cock?"

"No, I'm afraid I don't."

"I'm going to shove it up your ass!"

"Jesus, that's a relief. I thought you were going to hit me with it!"

A man who was to be investigated by the IRS asked his accountant for advice on what to wear.

"Wear your shabbiest clothing. Let him think you are a pauper," the accountant replied.

Then he asked his lawyer the same question, but got the opposite advice.

"Do not let them intimidate you. Wear your most elegant suit and tie."

Confused, the man told a friend of the conflicting advice, and asked him what he should do.

"Let me tell you a story," replied his friend.

"A woman, about to be married, asked her mother what to wear on her wedding night and was told 'Wear a heavy, long, flannel nightgown that goes right up to your neck.'

When she asked her best friend, she was told 'Wear your most sexy negligee, with a v-neck right down to your navel.'"

The man said, "What does all this have to do with my problem with the IRS?"

His friend replied, "No matter what you wear, you're going to get screwed."

A cop stops a guy leading a cow down the street.

He asks, "What are you doing with a cow in the middle of town?"

"I'm taking it home to keep it in my house."

"What about all the flies and shit?"

"It will just have to get used to them."

Q. What's green, slimy and smells like Miss Piggy?
A. Kermit's Finger.

There was a guy who worked at a dildo store, and it was his first day on the job. At about 12, the boss wanted to go out for lunch, so he said to the new guy, "I'm going out for lunch. I'm going to review the prices with you so that you won't make a bad sale. Now this is our nine-inch white dildo. It's $15."

The new guy says, "Nine-inch white, $15. Got it."

"This is the eleven-inch black dildo. It's $25."

"Eleven-inch black, $25. Got it." So the boss leaves.

A few minutes later, a very elegantly dressed woman walks in. "How much is that dildo there?" she asks the guy.

"Ah, that's our nine-inch white dildo, and it sells for $15."

"What about that black one there?"

"That's our eleven-inch black, it's $25."

"And how much for the plaid one over there?"

"Oh, that's the twelve-inch tartan dildo. It's...$50."

The woman looks at the selection again and decides to buy the tartan one. The guy wraps it for her and she leaves.

A few minutes later, the boss comes back from lunch. "How'd you do?" he asks the guy.

"Oh, great! I got $50 for my thermos flask!"

There were these two statues in a park, one of a nude man and one of a nude woman. They had been facing each other across a pathway for a hundred years, when one day, an angel comes down from the sky and with a single gesture brings the two to life.

The angel tells them, "As a reward for being so patient through the hundred blazing summers and dismal winters, you have been given life for thirty minutes to do what you've wished to do the most."

He looks at her, she looks at him, and they go running behind the shrubbery. The angel waits patiently as the bushes rustle and the giggling ensues. After fifteen minutes the two return, out of breath and laughing.

The angel tells them, "Um, you have fifteen minutes left. Would you care to do it again?"

He asks her, "Shall we?"

She eagerly replies, "Oh yes, let's! But let's change positions. This time, I'll hold the pigeon down and you shit on its head!"

Q: How do you know when you're really ugly?
A: Dogs hump your leg with their eyes closed.

A young boy went up to his father and asked him, "What is the difference between potentially and realistically?"

The father thought for a moment, then answered, "Go ask your mother if she would sleep with Robert Redford for a million dollars. Then ask your sister if she would sleep with Brad Pitt for a million dollars. Come back and tell me what you learn from that."

So the boy went to his mother and asked, "Would you sleep with Robert Redford for a million dollars?"

The mother replied, "Of course I would! I wouldn't pass up an opportunity like that."

The boy then went to his sister and asked, "Would you sleep with Brad Pitt for a million dollars?"

The girl replied, "Oh my God! I would just love to do that! I would be nuts to pass up that opportunity!"

The boy pondered for a while, then went back to his dad who asked him, "Did you find out the difference between potential and realistic?"

The boy replied, "No, sir," and tells his father the replies he'd been given.

"Well, son," the father replied. "Surely it's obvious: Potentially, we're sitting on two million dollars but, realistically, we're living with two sluts."

A man out shopping bought some new condoms. When he got home, his wife noticed the brand. "Olympic condoms? What makes them so special?" she asked.

"There are three colors," he replied. "Gold, silver and bronze."

"What color are you going to wear tonight?" she asked.

"Gold, of course," said the man.

"Really?" she said. "Why don't you wear silver—it would be nice if you came second for a change!"

A man walks into a pharmacy, buys a condom, then walks out of the store laughing hysterically. The pharmacist thinks this is weird but there are no laws preventing weird people from buying condoms. Who knows, maybe it's a good thing.

The next day, the same man comes back to the store, purchases yet another condom, and once again he leaves the store laughing wildly.

This piques the interest of the pharmacist. What could be so funny about buying a condom, anyway?

So he tells his clerk, "If that guy ever comes back, I want you to follow him to see where he goes."

Sure enough, the next day the same man is back. He buys the condom, and again starts cracking up with laughter, then leaves.

The pharmacist tells his clerk to go follow the guy. About an hour later, the clerk comes back to the store.

"Did you follow him? Where did he go?" asks the pharmacist.

The clerk replies, "Your house."

Q: What do you call a smart blonde?
A: A golden retriever.

One day a young man and woman were in their bedroom making love. All of a sudden, a bumble bee entered the bedroom window. As the young lady parted her legs the bee entered her pussy.

The woman started screaming, "Oh my god, help me, there's a bee in my pussy!"

The husband immediately took her to the local doctor and explained the situation.

The doctor thought for a moment and said, "Hmm, tricky situation. But I have a solution to the problem if the young man would permit."

The husband being very concerned agreed that the doctor could use whatever method to get the bee out. The doctor said, "OK, what I'm going to do is rub some honey over the top of my penis and insert it into your wife. When I feel the bee getting closer to the tip I shall withdraw it and the bee should hopefully follow it out."

The husband nodded and gave his approval. The young lady said, "Yes, yes, whatever, just get on with it."

So the doctor, after covering the tip of his penis with honey, slipped it into young lady. After a few gentle strokes, the doctor said, "I don't think the bee has noticed the honey yet. Perhaps I should go a bit deeper." So the doctor went deeper and deeper.

After a while the doctor began shafting the young lady very hard indeed.

The young lady began to quiver with excitement. She began to moan and groan aloud, "Oh, Doctor, Doctor!" she shouted.

The doctor, concentrating very hard, looked like he was enjoying himself. He then put his hands on the young lady's breasts and started making loud noises.

At this point the husband suddenly became very annoyed and shouted, "Now wait a minute. What the hell do you think you're doing?!"

The doctor, still concentrating, replied, "Change of plan, I'm going to drown the bastard!!"

A Catholic school girl is engaged to be married. A few days before the wedding she goes on a carriage ride with her mother. "Mom, my hands are cold."

"Stick them between your legs and they'll warm up," says her mother.

The following day she goes on a carriage ride with her fiancé, "My hands are cold," he says.

"Stick them between my legs and they'll warm up," she says.

The day after that they again go on a carriage ride. "My nose is cold," says the fiancé.

"Stick it between my legs and it'll warm up," says the girl.

The third day they are out on another carriage ride. "My penis is cold," says the boy.

"Stick it between my legs and it will warm up."

The girl returns home after the carriage ride and says, "Mom, do you know what a penis is?"

"Yes," answers the mother.

Then the girl tells her, "They sure do make a mess when they thaw out."

Q: What makes men chase women they have no intention of marrying?

A: The same urge that makes dogs chase cars they have no intention of driving.

A man was having problems with premature ejaculation. This was affecting marital relations with his wife so he decided to go to the doctor. He asked the doctor what he could do to cure his problem.

In response the doctor said, "When you feel the urge to ejaculate, try startling yourself."

On the way home the man went to a gun store and bought himself a starter pistol. All excited to try out this suggestion he ran home to his wife. When he got home he was surprised and delighted to find his wife in bed, already naked. He was so horny and excited to try out his new "system" that he didn't think twice and leapt on board.

After a few minutes of "slap and tickle" they found themselves in the "69" position. Sure enough, only moments later the man felt the sudden urge to come. Following the doctor's orders, he grabbed the starter pistol off the bedside table and fired it.

The next day, the man went back to the doctor. The doctor asked, "How did it go?"

The man answered, "Just great! When I fired the pistol, my wife crapped on my face and bit three inches off my dick, and my neighbor came out of the closet naked with his hands in the air!"

Little Johnny was supposed to have a "current event" every day for school.

He never did his homework and one day his teacher said, "Johnny, if you don't have a current event for class tomorrow you will fail and have to take this class again next year."

He went home, went to bed, and forgot all about it. The next morning on his way to school he remembered and thought to himself, Damn, I forgot to prepare my current event.

Then he saw a cat with two dogs chasing it run across the railway line. The cat made it across but a train hit the dogs.

When he got to school he yelled, "Teacher, teacher, I have my current event!"

She said, "OK what is it, Johnny?"

He told her, "This morning on my way to school I saw a cat run across the railway line and the two dogs that were chasing it got hit in the ass by a train."

She said, "Johnny! Don't use language like that. Say 'rectum.'"

He laughed and said, "Wrecked 'em, hell, it killed 'em both."

One Friday, a 5th grade teacher says, "Class, every Friday I am going to ask a question. Whoever gets the question right gets to skip school on Monday." So the class is very excited and can't wait until next Friday.

Friday comes around and the teacher says, "Okay, time for the question of the week. How many stars are in the sky?" Of course no one can answer it. Next week she asks, "How many grains of sand are there on the beach?" Still no one can answer.

One student, however, is fed up with this. When he gets home, he paints two ping-pong balls black. He puts them in a bag and goes to school. When Friday comes around he takes them to class. The teacher says, "Okay, class, time for the question of the week." The boy quickly drops the balls on the floor and they roll up to her feet.

The teacher says rudely, "Okay, who's the comedian with the black balls?"

Then the kid says quickly, "Bill Cosby. See you on Tuesday."

A man goes to the doctor and the visit goes like this.

MAN: Doc, I think I'm gay.

DOCTOR: What makes you think you're gay?

MAN: Well, my dad just announced to our family that HE'S gay.

DOCTOR: Just because your father is gay doesn't mean that you are. It's not hereditary.

MAN: But Doc, I have two uncles and they are BOTH gay.
DOCTOR: Well, that's just a coincidence. It's NOT hereditary.
MAN: But I have three brothers, and they are ALL gay.
DOCTOR: Dammit, son! Doesn't anyone in your family like pussy?!
MAN: Well, sure. My sister does!!

Ethel loved to speed around the nursing home in her wheelchair, taking corners on one wheel and getting up to maximum speed on the long corridors.

Because the poor woman was one sandwich short of a picnic, the other residents tolerated her, and some of the males actually joined in.

One day, Ethel was speeding up one corridor when a door opened and Mad Mickey stepped out with his arm outstretched.

"STOP!" he shouted in a firm voice. "Have you got a license for that thing?"

Ethel fished around in her handbag and pulled out a Kit-Kat wrapper, then held it up to him.

"OK," he said, and away Ethel sped down the hall.

As she took the corner near the TV lounge on one wheel Weird Harold popped out in front of her and shouted, "STOP! Have you got proof of insurance?"

Ethel dug into her handbag, pulled out a drink coaster, and held it up to him.

Harold nodded and said, "Carry on, ma'am."

As Ethel neared the final corridor before the front door, Crazy Craig stepped out in front of her, stark naked, holding a very sizable erection in his hand.

"Oh, good grief," said Ethel. "Not the breathalyzer again!"

A family is at the dinner table. The son asks his father, "Dad, how many kinds of 'boobies' are there?"

The father, surprised, answers, "Well, son, there are three kinds of breasts. In her twenties, a woman's breasts are like melons, round and firm. In her thirties to forties, they are like pears, still nice but hanging a bit. After fifty, they are like onions."

"Onions?" asked the son.

"Yes, you see them and they make you cry."

This infuriated his wife and daughter, so the daughter asked, "Mom, how many kinds of penises are there?"

The mother smiles and answers, "Well, dear, a man goes through three phases. In his twenties, his penis is like an oak tree, mighty and strong. In his thirties and forties, it's like a birch, flexible but reliable. After his fifties, it's like a Christmas tree."

"A Christmas tree?" queried the daughter.

"Yes, it's dead from the root up and the balls are for decoration only."

This old woman was in her attic with her cat (whom she loved very much) when she saw an old bottle. She started wiping the bottle and a genie appeared. The genie told her she would grant her three wishes. So the old woman wished to become a beautiful young woman and, POOF, she became a very beautiful young woman. Then she wished to have her house full of money from the floor to the ceiling and, POOF, her house filled up with money. Her last wish was for her beloved cat to become this gorgeous young hunk of a man, and, POOF, her cat became the biggest hunk she ever laid eyes on. She looked at the man and said, "I love you."

The man replied, "I love you too, but now don't you wish you hadn't had me neutered?"

Coming into the bar and ordering a double, the man leaned over and confided to the bartender, "I'm so pissed off!"

"What happened?" asked the bartender politely.

"See, I met this beautiful woman who invited me back to her home. We stripped off our clothes and jumped into bed and we were just about to make love when her goddamned husband came in the front door. So I had to jump out of the bedroom window and hang from the ledge by my fingernails!"

"Gee, that's tough!" commiserated the bartender.

"Right, but that's not what really got me aggravated," the customer went on. "When her husband came into the room he said 'Hey great! You're naked already! Let me just take a leak.' And damned if the lazy son of a bitch didn't piss out the window right onto my head."

"Yuk!" The bartender shook his head. "No wonder you're in a lousy mood."

"Yeah, but I haven't told you what really, really got to me. Next, I had to listen to them grunting and groaning and when they finished, the husband tossed his condom out of the window. And where does it land? My damned forehead!"

"Damn, that really is a drag!" said the bartender.

"Oh, I'm not finished. See what really pissed me off was when the husband had to take a dump. It turns out that their toilet is broken, so he stuck his ass out of the window and let loose right on my head!"

The bartender paled. "That would sure mess up my day."

"Yeah, yeah, yeah," the fellow rattled on, "but do you know what REALLY, REALLY, REALLY pissed me off? When I looked down and saw that my feet were only SIX inches off the ground!!"

A man is standing at the urinal in a public bathroom quietly going about his business when the door flies open and a big black guy runs in, whips out his dick and, letting out a sigh of relief, stands next to him. The black guy smiles at him and says "Just made it!!"

The first man takes a look at the black man's dick and says, "Shit! Could you make me one like that?"

Q. Why do so many gays have moustaches?
A. To hide the stretch marks.

A woman was in a coma. Nurses were in her room giving her a sponge bath when one of them noticed that there was a response on the monitor whenever her crotch was touched.

They went to her husband and explained what happened, telling him, "Crazy as this sounds, but maybe a little oral sex will do the trick and bring her out of the coma."

The husband was skeptical, but they assured him they'd close the curtains for privacy. The hubby finally agreed and went into his wife's room.

After a few minutes the woman's monitor flatlined. No pulse, no heart rate, nothing. The nurses ran into the room.

The husband, who was standing beside his wife's bed pulling up his pants, said, "Erm... I think she choked."

Two southern and VERY rural sisters, Georgia and Loreen, were sitting on the porch in rocking chairs discussing Loreen's recent trip to New York City.

Loreen says, "Sister, did you KNOW that in New York City there are women who kiss other women on the LIPS?!?!"

Georgia gasps and exclaims, "Oh, sister!!! What do they call them?"

"They call them lesbians," Loreen replies and drawls out the last word. "And, sister, did you know that in New York City there are MEN who kiss other men on the lips?"

"Oh, sister," says Georgia, fanning herself in a startled frenzy. "What do they call THEM?"

"They call them GAY," Loreen says. "And, SISTER, did you KNOW that in New York City there are MEN who kiss WOMEN on their PRIVATE PARTS???" Loreen whispers the last part.

To this, Georgia turns as red as the clay beneath the house and nearly falls out of her chair as she exclaims, "OHHH, sister! What do they call them?!?!?"

Loreen smiles a secretive smile and proudly announces, "Well, I don't know but when he looked up I called him Precious!"

New meanings...
SEAGULL MANAGER—A manager who flies in, makes a lot of noise, craps on everything, and then leaves.

SALMON DAY—The experience of spending an entire day swimming upstream only to get screwed and die.

PERCUSSIVE MAINTENANCE—The fine art of whacking the crap out of an electronic device to get it to work again.

AIRPLANE BLONDE—One who has bleached/dyed her hair but still has a black box.

AUSSIE KISS—Similar to a French kiss, but given down under.

BEER COAT—The invisible but warm coat worn when walking home after a booze cruise at 3 a.m.

BEER COMPASS—The invisible device that ensures you arrive home safely after a booze cruise, even though you're too drunk to remember where you live, how you got there, and where you've come from.

GREYHOUND—A very short skirt, only an inch from the hare.

One day a man goes to the doctor and says, "Doctor you have got to help me. I can not get an erection for anything, and it is ruining my marriage!"

The doctor thinks for a little while and then says, "I got just the solution for you. Go home tonight and wait until your wife is sound asleep, then reach over and put your fingers between her legs and get some of her juice and rub it under your nose. Keep on doing that and it should get you an erection."

So the guy thanks him and hurries on home. Later on that night he's lying in bed and his wife is fast asleep. So he reaches over and starts rubbing the juice under his nose. After about a minute he can feel himself getting hard. Excited he shakes his wife awake and says, "Look, honey, look what I've got!"

And she replies, "You woke me up at two in the morning to show me your bloody nose?!"

Three nuns were talking.

The first nun said, "I was cleaning in Father's room the other day and do you know what I found? A bunch of pornographic magazines."

"What did you do?" the other nuns asked.

"Well of course I threw them in the trash."

The second nun said, "Well, I can top that. I was in Father's room putting away laundry and I found a bunch of condoms!"

"Oh, my!" gasped the other nuns. "What did you do?"

"I poked holes in all of them!" she replied.

The third nun fainted.

A man is sitting on a train across from a busty blonde wearing a tiny miniskirt. Despite his efforts, he is unable to stop staring at the top of her thighs.

To his delight, he realizes she has no underwear. The blonde realizes he is staring and inquires, "Are you looking at my pussy?"

"Yes, I'm sorry," replies the man and promises to avert his eyes.

"It's quite alright," replies the woman. "It's very talented. Watch this, I'll make it blow a kiss to you."

Sure enough the pussy blows him a kiss. The man, who is completely absorbed, inquires what else the wonder pussy can do.

"I can also make it wink," says the woman. The man stares in amazement as the pussy winks at him. "Come and sit next to me," suggests the woman, patting the seat.

As the man moves over, the woman asks, "Would you like to stick a couple of fingers in?"

"Good God!" says the man. "Can it whistle too?"

Q: What's the difference between a blonde and a walrus?
A: One has whiskers and fishy flaps, and the other one's a walrus.

Little Johnny is taking a shower with his mother and says, "Mom, what are those things on your chest!?"

Unsure of how to reply she tells Johnny to ask his dad at breakfast tomorrow, quite certain the matter would be forgotten. Johnny didn't forget. The following morning he asks his father the same question.

His father, always quick with the answers, says, "Why, Johnny, those are balloons. When your mommy dies, we can blow them up and she'll float to heaven."

Johnny thinks that's neat and asks no more questions. A few weeks later, Johnny's dad comes home from work a few hours early. Johnny runs out of the house crying hysterically, "Daddy! Daddy! Mommy's dying!!"

His father says, "Calm down, son! Why do you think Mommy's dying?"

"Uncle Harry is blowing up mommy's balloons and she's screaming, 'Oh God, I'm coming!'"

A man has spent many days crossing the desert without water. His camel dies of thirst. He's crawling through the sands, certain that he has breathed his last, when all of a sudden he sees an object sticking out of the sand several yards ahead of him.

He crawls to the object, pulls it out of the sand, and discovers what looks to be an old brief case. He opens it and out pops a genie... But this is no ordinary genie. He is wearing an IRS ID badge and dull gray suit. There's a calculator in his pocket. He has a pencil tucked behind one ear.

"Well, kid," says the genie. "You know how it works. You have three wishes..."

"I'm not falling for this," says the man. "I'm not going to trust a person from the IRS."

"What do you have to lose? You've got no transportation, and it looks like you're a goner anyway!"

The man thinks about this for a minute, and decides that the genie is right.

"OK, I wish I were in a lush oasis with plentiful food and drink."
POOF

The man finds himself in the most beautiful oasis he has ever seen, and he is surrounded with jugs of wine and platters of delicacies.

"OK, kid, what's your second wish."

"My second wish is to be rich beyond my wildest dreams."
POOF

The man finds himself surrounded by treasure chests filled with rare gold coins and precious gems.

"OK, kid, you have just one more wish. Better make it a good one!"

After thinking for a few minutes, the man says, "I wish that no matter where I go beautiful women will want and need me."
POOF

He is turned into a tampon.

The moral of the story?

If the IRS offers you anything, there's going to be a string attached.

Three men with terrible addictions go and visit the doctor.

The alcoholic is the first to enter. "Well," says the doctor, "you have damaged your liver beyond repair—if you have one more drink, you will drop dead."

Shocked, the man leaves, vowing never to drink again.

The doctor's next patient is a heavy smoker. "Right," says the doctor, "your lungs are coated so heavily with tar that I'm afraid to say if you smoke one more cigarette, you will drop dead."

The man leaves, clearly shaken and promising himself to never puff on a cigarette again.

The doctor's final patient is a raging homosexual. "Well, I must say," says the doctor, "I'm afraid that if you give in to your addiction just one more time, you will also drop dead."

The homosexual leaves, resigned to the fact that he will never have sex again.

The three men are walking down the street when they pass a bar. The alcoholic can't help himself and runs inside for his final sip of beer—and drops dead.

The two remaining men are shocked but continue their walk down the road where they come across a whole burning cigarette lying in a doorway. The smoker stops to admire it—shaking.

As he's about to bend down and pick it up the homosexual turns to him and says,

"You do realize, if you pick that up we're both dead!"

Two guys were walking home from work one afternoon. "Shit," said the first guy, "as soon as I get home, I'm going to rip my wife's panties off!"

"What's the rush?" his friend asked.

"The fucking elastic in the legs is killing me," the guy replied.

A female TV reporter went to have an interview with a French farmer, seeking to find out the main cause of Mad Cow Disease.

The Lady: "Good evening, sir, we are here to collect information about the causes of Mad Cow Disease. Do you have any idea what might be the reason?"

The Farmer stared at the reporter and said: "Do you know that the bull fucks the cow once a year?"

The Lady (getting embarrassed): "Well, sir, that's a new piece of information, but what's the relation between this phenomenon and Mad Cow disease?"

The Farmer: "Well, Madam, do you know that we milk the cow four times a day?"

The Lady: "Sir, this is really valuable information, but what about getting to the point?"

The Farmer: "I am getting to the point, Madam. Just imagine, if I was playing with your tits four times a day and fucking you once a year, wouldn't YOU get mad?"

A rich man and a poor man were talking about what they got their wives for Christmas. The rich man told the poor man, "I got my wife a diamond ring and a Porsche."

The poor man asked why.

The rich man said, "If she does not like the ring she can take it back in her Porsche." The rich man then asks the poor man what he bought for his wife.

The poor man said, "A pair of slippers and a dildo."

The rich man asked "Why?"

The poor man said, "If she doesn't like the slippers she can go fuck herself."

Q. Did you hear about the flasher who was thinking of retiring?
A. He decided to stick it out for one more year!

A man was on the witness stand and the lawyer asked him, "What was my client doing that night?"

The witness said, "He was fucking!!!"

The judge told the witness, "You can't say fuck in court."

So the lawyer asked the man again, "What was my client doing on that night?"

"He was fucking!!!!"

The judge said to him again, "Listen, if you say fuck again, I am going to hold you for 30 days for contempt of court."

So the lawyer rephrased his question and said, "Could you describe what my client was doing on that night?"

The man thought for a moment and said this:

"His pants were down to his knees,

His ass was swinging in the breeze,

His you know what was in you know where,

And if that isn't fucking, you can give me the chair."

Washing a car is very much like making love to a beautiful woman.

You've got to caress the bodywork, breathe softly and gently, and give every inch of it your loving attention. And make sure you've got a nice wet sponge.

Mr. Smith owned a small business. He had two employees, Sarah and Jack. They were both extremely good employees, always willing to work overtime and chip in where needed.

Mr. Smith was looking over his books one day and decided that he wasn't making enough money to warrant two employees and he would have to lay someone off. But both Sarah and Jack were such good workers he was having trouble finding a fair way to do it. After much thought, he eventually decided that he would watch them work and the first one to take a break would be the one he would lay off.

So he sat in his office and watched them work. Suddenly, Sarah got a terrible headache and needed to take an aspirin. She got the aspirin out of her purse and went to the water cooler to get something to wash it down with.

Mr. Smith followed her to the water cooler, tapped her on the shoulder and said, "Sarah, I'm going to have to lay you, or Jack, off."

Sarah said, "You'll have to jack off—I have a headache!"

A dwarf with a lisp visits a stud farm.

"I'd like to buy a horth," he says to the owner of the farm.

"What sort of horse?" asks the owner.

"A female horth," the dwarf replies.

So the owner shows him a mare.

"Nithe horth," says the dwarf. "Can I thee her eyeth?"

So the owner picks up the dwarf to show him the horse's eyes and puts him down again.

"Nithe eyeth," says the dwarf. "Can I thee her teeth?"

Again the owner picks up the dwarf to show him the horse's teeth, and puts him down.

"Nithe teeth. May I now see her earth?" the dwarf asks.

By now the owner is getting a little fed up, but again picks up the dwarf to show him the horse's ears and then puts him down.

"Nithe earth," he says. "Now, can I see her twot?"

"With this, the owner picks the dwarf up, and, holding him by the scruff of his neck and the back of his belt, shoves his head deep inside the horse's vagina. He holds him there for a couple of seconds before pulling him out and putting him down.

The dwarf shakes his head and says, "Perhapth I should weefwaze that. Can I see her wun awound?!!"

Q: If you had sex 365 times in one year and melted the rubbers down to make a tire, what would you call it?

A: A fucking Goodyear!!!

One day, a young boy walks onto a city bus and sits directly behind the bus driver. He begins to shout at the top of his lungs saying, "If my mommy were a girl elephant and my daddy were a boy elephant, I'd be a baby elephant!" He goes on like this for half an hour when the bus driver finally reacts to the young boy's antics.

He slams on the brakes and turns around to the boy and yells, "If your mother were a prostitute and your father were gay, what would you be then?"

To which the boy replies with a large grin on his face, "A bus driver."

Q: What have working for the KGB and oral sex got in common?
A: One slip of the tongue and you're in deep shit.

This is called the rodeo: Get into the doggy style position, grab onto her breasts, tell her they feel just like her sister's, and then try holding on for eight seconds...

When Ralph first noticed his penis was growing longer and staying erect longer he was delighted, as was his wife. After several weeks his penis had grown to twenty inches. Ralph became quite concerned as he was having problems dressing and even walking. So he and his wife went to see a prominent urologist. After an initial examination the doctor explained to the couple that, though rare, Ralph's condition could be fixed through corrective surgery.

"How long will Ralph be on crutches?" the wife asked anxiously.

"Crutches? Why would he need crutches?" responded the doctor.

"Well," said Ralph's wife coldly, "you are going to lengthen his legs, aren't you?"

A Mexican is strolling down the street in Mexico City and kicks a bottle lying in the street.

Suddenly out of the bottle comes a genie. The Mexican is stunned. The genie says, "Hello, Master, I will grant you one wish—anything you want."

The Mexican begins thinking, Well, I really like drinking tequila.

Finally he says, "I wish to drink tequila whenever I want, so make me pee tequila."

The genie grants him his wish.

When the Mexican gets home, he gets a glass out of the cupboard and pees in it.

He looks at the glass and it's clear. It looks like tequila. Then smells the liquid. It smells like tequila.

So he takes a taste, and it is the best tequila he has ever tasted.

The Mexican yells to his wife, "Consuela, Consuela, come quickly!"

She comes running down the hall, and the Mexican takes another glass out of the cupboard and fills it.

He tells her to drink it. It is tequila, he says. Consuela is reluctant but goes ahead and takes a sip.

It is the best tequila she has ever tasted. The two drink and party all night.

The next night the Mexican comes home from work and tells his wife to get two glasses out of the cupboard. He proceeds to fill the two glasses. The result is the same. The tequila is excellent, and the couple drink until the sun comes up.

Finally Friday night comes and the Mexican comes home from work and tells his wife, "Consuela, grab one glass from the cupboard and we will drink tequila." His wife gets the glass from the cupboard and sets it on the table.

The Mexican begins to fill the glass, and when he fills it, his wife asks him, "But, Pancho, why do we need only one glass?"

Pancho raises the glass and says, "BECAUSE TONIGHT YOU DRINK FROM THE BOTTLE."

An attractive woman from New York is driving through a remote part of Texas when her car breaks down. A few minutes later, an Indian on horseback comes along and offers her a ride to a nearby town.

She climbs up behind him on the horse and they ride off. Every few minutes the Indian lets out a whoop so loud that it echoes from the surrounding hills.

When they arrive in town, he lets her off at a service station and yells one final "Yahoo!" before riding off.

"What did you do to get that Indian so excited?" the service station attendant asks.

"Nothing," she says, "I just sat behind him on the horse, put my arms around his waist and held on to his saddle horn so I wouldn't fall off."

"Lady," the attendant says, "Indians ride bareback."

Farmer Brown and his wife were working in the field one day around dusk. As they were heading back to the house they saw a bunch of strange lights way out in the field. Upon arriving, Farmer Brown and his wife saw a spaceship landing. They were approached by two aliens. The aliens said they were researching human sex life and wanted to know if they could partner switch. After talking it over Farmer Brown and his wife agreed. The next morning the aliens left.

Farmer Brown was dying to ask his wife what happened. Finally, he couldn't stand it any more and broke down and asked her what happened.

She replied that it was the best sex she'd ever had!!

"Why?" asked Farmer Brown.

"Well, when he took off his pants it was only an inch long and as big around as my little finger, but then he reached up and turned his left ear and it grew to 16 inches. Then he turned his right ear and it got as big around as a sausage."

Farmer Brown said, "Shit, no wonder that bitch was trying to rip my fucking ears off!!!"

Q. How do you turn a fox into an elephant?
A. Marry it.

A huge muscular man walks into a bar and orders a beer. The barman hands him the beer and says, "You know, I'm not gay but I want to compliment you on your physique. It really is phenomenal! I have a question though: Why is your head so small?"

The big guy nods slowly. He's obviously fielded this question many times.

"One day," he begins, "I was hunting when I got lost in the woods. I heard someone crying for help and finally realized that it was coming from a frog sitting next to a stream.

So I picked up the frog and it said, 'Kiss me. Kiss me and I will turn into a genie and grant you three wishes.'

So I looked around to make sure I was alone and gave the frog a kiss. POOF! The frog turned into a beautiful, voluptuous, naked woman.

She said, 'You now have three wishes.'

I looked down at my scrawny body and said, 'I want a body better than Arnold Schwarzenegger in his prime.'

She nodded, whispered a spell, and POOF! There I was, so huge that I ripped out of my clothes and was standing there naked!

She then asked, 'What will be your second wish?'

I looked hungrily at her beautiful body and replied, 'I want to make sensuous love with you here by this stream.' She nodded, lay down, held her arms out to me and we made mad passionate love!

Later, as we lay there next to each other, sweating from our glorious lovemaking, she whispered into my ear, 'You know, you do have one more wish, darling. What will it be?"

I looked in to her loving eyes and replied, 'How about a little head?'"

Tarzan and Jane are going to do it for the first time, but Tarzan tells Jane that he doesn't know how.

Jane says, "Look, it's very easy," and she explains what it is to make love.

Tarzan tells her, "Tarzan does it in tree trunk hole."

Jane tells him, "You've got it all wrong, you stick it in this hole," motioning to her crotch.

Tarzan and Jane get naked and Jane motions Tarzan to put it in her crotch. Tarzan goes to Jane and kicks her very hard in her crotch.

Jane, twitching with pain, asks Tarzan, "What was that for?"

Tarzan says, "Tarzan checks for Squirrels."

Q: What's grosser than gross?
A: Ten naked men running in a circle and the first one stops!

Q: Why did God create alcohol?
A: So ugly people could have sex, too.

The first grade teacher was starting a new lesson on multi-syllable words. She thought it would be a good idea to ask a few of the children examples of words with more than one syllable.

"Jane, do you know any multi-syllable words?"

After some thought Jane proudly replied with, "Monday."

"Great, Jane. That has two syllables, Mon...day."

"Does anyone know another word?"

"I do! I do!" replied Johnny.

Knowing Johnny's more mature sense of humor she picked Mike instead.

"OK, Mike, what is your word?"

"Saturday," said Mike.

"Great. That has three syllables..."

Not wanting to be outdone Johnny said, "I know a four syllable word. Pick me! Pick me!"

Not thinking he could do any harm with a word that large, the teacher reluctantly said, "OK, Johnny, what is your four syllable word?"

Johnny proudly said, "Mas...tur...ba...tion."

Shocked, the teacher, trying to retain her composure, said, "Wow, Johnny. Four syllables! That's certainly a mouthful."

"No, Ma'am, you're thinking of 'blow job', and that's only two syllables."

A woman in her forties went to a plastic surgeon for a facelift. The surgeon told her about a new procedure called "The Knob," in which a small knob is placed on the back of a woman's head and can be turned to tighten up her skin to produce the effect of a brand new face lift. Of course, the woman wanted "The Knob."

Over the years, the woman tightened the knob, and the effects were wonderful—the woman remained young-looking and vibrant.

After fifteen years, the woman returned to the surgeon with two problems.

"All these years, everything has been working just fine. I've had to turn the knob many times and I've always loved the results. But now I've developed two annoying problems: First, I have these terrible bags under my eyes and the knob won't get rid of them."

The doctor looked at her closely and said, "Those aren't bags. Those are your breasts."

She said, "Well, I guess there's no point in asking about the goatee."

Did you know that the most commonly used sexual position in the world is doggy style? You know, the one where the man sits up and begs and the women rolls over and plays dead.

A priest and a rabbi are sitting next to each other on an airplane. After a while the priest turns to the rabbi and asks, "Is it still a requirement of your faith that you do not eat pork?"

The rabbi responds, "Yes, that is still one of our beliefs."

The priest then asks, "Have you ever eaten pork?"

To which the rabbi replies, "Yes, on one occasion I did succumb to temptation and tasted a ham sandwich."

The priest nodded in understanding and went on with his reading.

A while later, the rabbi spoke up and asked the priest, "Father, is it still a requirement of your church that you remain celibate?"

The priest replied, "Yes, that is still very much a part of our faith."

The rabbi then asked him, "Father, have you ever fallen to the temptations of the flesh?"

The priest replied, "Yes, rabbi, on one occasion I was weak and broke with my faith."

The rabbi nodded understandingly. He was silent for about five minutes, and then he said, "Beats the hell out of a ham sandwich, doesn't it?"

A beautiful young woman walks into a dentist's office for some major work on her teeth. Sitting in the waiting room for a while, she is finally told the doctor will see her. She enters a small room and sits down in the chair and awaits the arrival of the dentist. After a few minutes or so the doctor comes and sits down to take a look. He asks the young woman to open her mouth so that he can take a look. To his surprise he notices that almost every tooth in her mouth is chipped, broken, and some are completely missing except for the roots. Even her tongue looks as if it has been beaten. She then asks the doctor what the problem could be, and he answers, "Well, Lois Lane..."

Q. What did the leper say to the prostitute?
A. Keep the tip!!

A guy is walking along the strip in Las Vegas and a knockout-looking hooker catches his eye. He strikes up a conversation and eventually asks the hooker, "How much do you charge?"

Hooker replies, "It starts at $500 for a hand job."

Guy says, "$500! For a hand job! Jesus Christ! No hand job is worth that kind of money!"

The hooker says, "Do you see that restaurant on the corner?"

"Yes."

"Do you see the restaurant about a block further down?"

"Yes."

"And beyond that, do you see that third one?"

"Yes."

"Well," says the hooker, smiling invitingly, "I own those. And, I own them because I give a hand job that's worth $500."

Guy says, "What the hell? You only live once. I'll give it a try." They retire to a nearby motel.

A short time later, the guy is sitting on the bed realizing that he's just experienced the hand job of a lifetime, worth every bit of $500. He is so amazed, he says, "I suppose a blow job is $1,000?"

The hooker replies, "$1,500."

"I wouldn't pay that for a blow job!"

The hooker replies, "Step over here to the window, big boy. Do you see that casino just across the street? I own that casino outright. And I own it because I give a blow job that's worth every cent of $1,500."

The guy, basking in the afterglow of that terrific hand job, decides to put off the new car for another year or so, and says, "Sign me up."

Ten minutes later, he is sitting on the bed more amazed than before. He can scarcely believe it but he feels he truly got his money's worth. He decides to dip into the retirement savings for one glorious and unforgettable experience. He asks the hooker, "How much for some pussy?"

The hooker says, "Come over here to the window, I want to show you something. Do you see how the whole city of Las Vegas is laid out before us, all those beautiful lights, gambling palaces, and showplaces?"

"Damn!" the guy says in awe. "You own the whole city?"

"No," the hooker replies, "but I would if I had a pussy."

Two old guys walk into a brothel and ask the madam behind the counter for her two best whores. The madam thinks, I'm not giving these men my two best whores. So she asks someone to put two blow up dolls in two separate rooms. The men go in and do their thing.

They come out when they are done and one says to the other, "How was your whore?"

"Mine was the best I ever had. How about yours?"

"I think mine was a witch."

"Why is that?" he asked.

"Well, I got to nibbling on her nipple and she let out a loud fart and flew out the window!!"

Back in the 1800s, a farmer and his daughter head into the market to sell that year's crop so they can survive the winter. They sell everything and have plenty of money to make it through the winter. On the way back, the father notices a pack of robbers behind them. He breaks down because he knows that they are planning to take all of the money.

The daughter says, "Quick, Dad, give me the money!"

Moments later the robbers take everything they can. The father begins to cry and the daughter says, "It's OK, Dad, I have the money still."

He replies, "Where did you hide it?"

She says, "In my pussy."

He replies, "Damn, if we had brought your mother we could have saved the horse and cart, too."

One day when the teacher walked to the black board, she noticed someone had written the word "penis" in tiny letters. She turned around and scanned the class looking for the guilty face. Finding none, she quickly erased it, and began her class.

The next day she went into the room, and she saw, in larger letters, the word "penis" again on the black board. Again, she looked around in vain for the culprit, but found none, so she proceeded with the day's lesson. Every morning for about a week she went into the classroom and found the same disgusting word written on the board, and each day the word was larger than the day before.

Finally, one day she walked in expecting to be greeted by the same word on the board, but instead found the words: "The more you rub it, the bigger it gets!"

A blonde and a brunette walk into a bar. As they sit down, the brunette notices a guy checking out the blonde. So the brunette decides to go and talk to this guy. She walks up to him and says, "I see you've been checking out my friend. You know, the blonde sitting over there. She's pretty isn't she?"

The guy responds, "Oh, man, she's just gorgeous, absolutely beautiful."

The brunette says, "Well, for $50 I can arrange for you to smell her crotch."

The guy says, "Well, yes, of course!" He pulls out the money and hands it to her.

She takes it and breathes in his face.

Q. What did the egg say to the boiling water?
A. How am I suppose to get hard if I just got laid 10 minutes ago?

A young man had been dating his girlfriend for over a year, and so they decided to get married. His parents, family and friends helped him in every way. There was only one thing bothering him, very much indeed, and that one thing was his fiancée's younger sister. She was twenty years of age, wore tight miniskirts and low-cut blouses. She would regularly bend down when near him and he had many a pleasant view of her underwear. It had to be deliberate. She never did it when she was near anyone else. One day, little sister called and asked him to come over to check the wedding invitations. She was alone when he got there. She whispered to him that soon he was to be married, but she had feelings and desires for him that she couldn't overcome—and didn't really want to overcome. She told him that she wanted to make love to him just once before he got married and committed his life to her sister. He was in total shock and couldn't say a word.

She said, "I'm going upstairs to my bedroom, and if you want to go ahead with it just come up and get me."

He was stunned. He was frozen in shock as he watched her go up the stairs. When she reached the top she pulled down her panties and threw them down the stairs at him. He stood there for a moment, then turned and went straight to the front door. He opened the door and stepped out of the house. He walked straight towards his car. His future father-in-law was standing outside. With tears in his eyes he hugged him and said,

"We are very happy that you have passed our little test. We couldn't ask for a better man for our daughter. Welcome to the family."

The moral of this story is:

Always keep your condoms in your car.

Q. What do toilets, a clitoris, and an anniversary have in common?
A. Men miss them all.

In a mental institution, a nurse walks into a room and sees a patient acting like he's driving a car.

The nurse asks him, "Charlie, what are you doing?"

Charlie replies, "Driving to Chicago!"

The nurse wishes him a good trip and leaves the room.

The next day the nurse enters Charlie's room just as he stops driving his imaginary car and asks, "Well, Charlie, how are you doing?"

Charlie says, "I just got into Chicago."

"Great," replies the nurse.

The nurse leaves Charlie's room and goes across the hall into Bob's room, and finds Bob sitting on his bed, furiously masturbating.

Shocked, she asks, "Bob, what are you doing?"

Bob says, "I'm screwing Charlie's wife while he's in Chicago."

A man picks up a hooker and takes her back to his room. She strips off all her clothes and all he does is stare at her.

"What, honey, is this the first pussy you seen since you crawled out of one?"

"No, it's just the first one I've seen big enough to crawl back into!"

One night a man got drunk, walked home from the bar, passed out in bed right next to his wife and started dreaming. He dreamed that he went to heaven and was at the Pearly Gates and saw Saint Peter waiting there. He walked up and said, "Am I in heaven?"

Saint Peter replied, "Yes, you're in heaven."

The drunk man asked how he died and Saint Peter said, "Umm, hold on, wait a little while and I'll get your records." While he was waiting, the drunken man saw a blonde angel pass and asked if he could have sex with her.

Saint Peter said, "Yes, do it behind the cloud." So he spent 30 minutes fucking the blonde and then she left. Shortly afterward, a brunette angel walked past him and he asked if he could have sex with her.

Saint Peter said, "Yes." So once again the drunk went behind the cloud and spent 30 minutes having sex before the brunette angel left. The same thing happened a third time, only it was a redhead angel who had sex with the drunk man. After all that sex he had to shit so he asked Saint Peter,

"Can I use the bathroom?"

Saint Peter said, "Yes, go over the edge of the cloud."

So he went over to the edge of the cloud and did what he had to do and wiped himself with a piece of cloud. Then he heard his name being called many times and wondered if Saint Peter had found out why he died. To his horror he woke with a start and realized it was actually his wife who was screaming his name.

She said, "You can fuck me three times and you can shit the bed, but there's no way you're going to wipe your ass with my pillow!!!"

To whom this may concern:

I have a serious issue. Do you mind me asking you a favor? Here's my dilemma. I've been wanting this for a long time. I've been craving it for so long! I mean, the memories of it going in hard and coming out soft—it's driving me insane! My tongue wrapped around it, licking up the juices. My mouth waters due to the strong urges. I can't help moan at the thought of each bite, for the flavor is too great! I need it, can't you see? So can you please help me? Well, now that I've chimed my heart out, here's my question:

Can I have some gum?

A woman walks into a tattoo parlor and tells the artist that she wants a tattoo of Santa Claus on her inner right thigh and a Thanksgiving turkey on her inner left thigh.

The artist says, "Ma'am, that's kind of a strange request ... Might I ask why you want those particular tattoos there?"

"Well," she says, "my husband's always bitching that there's nothing good in the house to eat between Thanksgiving and Christmas, so I thought I would fix that!"

Q. What's the difference between sin and shame?
A. It is a sin to put it in, but it's a shame to pull it out.

A teenage girl comes home from school and asks her mother, "Is it true what Rita just told me? That babies come out of the same place where boys put their dicks?"

"Yes, dear," replies her mother, pleased that the subject has finally come up and she won't have to explain it to her daughter.

"But when a baby's actually being born," responded the teenager, "how does it get past your teeth?"

Q. How do you hide an elephant in a cherry tree?
A. Paint its balls red.

Q. How did Tarzan die?
A. Picking cherries.

Three generations of prostitutes are discussing current financial conditions of their industry. The youngest one says, "I can't believe I only get $20 for a blow job."

Her mother says, "Girl, when I was your age I could barely get $5 for a blow job."

Grandma says, "When I was your age, we would give blow jobs for free just to have something warm in our stomach."

A woman walks down a street one day and runs into a man.

The man says, "Your hair smells good today."

The woman then says, "Yeah, OK."

The next day on her way home she runs into the same guy, and again he says, "Your hair smells good today."

By this time the girl was getting freaked out, so she went to the police station and told the police that she wanted to report the man on the street for harassment.

The policeman says, "OK, but what has he done?"

The lady says, "Well, everyday I go the same way home and I run into the man and he says that my hair smells good."

"Madam, I don't see a problem with that. He is just being nice," the officer says.

The woman gets mad and says, "Well, it's harassment when he is only waist high."

Jim Morrison is in one corner of a hotel room with the rest of his band, and in another corner are John Lennon, Paul McCartney, George Harrison and Ringo Starr. All are naked.

Monica Lewinsky walks in, squats seductively in front of Jim Morrison and begins to play the pink oboe. She gives him the presidential treatment, then moves on to his guitarist, drummer and keyboard player.

When she's finished, she licks her lips and wanders over to John Lennon and begins to do the same to him.

At that moment, there's a huge crash and Michael Caine smashes through a wall in a Mini Cooper. He jumps out, grabs her by the scruff of the neck and shouts . . . .

"Oi, you're only supposed to blow the Doors off!"

Q. What's the speed limit of sex?
A. 68, because at 69 you have to turn around.

One morning in December, a happily married couple rises from their night's rest. The husband rolls over to his beautiful wife and asks how her night was.

She replies, "It was great! I had the best dream in the world."

Intrigued, the husband urges her to go on.

"Well, I had a dream that I had the most beautifully decorated Christmas tree ever! It was covered with cocks: big ones, long ones, hard ones, smooth ones, every kind of dick you could imagine."

The husband, now gloating a little asks, "Was mine at the top for the shining star?"

"No, yours was at the bottom with the broken, wrinkly, tiny ones. How was your night, honey?"

Now pissed off, he replies, "Well, my dream was even better than yours! I dreamed that we had a Christmas tree decorated with the most beautiful vaginas ever: tight ones, pink ones, smooth ones, every kind of vagina."

"Was mine at the top for your shining star?"

Then the husband replies, "No, yours was holding up the fucking tree!"

A priest was getting ready to hear confessions one day when he got a terrible attack of diarrhea, so he asked the altar boy to take over for him.

"But I don't know how to hear confessions," said the altar boy.

"It's easy," said the priest. "You've seen me do it many times. Nobody will know the difference."

So the altar boy was in the confession booth when a man came in and sat down on the other side.

"Father, I don't know what to do," the man said. "Last night my wife and I were in bed. She was sleeping and I rolled her over and fucked her in the ass. I feel bad about it, but I don't know how to make it up to her."

"That's easy," said the altar boy. "Just give her milk and cookies like the priest gives me."

One day a priest went out to his farm to check his hens, but to his surprise there was no rooster! During mass he asked, "Has anyone here seen a cock?"

All the women stood up.

He then said, "I mean, has anyone got a cock?"

All the men stood up.

He said, "No, no, I mean has anyone seen a cock that does not belong to them?"

Half the women stood up.

"No, no, no, I mean has anyone seen my cock?"

All the choir boys stood up!

Little Johnny is in the middle of class and stands up and says, "I have to piss."

The teacher says, "Now, Johnny, the proper word is 'urinate' and while you're in the bathroom I want you to think of a sentence that has the word 'urinate' in it."

So Johnny goes, does his thing and comes back and the teacher asks, "Well, Johnny, did you think of a sentence?"

He says, "Yes...urinate, and if you had bigger tits you'd be a ten."

Q. Why is air a lot like sex?

A. Because it's no big deal unless you're not getting any.

Have you heard about the kid that was born last week? He was born with no eyelids. Apparently the doctors took the foreskin off his dick and made him eyelids. Now he's cockeyed.

One day Little Red Riding Hood was going to see her grandmother, so she put some provisions into a basket to take with her.

Just as she was going to leave, her mother turned to her and said, "Little Red Riding Hood, you had better look out for that Big Bad Wolf

THE GINORMOUS BOOK OF DIRTY JOKES

because he'll pull up your little red skirt, pull down your little red panties and fuck your little red socks off."

"Oh dear," said Little Red Riding Hood, as she went on her way.

About two hours later, she got to her grandmother's house and she was so pleased to see Little Red Riding Hood. Her grandmother invited her in and made some tea and they sat down and talked for hours. The grandmother suddenly noticed that it was 10 o'clock at night and said, "Oh dear, Little Red Riding Hood, it's getting late and you should be going."

So Little Red Riding Hood got ready and was just about to leave when grandma turned to her and said, "Little Red Riding Hood, you best beware of the Big Bad Wolf because he'll pull up your little red skirt, pull down your little red panties and fuck your little red socks off."

"Oh dear," said Little Red Riding Hood, as she set off for home. She got about half way through the woods when, all of a sudden, the Big Bad Wolf popped out from behind a bush. So Little Red Riding Hood pulled up her little red skirt, pulled down her little red panties and said to the big bad wolf, "Eat me like the story says!"

A woman and a man meet at a rapid dating service. The man sits down and says, "I've only got three questions."

"OK," replies the woman.

"Do you like to clean?" he asks.

"I love cleaning," she replies.

"Great. Do you like to cook for other people?"

"I love to cook," she says.

"Fantastic," says the man. "OK, last question. Do you like sex?"

"I like it infrequently," she replies.

The man then asks, "Is that one word or two?"

A man walks into a doctor's office and says, "Doctor, I think I have a slight discharge."

The female doctor says, "Alright, pull your pants down and stand over there."

The man pulls his pants down, and the doctor grabs his penis and starts massaging it gently. The man's head starts wobbling and he's got a big smile on his face.

After five minutes of this, the doctor says, "There's no discharge here."

The man replies, "I know, it's in my ear."

A rich, lonely widow decided that she needed another man in her life so she placed an ad, which read something like this:

Rich widow looking for man to share life and fortune.

Needs to have these qualifications:

1) Won't beat me up
2) Won't run away
3) Has to be great in bed

For several months, her phone rang off the hook; her doorbell was ringing constantly; she received tons of mail, etc., all to no avail. None seemed to match her qualifications.

Then one day the doorbell rang yet again. She opened the door to find a man with no arms and no legs lying on the doorstep.

Perplexed, she asked, "Who are you? And what do you want?"

"Hi," he said. "Your search is over, for I am the man of your dreams. I've got no arms so I can't beat you up and no legs so I can't run away."

"Well, then," she said, "what makes you think that you're so great in bed?"

To which he replied, "Well, I rang the doorbell, didn't I?"

Q. What is the first thing to come out of a penis when you kiss it?
A. The wrinkles.

One day, three sisters were at home and their mom said their boyfriends could stay the night.

That night, the mom was walking through the hallway and heard crying from the first daughter's room. Then, she heard laughter coming from the second daughter's room. However, there was no sound at all from the third daughter's room.

The next day after their boyfriends had left, the mother asked the first daughter why she was crying.

"Because it hurts the first time," she replied.

The mother asked the second daughter why she was laughing.

"Because it tickled the first time."

Then the mother asked the third daughter what she was doing as there was no sound from her room.

The daughter answered, "But, Mom, you always taught me not to talk with my mouth full!"

A man walks into a bordello in New Orleans and says to the madam of the house, "I would like to see Madelyn."

The madam says, "Madelyn is our most expensive woman at a $1,000 a night."

The guy says, "No problem!" and hands over $1,000 in cash. So the madam shows him up to Madelyn's room.

The next night, the man shows up and requests Madelyn again, throws down $1,000, and again he spends the night with the expensive hooker.

In the morning, Madelyn tries to make small talk and asks him where he's from.

The guy says, "I'm from Philadelphia."

Madelyn jumps up in surprise and says, "Really? Me too!!"

The guy says, "Yeah, I know. Your father just passed away and your brother wanted me to give you $2,000."

Q. Did you hear about the constipated mathematician?
A. He worked it out with a pencil.

A man feeling rather down in the dumps after splitting up with his girlfriend goes and sees his buddy.

His buddy has sympathy for him and says, "You can borrow my girlfriend, she's very frisky."

The other man replies, "Wow. Really?!"

Then his buddy says, "Oh, by the way, she can sing while giving a blow job but you have to turn out the light."

Later that night he turns out the light and she starts giving him a blow job and he hears singing in a wonderful voice.

The next day he asks his buddy, "How the hell does she do that?"

His buddy replies, "You can have her again tonight, but while she's giving you a blow job turn on the light."

That night he turns out the light and she starts giving him a blow job and the singing starts, so the guy reaches over and switches the lamp on. He then notices that on the bedside table next to the lamp is a GLASS EYE.

A man walks into a whorehouse and asks the madam, "Pardon me, madam, are you a union whorehouse?"

She replies, "No, we're not."

He says, "Then you can't have my business because I only shop at union businesses."

He walks into a second whorehouse and asks the madam, "Pardon me, madam, are you a union whorehouse?"

She replies, "No, we're not."

He says, "Then you can't have my business because I only shop at union businesses."

He then walks into a third whorehouse and asks the madam, "Pardon me, madam, are you a union whorehouse?"

She replies, "Why, yes, we are."

He says, "Then you have my business because I only shop at union businesses, and I'll take that pretty blonde in the corner."

The madam replies, "Oh, I'm sorry you can't have her. You have to take the fat, ugly one because she has seniority."

One day a little girl and a little boy were at the park with their pants pulled down. The little girl asked the little boy, "What is that?"

And the little boy said, "I don't know."

Then the little boy asked the little girl the same thing and she said she didn't know.

So that night the little girl asked her mom and her mom said, "That's your garage, and you must not let any big trucks go in."

Meanwhile, at the little boy's house, the little boy asked his dad what 'it' was and his dad said, "That's your big truck and you must not park it in any garage."

The next day the boy and the girl pulled their pants down again, but this time the girl went home with blood on her hands. Her mom screamed and asked why she had blood on her hands.

The girl said, "The boy tried to put his big truck in my garage so I pulled his two back tires off."

This guy walks into the bar and sees a gorgeous blonde sitting on a bar stool all alone. So the guy sits down next to her and pulls a small box from his pocket. He opens it and there's a frog inside.

The blonde says, "He's cute, but does he do tricks?"

The guy says, "Yes, he licks pussy."

So after talking with her for several minutes, he convinces her to come with him to his apartment.

They get there and she takes all of her clothes off, gets into the bed and spreads her legs. The guy sets the frog right between her legs and it just sits there not moving at all.

The blonde says, "Well? What's up?"

The frog still does not move.

So the guy leans over to the frog and says, "All right, I'm only going to show you how to do this one more time!"

Q. What does a female snail say during sex?

A. Faster, faster, faster!

Two old retirees are taking a trip down memory lane and have gone on vacation back to the place where they first met.

While sitting at a café the little old man says, "Remember the first time I met you over fifty years ago? We left this café, went around the corner behind the factory and I gave you one from behind."

"Why, yes, I remember it well, dear," replies the little old lady with a grin.

"Well, for old time's sake, let's go there again and I'll give you one from behind."

The two retirees pay their bill and leave the café. A young man sitting next to them has overheard the conversation and smiles to himself, thinking it would be quite amusing to see two old retirees going at it. He gets up and follows them. Sure enough, he sees the two retirees near the factory. The little old lady pulls off her panties and lifts up her dress. The old man pulls down his pants and grabs the lady's hips and the little old lady then reaches for the fence. Well, what follows is forty minutes of the most athletic sex the man has ever seen. The little old man is banging away at the little old woman at a pace that can only be described as phenomenal. Limbs are flying everywhere, the movement is a blur, and they do not stop for a single second. Finally, they collapse and don't move for an hour.

The man is stunned. Never in his life has he ever seen anything that equates to this, not in the movies, not from his friends, not from his own experiences.

Reflecting on what he has just seen, he says to himself, "I have to know his secret. If only I could fuck like that now, let alone in fifty years time!"

The two old retirees have by this time recovered and dressed themselves. Gathering the courage he approaches the older man.

He says, "Sir, in all my life I have never seen anybody screw like that, particularly at your age. What's your secret? Could you screw like that fifty years ago?"

The retiree replies, "Son, fifty years ago that fucking fence wasn't electric."

Q. What is foreplay for a blonde?
A. Thirty minutes of begging.

A social misfit walks into his local bar with a big grin on his face.

"What are you so happy about?" asks the bartender.

"Well, I'll tell you," replies the ugly guy. "You know I live by the railway. Well, on my way home last night I noticed a young woman tied to the tracks, like in the movies.

I, of course, went and cut her free and took her back to my place. Anyway, to cut a long story short, I scored big time! We made love all night, all over the house. We did everything, me on top, sometimes her on top!"

"Fantastic," exclaimed the bartender. "You lucky dog. Was she pretty?"

"I don't know. I never found her head."

One morning while making breakfast, a husband walked up to his wife, pinched her butt and said, "If you firmed this up, we could get rid of your control top pantyhose."

While this was on the edge of intolerable, she kept silent.

The next morning, the man woke his wife with a pinch on each of her breasts and said, "You know, if you firmed these up, we could get rid of your bra."

This was beyond a silent response, so she rolled over and grabbed him by his privates.

With a death grip in place, she said, "You know, if you firmed this up, we could get rid of the gardener, the postman, the pool man, and your brother!"

There was a man who enjoyed his sex life a lot, but sometimes had problems getting it up, so he went to see his doctor. His doctor said that to help it stay up he needed to masturbate a couple of hours before sex.

The man agreed but couldn't think of any good places to do this. He thought of the bathroom, but realized he may be heard. He thought of his office, but someone may walk in.

As he was driving home he thought of the perfect place. He pulled his car onto the side of the road, got out and lay down underneath the car. Pleased with the comfort and discretion, he shut his eyes and started to masturbate picturing his wife.

After about ten minutes, a policeman came and asked him what he was doing. His eyes still closed and masturbating he replied, "Erm, just checking everything's OK."

"Yeah, OK. Well while you're down there, you might want to check the brakes because your car rolled down the hill five minutes ago!"

There were two grannies sitting at bingo when one looked at the other and said, "Did you come on the bus?"

The other answered, "Well, yes I did actually, but I didn't think anyone heard me!"

A girl named Jane is in line to go to heaven and while she's at the Pearly Gates talking to St. Peter, she hears a drill and then a scream.

She asks, "What's that?"

St. Peter replies, "Oh, that's just an angel getting her halo fitted."

The woman thinks about it and then starts to talk to him again. Then she hears another scream and asks, "What's that?"

St. Peter smiles and says, "That's just an angel getting her wings fitted."

She says, "Fuck this, I'm going to Hell!"

St. Peter says, "But they rape you and sodomize you there."

She just smiles and says, "At least I have the holes for that."

Q. What do you call a virgin on a waterbed?

A. A cherry float.

A man goes to a brothel. He selects a girl, pays her $200 up front, and gets undressed. She's about to take off her sheer blue negligee when the fire alarm rings!

She runs out of the room with his $200 still in her hand. He quickly grabs his clothes and runs out after her. He's searching the building, but the smoke gets too heavy, so he runs outside looking for her.

By this time the firemen are there. He sees one of them and asks, "Did you see a beautiful blonde in a sheer blue negligee with $200 in her hand?"

The fireman says, "No!"

The man then says, "Well if you see her, screw her. It's paid for."

Early one summer, a six-year-old Arkansas boy and his family decided to take a trip to Sweden. During this trip, the six-year-old Arkansas boy stumbled upon a nudist camp. Noticing the adult men were different in appearance, the six-year-old wandered up to the most endowed male at the camp. "What is that?" the six-year-old asked.

"Dis is a penis," the Swedish man replied, "and da perfect penis, if I might add!!"

Upon arriving back in Arkansas, the six-year-old continued school with the second grade, and, for his first "show and tell," the six-year-old Arkansan removed his penis from his pants and said, "While in Sweden this summer, I learned that this is a penis...and it would be a perfect penis...if it were only 4 inches shorter!!"

A man walks in to the pharmacy and says "I need some birth control pills for my 12-year-old daughter."

The man behind the counter replies "Your 12-year-old daughter is already having active sex?!"

The dad says, "No, she just lies there like her mother!"

Some people are sitting in a bar when one guy says, "My name is Larry, and I am a SNAG."

A second guy says, "What's that?"

The first guy says, "That means I am a Single, New Age Guy."

Another one says, "My name is Gary, and I am a DINK."

A girl asks, "What's that?"

He says, "That means I am a Double Income, No Kids."

A lady says, "That's nice. My name is Gertrude, and I am a WIFE."

Larry says, "A WIFE? What's a WIFE?"

She says, "That means, Wash, Iron, Fuck, Etc."

A man had just bought a computer but he didn't know how to set it up so he got this girl to do it for him. When she asked him what his password was going to be, he said (trying to be funny), "Penis."

She didn't laugh at him, but she laughed at the response that came up: Password rejected—not long enough.

What do you call the extra skin around a pussy?
A woman.

A couple is working in the garden and the wife goes to take a shower. Her husband is looking for a rake and can't find it. He yells up to his wife, but she motions to him from the window that she can't hear.

So he points to his eye, hits his knee, and then makes raking motions. ("I need the rake.")

She replies by pointing to her eye, grabbing her left breast, slapping her butt, then rubbing her crotch.

The man is confused and runs upstairs.

"What? What was that?"

"Eye, left tit, behind, the bush."

Having therapy is very much like making love to a beautiful woman. You get on the couch, string 'em along with some half lies and evasions, probe some deep dark holes, and then hand over all your money.

A guy walks into the living room followed by a sheep and says, "This is the pig I've been fucking."

His wife, who is sitting on the sofa, says, "That's not a pig, stupid, it's a sheep."

The guy turns to his wife and says, "Shut up, bitch, I was talking to the sheep."

A 54-year-old accountant leaves a letter for his wife one Friday evening that reads:

"Dear Wife, I am 54 and by the time you receive this letter I will be at the Grand Hotel with my beautiful and sexy 18-year-old secretary."

When he arrives at the hotel there's a letter waiting for him that reads as follows:

"Dear Husband, I too am 54 and by the time you receive this letter I will be at the Breakwater Hotel with my handsome and virile 18-year-old boy toy. You being an accountant will appreciate that 18 goes into 54 many more times than 54 goes into 18."

A bright, young graduate joined the Internal Revenue Service. Anxious for his first investigation he was a bit dismayed when he was assigned to audit a Rabbi.

Looking over the books and taxes was pretty straightforward and the Rabbi was clearly very frugal, so he thought he'd make his day interesting by having a little fun with the Rabbi.

"Rabbi," he said, "I noticed that you buy a lot of candles."

"Yes," answered the Rabbi.

"Well, Rabbi, what do you do with the candle drippings?" he asked.

"A good question," noted the Rabbi. "We actually save them up, and when we have enough we send them back to the candle maker. And every now and then, they send us a free box of candles."

"Oh," replied the auditor somewhat disappointed that his unusual question actually had a practical answer.

So he thought he'd go on, in the traditional obnoxious way...

"Rabbi, what about all these cookie purchases? What do you do with the crumbs from the cookies?"

"Ah, yes," replied the Rabbi calmly, "we actually collect up all the crumbs from the cookies and when we have enough we send them in a box back to the manufacturer. Every now and then, they send a box of cookies."

"Oh," replied the auditor, thinking hard how to fluster the Rabbi.

"Well, Rabbi," he went on, "what do you do with all the foreskins from the circumcisions?"

"Yes, here too, we do not waste," answered the Rabbi. "What we do is save up all the foreskins and when we have enough we actually send them to the IRS."

"The IRS?" asked the auditor in disbelief.

"Ahh, yes," replied the Rabbi, "the IRS. And about once a year they send us a little prick like you."

A blonde girl is crossing the road when she gets hit by a car. As she is lying on the ground, the driver rushes out of the car to see if she is alright.

"I'm so sorry! I just didn't see you. Are you OK?" he blurts out.

"Everyfink is justa blur; I can't see a fing," she says tearfully.

Concerned, the man leans over the woman to test her eyesight. He asks, "How many fingers have I got up?"

"Ah, fuck!" she screams. "Don't tell me I'm paralyzed from the waist down, too!!!"

At a news conference a journalist said to a politician, "Your assistant said publicly that you have a small penis. Would you please comment on this?"

"The truth is," he replied, "my assistant has a big mouth."

A girl goes into the doctor's office for a checkup. As she takes off her blouse, he notices a red "H" on her chest. "How did you get that mark on your chest?" asks the doctor.

"Oh, my boyfriend went to Harvard and he's so proud of it that he never takes off his Harvard sweatshirt, even when we make love," she replies.

A couple of days later, another girl comes in for a checkup. As she takes off her blouse, the doctor notices a blue "Y" on her chest. "How did you get that mark on your chest?" asks the doctor.

"Oh, my boyfriend went to Yale and he's so proud of it that he never takes off his Yale sweatshirt, even when we make love," she replies.

A few days after, a third girl comes in for a checkup. As she takes off her blouse, the doctor notices a green "M" on her chest. "Do you have a boyfriend at Michigan?" asks the doctor.

"No, but I have a girlfriend at Wisconsin. Why do you ask?"

A husband and wife visit a marriage counselor. First, the wife speaks to the counselor alone. The counselor asks her, "You say you've been married 20 years. So what seems to be the problem?"

The wife replies, "It's my husband. He's driving me crazy! I'm going to leave him if he continues!"

"How does he drive you crazy?"

"For 20 years," she says, "he's been doing these stupid things. First, whenever we go out, he's always looking at the floor and refuses to go near anyone. It's very embarrassing."

The marriage counselor is amused, "Anything else?"

"He keeps picking his nose all the time! Even in public!"

"Hmm, anything else?"

The wife hesitates, "Whenever we're making love, he NEVER lets me be on top! Once in a while, I'd like to be in control!"

"Ah," says the counselor, "I think I'll talk to your husband now."

So the wife goes out of the room and the husband says to the counselor, "For years I've been loving and considerate and I've always given her what she wants! What could be the problem?"

The counselor explains, "She says you've got these habits that are driving her crazy. First, you're always acting strange in public—looking at the floor and never going near anyone else."

The husband looks concerned, "Oh, you don't understand! It's one of the few things my father told me to do on his deathbed and I swore I'd obey everything he said."

"What did he say?"

"He said that I should never step on anyone's toes!"

The counselor looks amused, "Actually, that means that you should not do anything that would cause anyone else to get angry."

The husband looks sheepish, "Oh. Okay."

The counselor continues, "And you keep picking your nose in public."

"Well, it's another thing my father specifically commanded me to do! He told me to always keep my nose clean."

The counselor smiles. "That just means you should stay out of trouble. And," he continued, "finally, she says that you never allow her to be on top during your lovemaking."

"This," says the husband, "is the last thing my father commanded me to do on his deathbed, and it's the most important thing."

"What did he say?"

The husband replies, "With his dying breath, he said, 'Don't screw up.'"

Q. What do bungee jumping and prostitutes have in common?

A. They both cost a hundred bucks and if the rubber breaks you're screwed.

Q. What's the best thing about a blow job?

A. Ten minutes of silence!

A man's walking home late at night when he sees a woman in the shadows.

"Twenty bucks," she says.

He's never been with a prostitute before, but he decides what the hell. They're going at it for a minute when all of a sudden a light flashes on them—it's a policeman.

"What's going on here, people?" asks the officer.

"I'm making love to my wife," the man answers indignantly.

"Oh, I'm sorry," says the cop, "I didn't know."

"Well," said the man, "to tell the truth neither did I until you shined that light on her face."

It was getting a little crowded in heaven, so God decided to change the admittance policy. The new law was that, in order to get into heaven, you had to have had a really bad day the day you died.

So the next day the first person came to the gates of heaven. The angel at the gate promptly asked the man to tell him about the day he died.

"Well, for some time now, I thought my wife was having an affair and that each day on her lunch hour she'd bring her lover home to our 25th floor apartment and have sex with him. So today I was going to come home too, and catch them. Well, I got there and busted in, and immediately began searching for this guy. My wife was half-naked and yelling at me as I searched the entire apartment. But, damn it, I couldn't find him! Just when I was about to give up, I happened to glance out onto the balcony and noticed that there was a man hanging off the edge by his fingertips! The nerve of that guy to think he could hide from me! Well, I ran out there and promptly stomped on his fingers until he fell to the ground. But, wouldn't you know it, he landed in some bushes that broke his fall, and he didn't die. This got me even more enraged so I went back inside to get the first thing I could get my hands on to throw at him, which turned out to be the refrigerator. I unplugged it, pushed it out onto the balcony and heaved it over the side. It plummeted 25 stories and crushed him!

The excitement of the moment was so great that I had a heart attack and died almost instantly."

The angel sat back and thought for a moment. Technically, the guy DID have a bad day. So he announced, "OK, sir, welcome to the kingdom of heaven," and let him in. A few seconds later the next guy came up. "OK, here's the rule. Before I can let you in, I need to hear about the day you died."

"Sure thing," the next man replied. "But you're not going to believe this. I was out on the balcony of my 26th floor apartment doing my daily exercises when I got a little carried away and accidentally fell over the side! Luckily I was able to catch myself by my fingertips on the balcony directly beneath mine, when, all of a sudden, this crazy man came running out of his apartment and started cussing and stomping on my fingers! Well, of course I fell. I hit some trees and bushes on the way down which broke my fall so I didn't die right away. As I lay there face up on the ground, unable to move and in excruciating pain, I saw the man push his refrigerator, of all things, over the ledge and it fell directly on top of me and killed me!"

The angel is quietly laughing to himself as the man finishes his story. "Very well," he announces. "Welcome to the kingdom of heaven," and lets the man enter.

A few seconds later a third man comes up to the gate. "Tell me about the day you died," says the angel.

"OK, picture this," says the man. "I'm naked inside a refrigerator..."

Q. Why do women pierce their belly button?
A. So they have a place to hang their air freshener.

This boy takes his girlfriend back to her house after being out together, and when they reach the front door he leans with one hand on the wall and says to her, "Sweetie, why don't you give me a blow job?"

"What? You're crazy!!!"

"Don't worry, it will be quick. No problem."

"No!! Someone may see. A relative, a neighbor..."

"At this time of night no one will show up."

"I've already said no, and I mean NO!"

"Honey, it's just a small blow job...I know you like it too."

"NO!!! I've said NO!!!"

"Baby...don't be like that."

At this moment the younger sister shows up at the door in nightgown with her hair all a mess, rubbing her eyes and says,

"Dad says either you blow him, I blow him, or he'll come down and blow the guy himself, but for God's sake tell your boyfriend to take his hand off the intercom."

Q. What's the difference between a lesbian and a Ritz cracker?

A. One's a snack cracker, and the other's a crack snacker!

The Pope had become very ill and was taken to many doctors, all of whom could not figure out how to cure him. Finally, he was brought to an old physician. After about an hour's examination he came out and told the cardinals that he had some good news and some bad news. The bad news was that the Pope had a rare disorder of the testicles. The good news was that all the Pope had to do to be cured was have sex.

Well, this was not good news to the cardinals, who argued about it at length. Finally, they went to the Pope with the doctor and explained the situation. After some thought, the Pope stated, "I agree, but under four conditions."

The cardinals were amazed and there arose quite an uproar. Over the noise a single voice asked, "And what are the four conditions?"

The room stilled. There was a long pause.

The Pope replied, "First, the girl must be blind, so that she cannot see who she is having sex with.

Second, she must be deaf, so that she cannot hear who she is having sex with.

And third, she must be dumb so that if somehow she figures out who she is having sex with, she can tell no one."

After another long pause a voice arose and asked, "And the fourth condition?"

The Pope replied, "Big tits."

A businessman met a beautiful girl and asked her to spend the night with him for $500. And she did. Before he left in the morning he told her that he did not have any cash with him, but that he would have his secretary write a check and mail it to her, calling the payment "RENT FOR APARTMENT." On the way to the office, he regretted what he had done, realizing that the whole event was not worth the price. So he had his secretary send a check for $250 and enclosed a note:

Dear Madam,

Enclosed find a check in the amount of $250 for rent of your apartment. I am not sending the amount agreed upon because when I rented the apartment I was under the impression that: (1) It had never been occupied before; (2) That there was plenty of heat; (3) That it was small enough to make me cosy and at home. Last night, however, I found out that it had been previously occupied, that there wasn't any heat, and that it was entirely too large.

Upon receipt of the note, the girl immediately returned the check for $250 with the following note:

Dear Sir,

First of all, I can not understand how you expect a beautiful apartment to remain unoccupied indefinitely. As for the heat, there is plenty of warmth if you know how to turn it on. Regarding the space, the apartment is indeed of regular size, but if you don't have enough furniture to fill it, please don't blame the landlord.

Bill worked in a pickle factory. He had been employed there for a number of years when he came home one day to confess to his wife that he had a tremendous urge to stick his penis into the pickle slicer.

His wife suggested that he should see a sex therapist to talk about it, but Bill indicated that he'd be too embarrassed. He vowed to overcome the compulsion on his own.

One day a few weeks later, Bill came home absolutely ashen. His wife could see at once that something was seriously wrong. "What's wrong, Bill?" she asked.

"Do you remember that I told you how I had this tremendous urge to put my penis into the pickle slicer?"

"Oh, Bill, you didn't."

"Yes, I did."

"My God, Bill, what happened?"

"I got fired."

"No, Bill. I mean, what happened with the pickle slicer?"

"Oh...she got fired too."

Q. How are a lawyer and a prostitute different?

A. The prostitute stops fucking you after you're dead.

It's Saturday morning. Bob's just about to set off on a round of golf when he realizes he forgot to tell his wife that the guy who fixes the washing machine is coming around at noon. So Bob heads back to the clubhouse and calls home.

"Hello?" says a little girl's voice.

"Hi, honey, it's Daddy," says Bob. "Is mommy near the phone?"

"No, Daddy. She's upstairs in the bedroom with Uncle Frank."

After a brief pause, Bob says, "But you haven't got an Uncle Frank, honey!"

"Yes I do, and he's upstairs in the bedroom with mommy!"

"Okay, then, here's what I want you do. Put down the phone, run upstairs and knock on the bedroom door and shout in to Mommy and Uncle Frank that my car's just pulled up outside the house."

"Okay, Daddy!"

A few minutes later, the little girl comes back to the phone. "Well, I did what you said, Daddy."

"And what happened?"

"Well, mommy jumped out of bed with no clothes on and ran around screaming. Then she tripped over the rug and fell through the upstairs window and now she's dead."

"Oh my god...and what about Uncle Frank?"

"He leapt out of bed with no clothes on, too, and he was so scared he jumped out of the back window into the swimming pool, but he must have forgotten that last week you took out all the water to clean it, so he hit the bottom of the swimming pool and now he's dead as well."

There is a long pause and then Bob says, "Swimming pool? Is this 554-7039?"

After the annual office Christmas party, John woke up with a pounding headache, cottonmouthed, and utterly unable to recall the events of the preceding evening. After a trip to the bathroom he was able to make his way downstairs, where his wife put some coffee in front of him.

"Louise," he moaned, "tell me what went on last night. Was it as bad as I think?"

"Even worse," she assured him in her most scornful tone. "You made a complete ass of yourself, succeeded in antagonizing the entire board of directors, and insulted the chairman of the company to his face."

"He's an arrogant, self-important prick. Piss on him!" said John.

"You did. All over his suit," Louise informed him. "And he fired you."

"Well, screw him," said John.

"I did. You're back at work on Monday."

A Pacific cruise ship sinks with only three survivors: David, Darren and Daisy.

They swim to a small island and live there for a couple of years doing what comes naturally.

Eventually Daisy feels so bad about having sex with both David and Darren that she kills herself. It's sad for David and Darren but they get over it and again nature takes it's course.

After year's time they feel really bad about what they are doing...

...so they bury her.

One night a guy goes to get a room in a hotel. "Hello, I want a single room for the night please."

"Fine, sir, here's one of our best rooms. Room 13," says the concierge and hands him the key.

The guy goes upstairs, takes a shower and gets straight into bed. At about 2 o'clock in the morning, two gorgeous naked women come in and slide under the covers. When he realizes what is going on, he starts screwing both of them. He can't believe what's happening. Next morning, still surprised by last night's events, he goes downstairs to settle the bill.

"How was your room sir?" asks the receptionist.

"Excellent, I will come back again. What do I owe you?" asks the man.

"Well…actually, sir, we are doing a promotional offer. Not only do you not have to pay but we give you $10 as a welcome gesture," says the receptionist.

"What?" says the guy, very surprised indeed. "That's amazing." He takes the ten-dollar bill and wanders off, debating whether his buddies will believe him or not. Needless to say, after a few days he's told all his friends and neighbors about room 13 and the amazing night of passion.

The next week one of his buddies goes to check out the room. "Room 13 please."

"Certainly, sir, here's your key."

After he gets in bed, at the same time, 2 o'clock, three girls this time, extremely horny, get in bed and screw his brains out. The next morning, not only does he not have to pay, but he too gets $10.

After a month, everyone knows this hotel and especially room 13. Everyone that stays in room 13 gets the same treatment: a good screw and a ten bucks.

After a few weeks, the story reaches an archbishop. The archbishop decides to check the story out for himself. He visits the hotel and asks for room 13. He gets the keys and goes upstairs. After a couple of drinks he gets in bed waiting patiently for the naked girls to appear. Indeed at about 2 o'clock in the morning two naked ladies come to bed. They are as horny and wild as all the stories the archbishop has heard. The archbishop gets his pecker out and screws the both of them all night long. This is the night of his life.

Next morning he goes to reception and when he asks how much the bill is, the receptionist says, "Nothing to pay, sir. Actually, we are doing an introductory offer. Here's $50 as a welcome gesture."

Curious, the archbishop asks the receptionist,

"Well, that's strange. Everyone else who comes here gets $10. Why do I get $50?"

"Well, sir," says the receptionist. "This is the first time we've filmed a porn movie with an archbishop in it!"

An elderly couple, a middle-aged couple and a young newly-wed couple wanted to join a church. The priest said, "We have special requirements for new parishioners. You must abstain from having sex for two weeks."

The couples agreed and came back at the end of two weeks.

The pastor went to the elderly couple and asked, "Were you able to abstain from sex for the two weeks?"

The old man replied, "No problem at all, Priest."

"Congratulations! Welcome to the church!" said the priest.

The priest went to the middle-aged couple and asked, "Well, were you able to abstain from sex for the two weeks?"

The middle-aged man replied, "The first week was not too bad. The second week I had to sleep on the couch for a couple of nights but, yes, we made it."

"Congratulations! Welcome to the church," said the priest.

The priest then went to the newlywed couple and asked, "Well, were you able to abstain from sex for two weeks?"

"No Pastor, we were not able to go without sex for the two weeks," the young man replied sadly.

"What happened?" inquired the priest.

"My wife was reaching for a can of corn on the top shelf and dropped it," said the young man. "When she bent over to pick it up, I was overcome with lust and took advantage of her right there."

"You understand, of course, this means you will not be welcome in our church," stated the priest.

"We know," said the young man. "We're not welcome at the supermarket anymore either."

This farmer has about 200 hens, but no rooster, and he wants chicks. So, he goes down the road to the next farmer and asks if he has a rooster. The other farmer says, "Yeah, I've got this great rooster named Randy. He'll service every chicken you've got. No problem."

Well, Randy the rooster is a lot of money, but the farmer decides he'll be worth it. So, he buys Randy. The farmer takes Randy home and sets him down in the farmyard, giving the rooster a pep talk.

"Randy, I want you to pace yourself now. You've got a lot of chickens to service here and you cost me a lot of money and I'll need you to do a good job. So, take your time and have some fun," the farmer says with a chuckle.

Randy seems to understand, so the farmer points towards the hen house and Randy takes off like a shot—WHAM—he nails every hen in there THREE or FOUR times, and the farmer is just shocked. Randy runs out of the hen house and sees a flock of geese down by the lake—WHAM—he gets all the geese. Randy's up in the pigpen. He's in with the cows. Randy is jumping on every animal the farmer owns.

The farmer is distraught, worried that his expensive rooster won't even last the day. Sure enough, the farmer goes to bed and wakes up the next day to find Randy dead as a dodo in the middle of the yard. Buzzards are circling overhead.

The farmer, saddened by the loss of such a colorful animal, shakes his head and says, "Oh, Randy, I told you to pace yourself. I tried to get you to slow down. Now look what you've done to yourself."

Randy opens one eye, nods towards the sky and says, "Shhh. They're getting closer..."

Q. What's the difference between oral sex and anal sex?
A. Oral sex makes your day; anal sex makes your hole weak.

Jack is one horny guy. He reaches into his pocket and pulls out a $10 bill. He walks down the street to the local brothel and knocks on the door. The madam opens the door and invites Jack in.

"I'm really horny but I only have a $10 bill. What can you do for me?" Jack asks the madam.

She looks over this fellow and tells him, "Don't worry, we can take care of you. No problem."

She leads Jack into a room, and there is a chicken in the corner. Jack thinks about this a second and figures it can't be that bad. He gives the madam the $10 note, and she closes the door behind her.

Jack undresses and has the time of his life. When he's done, he can't remember when he has had such a pleasurable experience.

One week later, and horny again, Jack has saved up $20. Being a satisfied customer he goes back to the same madam and asks what she can do for him for $20.

"Well, for $20 we have a special show," the madam replies.

She leads him into a different room where there are several other people sitting on benches.

"Sit back and enjoy the show, Jack," the madam tells him.

Jack gives the money to the madam and takes a seat. Soon after, the lights dim and the blinds open revealing another room on the other side of a two way mirror where two women begin to undress each other.

Jack is very impressed. Clearly these women are unaware anyone is watching as they begin to make love to each other passionately.

Apparently there is nothing they won't do to each other. Jack once again feels like he is getting his money's worth.

He turns to the person beside him and says, "This is a pretty good show for twenty bucks, eh?!"

The guy turns to Jack and says, "This is nothing...last week we saw a man screw a chicken."

A lady called her gynecologist and asked for an "emergency" appointment. The receptionist said to come right in. She rushed to the office, and was ushered right into an examination room. The doctor came in and asked about her problem.

She was very shy about her emergency problem, and asked the gynecologist to please examine her vagina.

So the doctor started to examine her. He stuck up his head after completing his examination. "I'm sorry, Miss," he said, "but removing that vibrator is going to involve a very lengthy, delicate and expensive surgical operation."

"I'm not sure I can afford it," sighed the young woman. "But while I am here could you just replace the batteries?"

Three friends—two straight guys and a gay guy—and their significant others were on a cruise. A tidal wave came up and swamped the ship. Everyone drowned, and soon they were standing before St. Peter.

First came one of the straight guys and his wife. St. Peter shook his head sadly, and said, "I can't let you in. You loved money too much. You loved it so much, you even married a woman named Penny."

Next in line was the second straight guy and his wife. "Sorry, I can't let you in, either. You loved food too much. You loved to eat so much, you even married a woman named Candy!"

The gay guy turned to his boyfriend and whispered nervously, "It doesn't look good, Dick."

Q. What has one hundred balls and screws old ladies?
A. Bingo.

A guy is walking along a beach when he comes across a lamp partially buried in the sand. He picks up the lamp and gives it a rub. Two genies appear and they tell him he has been granted three wishes.

The guy makes his three wishes and the genies disappear. The next thing he knows he's in a bedroom in a mansion surrounded by 50 beautiful women. He makes love to all of them and begins to explore the house. Suddenly, he feels something soft under his feet. He looks down and the floor is covered in $50 bills.

Then, there is a knock at the door. He answers the door and standing there are the two genies. They drag him outside to the nearest tree, throw a rope over a limb and hang him by the neck until he is dead.

As the genies walk off, one genie says to the other one, "Hey, I can understand the first wish having all these beautiful women in a big mansion to make love to. I can also understand him wanting to be a millionaire. But to be well-hung is beyond me!"

A woman could never get her husband to do anything around the house. He would come home from work, sit in front of the TV, eat dinner, and sit some more. He would never do those little household repairs that most husbands take care of. This frustrated the wife quite a bit.

One day, the toilet blocked up. So when her husband got home, she said sweetly, "Honey, the toilet is clogged. Would you look at it?"

Her husband snarled, "Who do I look like, a plumber?" and sat down on the sofa.

The next day, the garbage disposal wouldn't work. Again, when her husband got home, she said very nicely, "Honey, the disposal has broken. Would you try to fix it for me?"

Once again, he growled, "Who do I look like, the plumber?"

The next day, the washing machine was out of order. When her husband got home, she worked up her courage and said, "Honey, the washing machine isn't working. Would you check it?"

And again she was met with a snarl, "Who do I look like, the repairman?"

Finally, she had enough. The next morning, the woman called three repairmen to fix the toilet, the garbage disposal, and the washing machine. When her husband got home, she said, "Honey, I had the repairmen out today."

He frowned, "How much is that going to cost?"

"Well, honey, they all said I could pay them by baking them a cake or having sex with them."

"Well, what kind of cakes did you bake them?" he asked.

She smiled.

"Who do I look like? Sara Lee?"

Women are just like cartons of orange juice.

It's not the shape or size that matters or even how sweet the juice is—it's getting those fucking flaps open!!

A farmer ordered a high-tech milking machine.

It happened that the equipment arrived when his wife was away, so he decided to test it on himself first. He inserted his penis into the equipment, turned the switch on and voila, everything else was automatic!!

He really had a good time because the equipment provided him with as much pleasure as his wife did. When the fun was over, he found that he could not take the instrument off.

He read the manual but did not find any useful information. He tried every button on the instrument. Some made the equipment squeeze, shake, or suck harder or softer, but still without success.

Panicking, he called the supplier's Customer Service Hot Line.

"Hello, I just bought a milking machine from your company. It's fantastic. But how can I take it off the cow's udder?"

Customer Service replied, "Don't worry. The machine was programmed to release automatically after collecting about two gallons of milk."

The last time the circus came to town, an ad for an animal trainer was placed in the local paper.

Only two applicants showed up, a male and a female.

The owner said he could only afford one animal trainer so he would choose the one with the best act.

At first glance it appeared that the female was much better prepared because she came to the interview with a very long flowing cape, a whip and chair. The man showed up with a cigar. She looked more like a model than a trainer.

The owner asked who would like to go first, and the man said, "Ladies first."

The female asked for her special music to be played and once the music started she entered the cage with a flurry of whip-snapping. She motioned the attendant to release the tiger.

The tiger leaped into the cage snarling. The young lady threw aside her whip, flung back her cape and sat on the chair as naked as the day she was born.

Our tiger now circled her sniffing the air and suddenly bounded to her, put its face between her legs and started licking. She threw back her head moaning, holding the tiger by the ears.

125

The owner looked at the man and said, "That's quite an act. Think you can do better that that?"

The man said, "No problem, just get that tiger out of the cage first."

A man meets a gorgeous woman in a bar. They talk, they connect, and they end up leaving together.

They go back to her place, and as she shows him around her apartment, he notices that her bedroom is completely packed with teddy bears. Hundreds of small bears are on a low shelf, medium-sized ones on a shelf a little higher and huge bears on the top shelf.

The man is kind of surprised that this woman would have a collection of teddy bears, especially one that's so extensive, but he decides not to mention this to her.

After a night of passion, as they are lying together in the afterglow, the man rolls over and asks, smiling, "Well, how was it?"

The woman says, "You can have any prize from the bottom shelf."

A man goes into a greasy spoon restaurant and orders a bowl of chicken soup. "What's this?!?!?" he screams. "There's a pubic hair in my soup! I'm not paying for it!" And he storms out.

The waitress gets very upset at this, follows him out and sees him go into the whorehouse across the street. He pays the madam and retires to a room with a lovely blonde and goes down on her with gusto. The waitress bursts in and yells, "You complain about a hair in your soup and then come over here and do THIS!???"

He lifts his head, turns to her and says, "Yeah! And if I find a noodle in here, I'm not paying for it EITHER!!!"

A young couple had been married for a couple of weeks, but the man was always asking his wife to quit smoking.

One afternoon, she lit up after some lovemaking, and he said, "You really should quit."

She, getting tired of his nagging, said, "I really enjoy a good cigarette after sex."

He replied, "But they stunt your growth."

She asked if he ever smoked, and he replied that he never had.

Smiling and lifting her gaze to his groin, she said, "So, what's your excuse?"

After years of frustration, the Smiths had no children and decided to use a proxy father to start their family. On the day the proxy father was to arrive, Mr. Smith kissed his wife and said, "I'm off. The man should be here soon."

Half an hour later, just by chance, a door-to-door baby photographer rang the doorbell, hoping to make a sale. "Good morning, madam. You don't know me, but I've come to..."

"Oh, no need to explain. I've been expecting you," Mrs. Smith cut in.

"Really?" the photographer asked. "Well, good! I've made a speciality of babies."

"That's what my husband and I had hoped. Please come in and have a seat. Just where do we start?" asked Mrs. Smith, blushing.

"Leave everything to me. I usually try two in the bathtub, one on the couch and perhaps a couple on the bed. Sometimes the living room floor is fun, too—you can really spread out."

"Bathtub, living room floor? No wonder it didn't work for Harry and me."

"Well, madam, none of us can guarantee a good one every time. But if we try several different positions and I shoot from six or seven angles, I'm sure you'll be pleased with the results."

"I hope we can get this over with quickly," gasped Mrs. Smith.

"Madam, in my line of work, a man must take his time. I'd love to be in and out in five minutes, but you'd be disappointed with that, I'm sure."

"Don't I know!!" Mrs. Smith exclaimed.

The photographer opened his briefcase and pulled out a portfolio of his baby pictures. "This was done on the top of a bus in New York."

"Oh my god!!" Mrs. Smith exclaimed, tugging at her handkerchief.

"And these twins turned out exceptionally well when you consider their mother was so difficult to work with."

The photographer handed Mrs. Smith the picture. "She was difficult?" asked Mrs. Smith.

"Yes, I'm afraid so. I finally had to take her to Central Park to get the job done right. People were crowding around in large numbers, pushing to get a good look."

"In large numbers?" asked Mrs. Smith, eyes widened in amazement.

"Yes," the photographer said. "And for more than three hours, too. The mother was constantly squealing and yelling. I could hardly concentrate. Then darkness approached and I began to rush my shots. Finally, when the squirrels began nibbling on my equipment, I just packed it all in."

Mrs. Smith leaned forward. "You mean they actually chewed on your, uh ...equipment?"

"That's right. Well, madam, if you're ready, I'll set up my tripod so that we can get to work."

"Tripod??" Mrs. Smith looked extremely worried now.

"Oh yes, I have to use a tripod to rest my Canon on. It's much too big for me to hold while I'm getting ready for action. Madam? Madam?... Good Lord, she's fainted!!"

Tommy O'Connor went to confession and said, "Forgive me, Father, for I have sinned."

"What have you done Tommy O'Connor?"

"I had sex with a girl."

"Who was it, Tommy?"

"I cannot tell you, Father. Please forgive me for my sin."

"Was it Mary Margaret Sullivan?"

"No, Father, please forgive me for my sin but I cannot tell you who it was."

"Was it Catherine Mary McKenzie?"

"No, Father, please forgive me for my sin."

"Well, then it has to be Sarah Martha O'Keefe."

"No, Father, please forgive me, I cannot tell you who it was."

"Okay, Tommy, say five Hail Marys and four Our Fathers and you will be abolished of your sin."

So Tommy walked out to the pews where his friend Joseph was waiting.

"What did you get?" asked Joseph.

"Well, I got five Hail Marys, four Our Fathers, and three good leads."

Q. If the dove is the bird of peace, what is the bird of true love?
A. The swallow.

After his day of sightseeing, an American touring Spain stopped at a local restaurant. While sipping his wine, he noticed a sizzling, scrumptious-looking platter being served at the next table. Not only did it look good, but the smell was wonderful.

He asked the waiter, "What is that you just served?"

The waiter replied, "Ah, señor, you have excellent taste! Those are bull's balls from the bull fight this morning. A delicacy!"

The American, though momentarily daunted when he learned the origin of the dish, said, "What the hell, I'm on vacation! Bring me an order!"

The waiter replied, "I am so sorry, señor. There is only one serving a day since there is only one bull fight each morning. If you come early tomorrow and place your order, we will be sure to serve you this delicacy!"

The next morning the American returned and placed his order. That evening he was served the one and only special delicacy of the day. After a few bites, and inspecting the contents of his platter, he called to the waiter and said, "These are much, much smaller than the ones I saw you serve yesterday!"

The waiter promptly replied, "Si, señor! Sometimes the bull wins!

When nuns are admitted to heaven, they go through a special gate and are expected to make one last confession before they become angels. Several nuns are lined up at this gate waiting to be absolved of their last sins before they are made holy.

"And so," says St. Peter, "have you ever had any contact with a penis?"

"Well," says the first nun in line, "I did once just touch the tip of one with the tip of my finger."

"OK," says St. Peter. "Dip your finger in the holy water and pass on into heaven."

The next nun admits, "Well, yes, I did once get carried away and I, you know, sort of massaged one a bit."

"OK," says St. Peter. "Rinse your hand in the holy water and pass on into heaven."

Suddenly there is some jostling in the line and one of the nuns is trying to cut in front.

"Well now, what's going on here?" asks St. Peter.

"Well, your excellency," says the nun who is trying to improve her position in line, "if I'm going to have to gargle that stuff, I want to do it before Sister Mary Thomas sticks her ass in it."

A priest was driving along and saw a nun on the side of the road. He stopped and offered her a lift, which she accepted. She got in and crossed her legs, forcing her gown to open and reveal a lovely leg.

The priest took a look and nearly had an accident. After regaining control of the car, he stealthily slid his hand up her leg.

The nun looked at him and immediately said, "Father, remember Psalm 129?"

The priest was flustered and apologized profusely. He forced himself to remove his hand. However, he was unable to remove his eyes from her leg.

Further on, while changing gear, he let his hand slide up her leg again. The nun once again said, "Father, remember Psalm 129?"

Once again the priest apologized. "Sorry, sister, but the flesh is weak." Arriving at the convent, the nun got out, gave him a meaningful glance and went on her way. On his arrival at the church, the priest rushed to retrieve a Bible and looked up Psalm 129.

It said, "Go forth and seek, further up you will find glory."

A man was in a terrible accident and his "manhood" was mangled and torn from his body. His doctor assured him that modern medicine could give him back his manhood, but that his insurance wouldn't cover the surgery, since it was considered cosmetic.

The doctor said the cost would be $3,500 for small, $6,500 for medium, $14,000 for large.

The man was sure he would want a medium or large, but the doctor urged him to talk it over with his wife before he made any decision.

The man called his wife on the phone and explained their options. The doctor came back into the room, and found the man looking dejected.

"Well, what have the two of you decided?" asked the doctor.

The man answered, "She'd rather have a new kitchen."

Doctors say penis is the greatest breakfast because it has a mushroom head, a hotdog, two eggs and cream, which provides all the nutrients necessary to make a woman healthy.

One day a little cat was walking through the park when he came across a pond. He peered into the pond and noticed that at the bottom of the pond there was a little cocktail sausage. The cat was feeling quite happy, so since the water wasn't that deep, he reached in with his little paw, hooked the sausage out and ate it.

The next day the cat was walking through the park again and peered into the pond. There was another sausage in the pond but this time it was a normal sized one, so the cat reached in. This time he had to put both front legs into the pond. The cat hooked the sausage out and ate it.

The next day things go basically the same and the cat again looks into the pond. There he found an enormous sausage at the bottom of the pond. It looked so delicious but it was so deep that he had to really stretch to get it, and then SPLASH—he fell in.

The moral of the story: The bigger the sausage, the wetter the pussy!

A man comes home drunk in the wee hours of the morning to find his wife angry and waiting for him at the door.

"Out drinking again!?" she says. "How much money did you spend this time?"

"$200," answers the man.

"$200!" she shouts. "That's ridiculous, spending so much in one night!"

"Easy for you to say," he replies. "You don't smoke, you don't drink, and you have your own pussy."

Pierre, a brave French fighter pilot, takes his girlfriend, Marie, out for a pleasant little picnic by the River Seine. It's a beautiful day, and love is in the air. Marie leans over to Pierre and says, "Pierre, kiss me!"

Our hero grabs a bottle of Merlot wine and splashes it on Marie's lips. "What are you doing, Pierre?" asks the startled Marie.

"I am Pierre the fighter pilot! When I have red meat, I have red wine!"

She smiles and they start kissing. When things began to heat up a little, Marie says, "Pierre, kiss me lower."

Our hero tears her blouse open, grabs a bottle of Chardonnay and starts pouring it all over her breasts.

"Pierre! What are you doing?" asks the bewildered Marie.

"I am Pierre the fighter pilot! When I have white meat, I have white wine!"

They resume their passionate interlude and things really steam up. Marie leans close to his ear and whispers, "Pierre, kiss me lower!"

Our hero rips off her underwear, grabs a bottle of Cognac and pours it in her lap. He then strikes a match and lights it. Marie shrieks and dives into the river. Standing waist deep in the water, Marie throws her arms upwards and screams furiously, "PIERRE, WHAT IN THE HELL DO YOU THINK YOU'RE DOING?"

Our hero stands up defiantly and says, "I am Pierre the fighter pilot! If I go down, I go down in flames!"

A salesman decides to try for a new job in a department store.

The manager says, "Do you have any sales experience?"

The man says, "Yeah, I've been a salesman all my life."

The boss liked him, so he gave him the job. "You start tomorrow. I'll come down after we close and see how you did."

His first day on the job was rough but he got through it. After the shop was locked up, the boss came down. "How many sales did you make today?"

The salesman says, "One."

The boss says, "Just one? Our sales people average 20 or 30 sales a day. How much was the sale for?"

"$50,237.64."

"$50,237.64?? What the hell did you sell him?"

"First, I sold him some fish hooks. Then I sold him a new fishing rod. Then I asked him where he was going fishing, and he said 'down at the coast', so I told him he was going to need a boat, so we went down to the boat department, and I sold him that big twin engine job. Then he said he didn't think his Honda Civic would pull it, so I took him down to the car department and sold him a 4x4 Land Rover."

The boss said, "Somebody came in here to buy fish hooks and you sold him a boat and a 4x4?"

"No, he came in here to buy a box of tampons for his wife, and I said, 'Well, since your weekend's fucked, you may as well go fishing.'"

An attractive young woman had finished taking golf lessons from the club pro. She'd just started playing her first round of golf when she got a bee sting. The pain was so intense she decided to return to the clubhouse.

Her golf pro saw her come into the clubhouse and asked, "Why are you back so early? What's wrong?"

"I was stung by a bee," was her reply.

"Where?" he asked.

"Between the first and second hole."

He nodded knowingly and said, "Then your stance is too wide."

A man walks into a bar and says "G-g-gimme a b-b-beer."

The bartender says, "Seems as though you've got a major stuttering problem."

The man replies, "N-n-no k-k-k-idding!"

The bartender says, "I used to stutter, but my wife cured me. One afternoon she gave me oral sex three times in a row, and I haven't stuttered since!"

The man says, "W-w-wow, th-th-that's great to kn-kn-know..."

A week later, the same man walks in to the bar, and says, "G-g-gimme a b-b-beer."

The bartender says, "Why didn't you try what I told you?"

"I d-d-did!" said the man. "It j-j-just d-d-didn't w-w-work... ....b-b-but I m-m-must say, you have a r-r-really n-n-nice apartment!"

A middle-aged wife had just returned to the house on Saturday afternoon after a shopping trip. She was quite agitated, and proceeded to tell her husband about a certain shoe salesman who had been rude.

It seems she was sitting down while he helped her try on various shoes, and happened to glance up and notice that she was not wearing any panties. Without even thinking, he just blurted out, "If that thing was full of ice cream, I'd eat every bite."

Well, she was understandably insulted, and now wanted to know what her husband was going to do about it.

The husband just sat there, watching football on TV, and grunted. The wife became hysterical, and insisted on knowing why he didn't go down to the shop and punch the rude salesman right in the nose.

"Well," the husband replied, "there are three reasons I won't punch that guy in the nose. First of all, you shouldn't have even been shopping for shoes, since you have a whole wardrobe full of them. Secondly, you have no business going shopping with no panties on. But most of all, I'm not going to punch anyone who's big enough to eat that much ice cream!"

Humpty Dumpty sat on his bed,
As Little Bo Beep was giving him head,
Just as he came she began to weep,
She could tell by the taste,
He'd been screwing her sheep!!

This girl who is a total Beatles fanatic decides to get John Lennon and Paul McCartney tattooed onto her inner thighs. She takes their pictures to the tattoo artist who says he can do a perfect job of reproducing their images in ink on her inner thighs. Hours later, the job is done. The tattoo artist hands her a mirror, and she is shocked!

"That sucks...It doesn't look anything like John or Paul!"

The tattoo artist is offended. "Of course it does. That looks just like them! Tell you what, ask the first person you see, and I'll bet you $10 that they say they look just like John and Paul."

She takes him up on it, but the place is empty and the first person she finds is an old wino sitting outside on the sidewalk. They call the wino inside. She sits in the chair, spreads her legs and points to the tattoos, "Does this look like John Lennon and Paul McCartney to you?"

The old wino squints, scratches his head, burps, and slurs, "Well, lady, I don't know about John Lennon and Paul McCartney, but that guy in the middle looks just like Willie Nelson."

A man goes to the doctor and says, "Doc, you've got to help me. My dick's gone orange."

The skeptical doctor pauses to think and asks the guy to drop his pants so he can check. Sure enough the guy's dick is bright orange.

Doc tells the guy, "This is very strange. Sometimes things like this are caused by a lot of stress in a person's life." Probing as to the causes of possible stress, the doctor asks the guy, "How are things going at work?"

The guy responds that he was fired about six weeks ago and the doctor tells him that this must be the cause of the stress.

The guy responds, "No. The boss was a bastard. I had to work 20-30 hours of overtime every week and I had no say in anything that was happening. I found a new job a couple of weeks ago where I can set my own hours. I'm getting paid double what I got on the old job and my new boss is really great."

So the doc asks the guy, "How's your home life?"

The guy says, "Well, I got divorced about eight months ago."

The doc figures that this has got to be the reason for all of the guy's stress.

The guy says, "No. For years all I listened to was nag, nag, nag. God, am I glad to be rid of that old bitch."

So the doctor takes a few minutes to think a little longer. He inquires, "Do you have any hobbies or a social life?"

The guy replies, "No, not really. Most nights I sit at home, watch porno films and eat cheese puffs."

There are three women who always hang their laundry out in the back garden. When it rains, of course, the laundry always gets wet—all the laundry except for Brenda's. The other two women wonder why Brenda never has her laundry out on the days that it rains.

So one day they are all out in their back gardens putting their clothes on the line, when one of the women says to Brenda, "How come when it rains your laundry is never out?"

"Well," says Brenda, "when I wake up in the morning I look over at Paul. If his prick is hanging over his right leg, I know it's going to be a great day and I can hang the laundry outside. If his prick is hanging over his left leg, I know it's going to rain, so I don't hang it out."

"What if it is pointed up?" asks one of the women.

"Well," says Brenda, "on a day like that you don't do the laundry!"

Three guys are drinking in a bar when a drunk comes in, staggers up to them and points at the guy in the middle, shouting, "Your mom's the best sex in town!"

Everyone expects a fight but the guy ignores him, so the drunk wanders off and bellies up to the bar at the far end. Ten minutes later, the drunk comes back, points at the same guy and says, "I just screwed your mom, and it was s-w-e-e-t!"

Again the guy refuses to take the bait, and the drunk goes back to the far end of the bar. Ten minutes later, he comes back and announces, "Your mom loved it!"

Finally, the guy just can't take it anymore. He looks at the drunk and yells, "Go home, Dad! You're drunk again!"

After having their 11th child, a redneck couple decided that was enough. They could not afford a larger house so the husband went to his doctor (who also treated mules) and told him that he and his wife/cousin didn't want to have any more children.

The doctor told him that there was a procedure called a vasectomy that could fix the problem.

The doctor instructed him to go home, get a cherry bomb (small firework), light it, put it in a beer can, then hold the can up to his ear and count to 10.

The redneck said to the doctor, "I may not be the smartest man but I don't see how putting a cherry bomb in a beer can next to my ear is going to help me."

So, the couple drove to get a second opinion. The second doctor was just about to tell them about the medical procedure for a vasectomy, when he realized how truly backward these people were. This doctor instead told him to go home and get a cherry bomb, light it, place it in a beer can, hold it to his ear and count to 10.

Figuring that both physicians couldn't be wrong, the man went home, lit a cherry bomb and put it in a beer can. He held the can up to his ear and began to count "1...2...3...4...5..." at which point he paused, placed the beer can between his legs and resumed counting on his other hand...

A woman walks into the doctor's office but doesn't like the way he's looking at her.

When he tells her to undress, she asks him to turn out the lights before she disrobes. After he turns out the lights she says, "Where will I put my clothes?"

"Hang them up over here," he says. "Next to mine."

At the end of a long work week, a group of coal miners discovered that one of them, young Billy, was a virgin. Well, they decided this wasn't right, and pooled their money to remedy the situation. They talked him into going out for a night on the town, got him all cleaned up, and drove to the local brothel.

Upon entering, the ring leader went to the madam, explained the situation and gave her $100. She assured him she would sort Billy out and they all left Billy there to enjoy himself.

Being naive, Billy asked the madam what was going on. She explained to him that he was about to become a man, courtesy of his friends.

"All you have to do is choose one of my girls and she will take care of you."

Well, Billy looked around at the group of women before him and, after several minutes of pondering, picked a likely looking girl to take upstairs.

Once they were in their room, the girl said to Billy, "I hear you're a virgin boy. So what's your pleasure? You want missionary, Greek, doggy style, 'round the world', 69 or what?"

Billy said, "Gosh, ma'am, give me what you think I ought to have."

"No, boy, I'm a professional. You need to tell me what you want."

Billy decided a 69 sounded pretty good, so they settled into the proper position. After several minutes of missing the target, Billy finally got it right and was starting to enjoy it. Sadly, the whore had beans for dinner and let loose a little fart in his face.

Billy shook his head, thinking it was part of the fun, and continued licking away.

A little while later, she passed wind again.

Billy still thought it was part of the fun and dived back in with a vengeance, licking like there was no tomorrow.

A few minutes later, she really let loose with a fart that curled Billy's eyebrows.

He pushed her off his face and said, "I don't want you to think I'm not enjoying myself or anything, but I'll be dammned if I can take another 66 of those."

A commercial traveler was driving through the Scottish Highlands when his car broke down. There was a cottage near by so he went up to it and knocked on the door. The door opened to reveal a burly Highlander. "My car has conked out," said the traveler. "Where can I spend the night?"

"Why, right here of course!" said the Scot. "Come in and avail yourself of our world famous hospitality."

The traveler duly entered the humble but cosy residence.

"Jeannie," shouted the host in the direction of the kitchen, and in response to his call his beautiful daughter appeared. "Jeannie, make a meal for the gentleman and remember to uphold our great tradition of Highland hospitality."

The traveler was soon tucking into an appetizing meal. The girl had indeed spared no effort to extend Highland hospitality to the guest.

"And now," said the Highlander, "I'm afraid I must go out and milk the cows, but just make yourself at home and take full advantage of our world-famous Highland hospitality."

No sooner had the door closed behind him than the traveler set about seducing the lovely daughter. In no time at all he had her on the floor and was on the job. Suddenly, the door opened and there stood the Highlander. He took one look at what was going on and his face turned purple with rage. He dropped his two buckets of milk with a crash and gave verbal vent to his wrath.

"After all I have been saying about the Highland hospitality," he roared. "Arch your back, woman, and take the poor man's balls off the cold floor."

A missionary is sent into deepest, darkest Africa, and goes to live with a tribe there. He spends years with the people, teaching them to read and write, and the good Christian ways of the white man. One thing that he particularly stresses is the evil of sexual sin.

"Thou must not commit adultery or fornication!!!"

One day, the wife of one of the tribe's noblemen gave birth to a white child. The village is shocked, and the chief is then sent by his people to talk with the missionary.

"You have taught us of the evils of sexual sin, yet here a black woman gives birth to a white child. You are the only white man that has ever set foot in our village. I know what you've done!"

The missionary replies, "Oh no, my good man, you are mistaken. What you have here is a natural occurrence called an albino. Look in yonder field! You see a field of white sheep, yet amongst them is one black sheep. Nature does this on occasion."

The chief pauses a moment, and then says, "Tell you what... you don't say anything about the sheep, and I won't say anything about the kid."

A ventriloquist walked up to a farmer and said, "I'll bet I can make your horse talk."

Farmer: "Horses don't talk."

Ventriloquist: "Watch this. Hi, horse. How does your master treat you?"

Horse: "Oh, he is good to me. He gives me food, water and he keeps me out of the sun."

Ventriloquist: "I'll bet I can make your dog talk."

Farmer: "Dogs can't talk."

Ventriloquist: "Watch this. Dog, how are you? Does your master treat you well?"

Dog: "Oh! He treats me well. He gives me food, water and he plays ball with me."

Ventriloquist: "I'll bet I can make your sheep talk."

Farmer: "Sheep, lie! Sheep, lie!"

Three sisters, Monica, Phoebe and Fanny, are all invited to a party, so they go to buy new dancing shoes. Monica comes home with a new pair of size 9 stilettos, Phoebe buys a pair of size 10 strappy sandals but poor Fanny, who takes a manly size 14, is forced to go in men's wingtips. At the party, Fanny sits alone in the corner watching her sisters cut a rug on the dance floor.

While the two sisters are dancing, two men approach and point down at their feet, "Wow, those are huge feet!" one of the men exclaims.

"If you think those are big," replies Monica proudly, "wait till you see our Fanny's!"

A man and a woman are sitting beside each other on a flight to New York.

The woman sneezes, takes out a tissue, gently wipes her nose and then visibly shudders for about ten seconds.

A few minutes later the woman sneezes again. Once more, she takes a tissue, wipes her nose and then shudders.

A few more minutes pass before the woman sneezes and violently shudders again.

Curious, the man says, "I can't help noticing that you shudder every time you sneeze. Are you OK?"

"I'm so sorry if I'm disturbing you," says the woman. "I'm suffering from a very rare medical condition. Whenever I sneeze, I have an orgasm."

"Are you taking anything for it?" he asks.

"Yes," says the woman. "Pepper."

A guy walks into a bar and sits on a stool. In front of him he sees a big jar full of change and a little card that reads:

If you would like to win all of this money you have to make the horse at the end of the bar laugh.

COST $5.

So he puts in five dollars and takes the horse into the bathroom. Two minutes later they come out and the horse is laughing so hard that he pisses on the floor. So the guy takes the money and leaves.

The next day the same guy walks in the bar again and sees the horse and the jar. This time it says:

You can win all of this if you make the horse cry.

COST $10.

So he puts in ten dollars and takes the horse into the bathroom. Four minutes later they come out and the horse is crying like nobody ever has.

So the guy takes the jar but before he could leave the bartender asks, "How did you do that?"

The guy says, "The first time I told him my dick was bigger than his and the second time I showed him!"

Q. What's the definition of a Yankee?
A. Same thing as a "quickie," only you do it yourself.

Anagrams
Mel Gibson —Big melons
Gloria Estefan—Large fat noise
Martina Navratilova—Variant rival to a man
Gabriela Sabatini—Insatiable airbag
Irritable Bowel Syndrome—O my terrible drains below
Evangelist—Evil's Agent
Desperation—A Rope Ends It
The Morse Code—Here Come Dots
Mother-in-law—Woman Hitler

Little Johnny had become a real nuisance while his father tried to concentrate on his Saturday afternoon poker game with friends and relatives. His father tried every way possible to get Johnny to occupy himself: television, ice cream, homework, and video games, but the youngster insisted on running back and forth behind the players and calling out the cards they held.

The other players became so annoyed that they threatened to quit the game and go home. At this point, the boy's uncle stood up, took Johnny by the hand and led him out of the room. The uncle soon returned back to the poker table without Johnny, and without comment the game resumed. For the rest of the afternoon, little Johnny was nowhere to be seen and the card players continued without any further interruptions.

After the poker game ended, the father asked Johnny's uncle, "What in the world did you say to Johnny? I haven't heard a peep from him all day!"

"Not much," the boy's uncle replied. "I just showed him how to masturbate."

Going fishing is very much like making love to a beautiful woman.

First, you clean and inspect your tackle, then carefully pull back your rod cover and remove any dirt or grunge that may have built up while not in use. Then you extend your rod to its full length and check that there are no kinks or any wear, particularly at the base where the grip is usually applied.

Make sure you've got a decent float, the appropriate bait, and that there's plenty of weight in your sack.

Q. How many yuppies does it take to screw in a light bulb?
A. None, yuppies only do it in jacuzzis.

Police are warning all men who frequent clubs, parties and local bars to be alert and stay cautious when offered a drink by a woman. Many females use a date rape drug on the market called "Beer."

The drug is found in liquid form and is available anywhere. It comes in bottles, cans, or from taps and in large "kegs." Beer is used by female sexual predators at parties and bars to persuade their male victims to go home and sleep with them. A woman needs only to get a guy to consume a few units of Beer and then simply ask him to come home with her for no strings attached sex.

Men are rendered helpless against this approach. After several beers, men will often succumb to the desires to sleep with horrific-looking women who they would never normally be attracted to. After drinking Beer, men often awaken with only hazy memories of exactly what happened to them the night before, often with just a vague feeling that "something bad" occurred.

At other times these unfortunate men are swindled out of their life's savings, in a familiar scam known as "a relationship." In extreme cases, the female may even be shrewd enough to entrap the unsuspecting male into a longer term form of servitude and punishment referred to as "marriage." Men are much more susceptible to this scam after Beer is administered and sex is offered by the predatory females.

Please! Forward this warning to every male you know. If you fall victim to this "Beer" scam and the women administering it, there are male support groups where you can discuss the details of your shocking encounter with similarly victimized men. For the support group nearest you, just look up "Golf Courses" in the phone book.

Q. What does a blonde put behind her ears to make her more attractive?

A. Her ankles.

Three Englishmen are out drinking one night and decide to pick a fight. They stagger through town looking for a victim, until they come across an Irishman sitting alone in a pub.

"Watch this," says the first Englishman, heading over to the guy. "I hear that St. Patrick was a fag."

"Really?" says the Irishman, calmly continuing to drink.

With that the second English guy decides to join in, "Yeah, and he was a pervert, too."

"Is that so?" the still calm Irishman responds.

Determined to rouse him, the third Englishman staggers up and slurs, "Hey, did you know St. Patrick was really an Englishman?"

The Irish guy casually looks up and says, "Yeah, so your friends were telling me."

A very attractive blonde arrives at a casino and bets $20,000 on a single roll of the dice.

"I hope you don't mind," she says, "but I feel much luckier when I am completely naked."

With that, she strips from the neck down, rolls the dice and yells out, "Yes! I've won! I've won!" She jumps up and down, hugs each of the dealers, scoops up all the chips on the table as well as her clothes and then quickly departs.

The dealers stare at each other utterly dumbfounded.

Finally, one of them asks, "So, what did she roll?"

"No idea," replies the other. "I thought you were watching the dice."

A sign over a gynecologist's office: Dr. Jones, at your cervix.

Q. What do blondes and spaghetti have in common?
A. They both wriggle when you eat them.

Q. Why is marriage a three-ring circus?
A. First the engagement ring, then the wedding ring and then the suffering.

A man returns home early from work one afternoon to find his wife spread out on the bed naked, puffing and panting.

"What are you doing?" the man inquires.

"Err," she stammers back. "I… um… I think I'm having a heart attack!"

"Oh," cries the gullible husband, "quick, I'll call an ambulance!"

He runs downstairs, picks up the phone and begins dialing 911, when his son Johnny appears, sobbing his little heart out.

"What's the matter, son?" asks the father.

"Uncle James is in the closet with no clothes on, Daddy," replies his tearful toddler.

Enraged, the man runs back upstairs, flings open the wardrobe and finds his brother there absolutely naked, just as his son had said.

"You bastard, Jim," screams the man. "My wife is over there having a heart attack and you're running around naked scaring Johnny!"

How to impress a woman: Compliment her, cuddle her, kiss her, caress her, love her, tease her, comfort her, protect her, hug her, hold her, spend money on her, wine and dine her, care for her, stand by her, support her, go the ends of the earth for her.

How to impress a man: Turn up naked with beer.

A young man is out walking his dog in the park, when a beautiful young woman stops to admire the animal.

"What's your dog's name?" she asks flirtatiously.

"Herpes," replies the dog's owner.

"How odd!" exclaims the woman. "Why in the world did you name your dog Herpes?"

The young man replies, "Because he just won't heel."

Patrick O'Malley raised his beer and said, "Here's to spending the rest of my life between the legs of my wife!" And he took home the top prize for the best toast of the night.

In bed later that night, he told his wife, "Mary, I won the prize for the best toast of the night."

She said, "What was your toast?"

So he told her, "Here's to spending the rest of my life sitting in church beside my wife."

"Oh," she said, "that is very nice, dear."

The next day, Mary ran into one of Patrick's drinking partners in the street. Mischievously, the man said, "Did you hear about your husband winning a prize in the pub the other night for a toast about you, Mary?"

She replied: "Yes—and I was a bit surprised. 'Til now, he's only been down there twice. Once he fell asleep, and the other time I had to pull him by the ears to make him come."

A man staying at a nice London hotel finds a card in the telephone box offering sexual services.

He calls the number and says, "I'd like some doggy-style, some sixty-nining and some mild bondage—is that OK?"

"It all sounds very interesting, sir," the lady replies, "but you might like to dial 9 for an outside line first."

A husband walks into the bedroom holding two aspirin and a glass of water. His wife asks, "What's that for?"

"It's for your headache."

"I don't have a headache."

"Gotcha!"

A man and his wife are sound asleep in bed when the phone rings.

The man picks up, listens for a second and says, "How the hell would I know, you idiot? I'm not a weatherman," before slamming down the receiver.

"Who was that?" asks his wife.

"Wrong number. It was some idiot asking if the coast was clear."

Q. How do you know when you are getting old?
A. When you start having dry dreams and wet farts.

A man walks into a bar and orders a 12-year-old scotch. The bartender, believing that the customer won't be able to tell the difference, pours him a shot of the cheap three-year-old house scotch instead.

The man takes a sip, spits the scotch out on the bar and screams at the bartender, "This is the cheapest three-year-old scotch you can buy. I'm not paying for it. Now, give me a good 12-year-old scotch."

The bartender, now enjoying the challenge, pours the man a slightly better six-year-old scotch. Again, the man takes a sip and spits it out on the bar. "This is only six-year-old scotch. I won't pay for this. I insist on a good, 12-year-old scotch."

The bartender finally relents and serves the man his best quality 12-year-old scotch.

At that point, an old drunk who has witnessed the entire episode from the end of the bar walks up to the expert scotch drinker and sets a glass down in front of him.

"What do you think of this?" he asks.

The guru takes a sip, and, in disgust, spits out the yellow liquid, yelling, "It tastes like piss!"

"That's right," says the drunk, "now tell me how old I am."

A blonde, a brunette and a redhead all work at the same office for a female boss who always goes home early.

"Hey, girls," says the brunette one day, "let's go home early tomorrow. She'll never know."

So the next day they all leave right after the boss does. The brunette gets some extra gardening done, the redhead goes to a bar, and the blonde goes home to find her husband having sex with the female boss.

She quietly sneaks out of the house and vows to return home at her normal time the next day.

In the morning, the brunette says, "That was fun, we should do it again sometime."

"No way," says the blonde. "I almost got caught."

Q. Why are hurricanes named after women?

A. Because when they come, they're wild and wet, and when they go they take your house and car with them.

A man lies on his deathbed surrounded by his family, a weeping wife and four children.

Three of the children are tall, good-looking and athletic, but the fourth and the youngest is an ugly runt.

"Darling wife," the husband whispers, "assure me that the youngest child really is mine. I want to know the truth before I die. I will forgive you if..."

The wife gently interrupts him. "Yes, my dearest, absolutely, no question. I swear on my mother's grave that you are his father."

The man dies happy.

The wife mutters under her breath, "Thank God he didn't ask me about the other three!"

Q. How do you get a nun pregnant?
A. Dress her up as an altar boy.

A priest who has to spend the night in a hotel asks the girl in reception to come up to his room for dinner.

After a while he makes a pass at her, but she stops him and reminds him that he is a holy man.

"It's OK," he replies, "it's written in the Bible." After a wild night of sex she asks to see where in the Bible it says it's OK.

The priest rolls over, takes Gideon out of the desk by the bed and shows her the first page. On it, someone has scrawled, "The girl in reception will fuck anyone."

Mr. Bear and Mr. Rabbit didn't like each other very much. One day, while walking through the woods, they came across a golden frog.

They were amazed when the frog talked to them. The golden frog admitted that he didn't often meet anyone, but when he did he always granted them wishes. He told them that they could have three wishes each.

Mr. Bear immediately wished that all the other bears in the forest were females.

The frog granted his wish. Mr. Rabbit, after thinking for a while, wished for a crash helmet.

One appeared immediately, and he placed it on his head. Mr. Bear was amazed at Mr. Rabbit's wish, but carried on with his second wish.

He wished that all the bears in the neighboring forests were females as well, and the frog granted his wish.

Mr. Rabbit then wished for a motorcycle. It appeared before him, and he climbed on board and started revving the engine.

Mr. Bear could not believe it and complained that Mr. Rabbit had wasted two wishes that he could have had for himself.

Shaking his head, Mr. Bear made his final wish, that all the other bears in the world were females as well, leaving him as the only male bear in the world.

The frog replied that it had been done, and they both turned to Mr. Rabbit for his last wish.

Mr. Rabbit revved the engine, thought for a second, then said, "I wish that Mr. Bear was gay!" and rode off as fast as he could.

Q. Why don't witches wear panties when flying on their broomsticks?
A. Better traction.

A woman walks into her accountant's office and tells him that she needs to file her taxes.

The accountant says, "Before we begin, I'll need to ask a few questions."

He gets her name, address, social security number, etc., and then asks, "What is your occupation?"

The woman replies, "I'm a whore."

The accountant balks and says, "No, no, no. That will never work. That is much too crass. Let's try to rephrase that."

"OK, I'm a prostitute."

"No, that is still too crude. Try again."

They both think for a minute, then the woman says, "I'm a chicken farmer."

The accountant asks, "What does chicken farming have to do with being a whore or a prostitute?"

"Well, I raised over 5,000 cocks last year."

Q. Why do blondes wear panties?
A. To keep their ankles warm.

One day a husband comes home to his wife and she says to him, "I need $20, dear. I have to go out and buy some meat."

"$20! Are you crazy? Come upstairs to the bathroom and let me show you something."

They run up to the bathroom and he stands in front of the mirror and pulls out a twenty-dollar bill and says, "You see that $20 in the mirror? That one's yours and this one's mine."

He goes to work the next day and when he comes home he finds the kitchen table packed full of meat from one end to the other.

He looks over to his wife and says, "Where the hell did you get all this meat?"

"Well," she replies. "Come upstairs to the bathroom and let me show you something."

They run up to the bathroom and she stands in front of the mirror, lifting up her skirt.

"You see that in the mirror? Well, that one's yours and this one's the butcher's."

One day the sheriff sees Billy Bob walking around town with nothing on except his gun belt and his boots.

The sheriff says, "Billy Bob, what the hell are you doing walking around town dressed like that?"

Billy Bob replies, "Well, sheriff, it's a long story!"

The sheriff says he isn't in a hurry and that Billy Bob should tell the story.

Billy Bob continues, "Well, sheriff, me and Mary Lou were down on the farm and we started cuddling. Mary Lou said we should go in the barn and we did.

Inside the barn we started kissing and cuddling and things got pretty hot and heavy. Well Mary Lou said that we should go up on the hill so we did.

Up on the hill we started kissing and cuddling and then Mary Lou took off all her clothes and said that I should do the same. Well, I took off all my clothes except my gun belt and my boots.

Then Mary Lou lay on the ground and opened her legs and said, "Okay, Billy Bob, go to town..."

At 85 years of age, Morris marries Lou Anne, a lovely 25-year-old.

Since her new husband is so old, Lou Anne decides that after their wedding she and Morris should have separate bedrooms, because she is concerned that her new, but aged, husband may overexert himself if they spend the entire night together.

After the wedding festivities, Lou Anne prepares herself for bed and the expected "knock" on the door. Sure enough the knock comes, the door opens and there is Morris, her 85-year-old groom ready for action. They unite as one.

All goes well. Morris takes leave of his bride, and she prepares to go to sleep. After a few minutes, Lou Anne hears another knock on her bedroom door, and it's Morris. Again he is ready for more action.

Somewhat surprised, Lou Anne consents for more coupling. When the newlyweds are done, Morris kisses his bride, bids her a fond goodnight and leaves.

She is ready to go to sleep again, but you guessed it, Morris is back again rapping on the door, fresh as a 25-year-old and ready for more action. And, once again they enjoy each other.

But as Morris gets set to leave again, his young bride says to him, "I am thoroughly impressed that at your age you can perform so well and so often. I have been with guys less than a third of your age who were only good once. You are truly a great lover, Morris."

Morris, somewhat embarrassed, turns to Lou Anne and says, "You mean I was here already?"

"Hello, darling," breathed the obscene phone caller. "If you can guess what's in my hand, I'll give you a piece of the action."

"Listen, honey," drawled the lady, "if you can hold it in one hand, I'm not interested."

Two gay men decide that they want to have a baby, but they don't want to adopt because they want the baby to be as close to their own as possible.

So they both masturbate into a cup and have a doctor use their sperm to impregnate a female friend of theirs.

Nine months later, the two gays are looking at their baby in the hospital nursery. All of the babies are crying and screaming except for theirs.

"Wow," one of the gay men says, "our baby is the most well-behaved one in here."

A nurse who happens to be walking by says, "Now he's quiet, but wait until we take the pacifier out of his ass."

Q. How can you tell which is the head nurse?
A. The one with the dirty knees.

Women were asked what they would do if they had a penis for a day. These were the responses:

I would:

Write my name in the snow

Pee off a tall building

Check out my boyfriend's reflexes

Pin my boyfriend down and slap him in the face with it

See how many donuts I could carry with it

I would want a big one and show it off to everyone

I would grab myself in public and not be embarrassed

I would not lift the toilet seat while peeing

I would love it and squeeze it and play with it all day

I would get it kicked to see if it really hurts

I would get it removed

I would see what a woman felt like on the other end

Go to an adult store and try out all kinds of stimulants to see what was the best

Stand up and jump up and down and watch it swing around

I would measure it both ways

I would play with him and make him roll over into the wet spot

I would go into my boss' office and lay it on his desk and say, "Where's my raise?"

I would find my ex-boyfriend and go to bed with him and tell him to roll over and try something new

Demonstrate to my boyfriend that it is possible to hit the water and not pee all over everything

I would prod him all night long with it

Mick was fixing a door and he found that he needed a new hinge, so he sent Mary to the hardware store.

At the hardware store Mary saw a beautiful teapot on a top shelf while she was waiting for Joe to finish serving a customer.

When Joe was finished, Mary asked, "How much for the teapot?"

Joe replied, "That's silver and it costs $100!"

"My goodness, that's a lot of money!" Mary exclaimed. She then proceeded to describe the hinge that Mick had sent her to buy and Joe went to the backroom to find a hinge.

From the backroom Joe yelled, "Mary, you wanna screw for that hinge?"

To which Mary replied, "No, but I will for the teapot."

Q. How does a man show that he is planning for the future?
A. He buys two cases of beer instead of one.

A man with a stuttering problem tries everything he can to stop stuttering, but he can't. Finally, he goes to a world-renowned doctor for help.

The doctor examines him and says, "I've found your problem. Your penis is 12 inches long. It weighs so much it is pulling on your lungs, causing you to stutter."

So the man asks, "What's the cure, Doctor?"

To which the doctor replies, "We have to cut off 6 inches."

The man thinks about it, and, eager to cure his stuttering, agrees to the operation. The operation is a success, and he stops stuttering.

Two months later he calls the doctor and tells him that since he had the 6 inches cut off, all of his girlfriends have dumped him, and his love life has gone down the tubes.

He wants the doctor to operate to reattach the six inches. Not hearing anything on the line, he repeats himself, "Hey, Doc, didn't you hear me? I want my 6 inches back!"

Finally, the doctor responds, "F-f-f-f-f-fuck y-y-you!"

A woman was having a daytime affair while her husband was at work. One wet and lusty day she was in bed with her boyfriend when, to her horror, she heard her husband's car pull into the driveway.

"Oh, my God, hurry! Grab your clothes and jump out the window. My husband's home early!"

"I can't jump out of the window. It's raining out there!"

"If my husband catches us in here, he'll kill us both!" she replied. "He's got a hot temper and a gun, so the rain is the least of your problems!"

So the boyfriend scoots out of bed, grabs his clothes and jumps out the window.

As he ran down the street in the pouring rain, he quickly discovered he had run right into the middle of the town's annual marathon, so he started running along beside the others, about 300 of them. Being naked with his clothes tucked under his arm, he tried to blend in as best he could, but after a little while a small group of runners who had been watching him with some curiosity jogged closer.

"Do you always run in the nude?" one asked.

"Oh yes!" he replied, gasping in air. "It feels so wonderfully free!"

Another runner moved alongside. "Do you always run carrying your clothes with you under your arm?"

"Oh, yes," our friend answered, thinking quickly. "That way I can get dressed right at the end of the run and get in my car to go home!"

Then a third runner cast his eyes a little lower and queried, "Do you always wear a condom when you run?"

"Nope... only when it's raining."

Q. How is being at a singles bar different from being at the circus?
A. At the circus, the clowns don't talk.

Q. What did the elephant say to the naked man?
A. "How do you breathe through something so small?"

Miss Bea, the church organist, was in her eighties and had never been married. She was much admired for her sweetness and kindness to all.

One afternoon, the pastor came to call on her, and she showed him into her living room. She invited him to have a seat while she prepared some tea.

As he sat facing her old pump organ, the young minister noticed a cut glass bowl sitting on top of it, filled with water. In the water floated, of all things, a condom!

When she returned with tea and cookies they began to chat. The pastor tried to stifle his curiosity about the bowl of water and its strange contents, but soon it got the better of him and he could no longer resist.

"Miss Bea," he said, pointing to the bowl, "I wonder if you would tell me about this?"

"Oh, yes," she replied, "isn't it wonderful? I was walking through the park a few months ago and I found this little package on the ground. The directions said to place it on the organ, keep it wet, and it would prevent the spread of disease. And you know, I haven't had a cold all winter."

A sweet, beautiful young would-be starlet comes to Hollywood to seek her fame and fortune. At her first power cocktail party she goes to the host and asks him, "Who's the most powerful man in the room?"

"That would be Jerry over there by the caviar," he says.

The young woman walks over to Jerry and says, "Excuse me, Jerry, would you mind stepping back behind this column? I'd like to talk to you."

Jerry and the girl step behind the column and she says, "Jerry, I'm going to unzip your fly, take out your cock, and give you the best blow job you've ever had!"

Jerry smiles slightly and says, "Well, okay. But what's in it for me?"

Two hunters went moose hunting every winter without success. Finally, they came up with a foolproof plan. They got a very authentic female moose costume and learned the mating call of a female moose.

The plan was to hide in the costume, lure the bull, then come out of the costume and shoot the bull. They set themselves up on the edge of a clearing, put on their outfit and began to give the moose love call.

Before long their call was answered as a bull came crashing out of the forest and into the clearing. When the bull was close enough, the guy in front said, "Okay, let's get out and get him."

After a moment that seemed like an eternity, the guy in the back shouted, "The zipper is stuck! What are we going to do!?"

The guy in the front says, "Well, I'm going to start nibbling grass, but you'd better brace yourself."

A man was approached by a co-worker at lunch who invited him out for a few beers after work.

The man said that his wife would never go for it, that she didn't allow him to go drinking with the guys after work. The co-worker suggested a way to overcome that problem.

"When you get home tonight, sneak into the house, slide down under the sheets, gently pull down your wife's panties, and give her oral sex.

Women love it, and believe me, she'll never mention that you were out late with the boys."

So the man agreed to try it, and went out and enjoyed himself.

Late that night, he sneaked into the house, slid down under the sheets, gently slid down his wife's panties, and gave her oral sex. She moaned and groaned with pleasure, but after a little while, he realized he had to take a leak, so he told her he'd be right back. He got out of bed and walked down the hall to the bathroom.

When he opened the door and went in, he was very surprised to see his wife sitting on the toilet.

"How did you get in here?" he asked.

"Shhhhh!!!" she replied. "You'll wake my mother!"

John and Nancy decided that the only way to pull off a Sunday afternoon quickie with their six-year-old son in the apartment was to send him out on the balcony and order him to report on all the neighborhood activities.

The boy began his commentary as his parents put their plans into operation.

"There's a car being towed from the parking lot," he said. "An ambulance just drove by." A few moments passed. "Looks like the Smiths have company," he called out. "Matt's riding a new bike and the Sanders are having sex."

Mom and Dad shot up in bed. "How do you know that?" the startled father asked.

"Their kid is standing out on the balcony, too," his son replied.

A woman woke in the middle of the night to find her husband missing from their bed. In the stillness of the house, she could hear a muffled sound downstairs. She went downstairs and looked all around, finally finding her husband in the basement, crouched in the corner, facing the wall and sobbing.

"What's wrong with you?" she asked him.

"Remember when your father caught us having sex when you were sixteen?" he replied. "And remember he said I had two choices: I could either marry you or spend the next twenty years in prison."

Baffled, she said, "Yes, I remember. So what?"

"I would have been a free man today."

On their first night together, a newly-wed couple gets ready for bed. The new bride comes out of the bathroom, all showered and wearing a beautiful robe. The proud husband says, "My dear, we are married now. You can open your robe."

The beautiful young woman opens her robe, and he is astonished with her beauty.

"Oh, oh, aaaahhh," he exclaims. "Oh my goodness, you are so beautiful. Let me take your picture."

Puzzled she asks, "My picture?"

He answers, "Yes, my dear, so I can carry your beauty next to my heart forever." She smiles and he takes her picture, and then he heads into the bathroom to shower.

He comes out wearing his robe and the new wife asks, "Why are you wearing a robe? We are married now."

The man opens his robe and she exclaims, "Oh, oh, oh, my, let me get a picture."

He beams and asks, "Why?"

She answers, "So I can get it enlarged!"

A man's wife asks him to go to the store to buy some cigarettes, so he walks down to the store only to find it closed. So he goes into a nearby bar to use the vending machine. At the bar he sees a beautiful woman and starts talking to her. They have a couple of beers and one thing leads to another and they end up in her apartment.

After they've had their fun, he realizes its 3 a.m. and says, "Oh no, it's so late, my wife's going to kill me." He takes his shoes outside and rubs them in the grass and mud, then proceeds home.

His wife is waiting for him in the doorway and she is pretty pissed off. "Where the hell have you been?!?!"

"Well, honey, it's like this. I went to the store like you asked, but they were closed. So I went to the bar to use the vending machine. I saw this great-looking chick there and we had a few drinks and one thing led to another and I ended up in bed with her."

She sees his shoes are covered with grass and says, "You lying bastard!!! You've been fishing again!!!"

Q. Why do men find it difficult to make eye contact?
A. Breasts don't have eyes.

A big shot businessman had to spend a couple of days in the hospital. He was a royal pain to the nurses because he bossed them around just like he did his employees.

None of the hospital staff wanted to have anything to do with him. The head nurse was the only one who could stand up to him. She came into his room and announced, "I have to take your temperature."

After complaining for several minutes, he finally settled down, crossed his arms and opened his mouth.

"No, I'm sorry," the nurse stated, "but for this reading I cannot use an oral thermometer."

This started another round of complaining, but eventually he rolled over and bared his rear end.

After feeling the nurse insert the thermometer, he heard her announce, "I have to get something. Now you stay JUST LIKE THAT until I get back!"

She left the door to his room open on her way out. He cursed under his breath as he heard people walking past his door laughing. After almost an hour, the man's doctor came into the room.

"What's going on here?" asked the doctor.

Angrily, the man answered, "What's the matter, Doc? Haven't you ever seen someone having their temperature taken?"

After a pause, the doctor confessed, "Well, no. I guess I haven't... Not with a carnation anyway."

Q. How can you tell if you're making love to a teacher, a nurse or an airline stewardess?

A. The teacher says, "We've got to do this over and over again until we get it right."

The nurse says, "Hold still; this won't hurt at all."

And the airline stewardess says, "Put this over your mouth and nose and breathe normally."

A farmer is sitting in the neighborhood bar getting drunk. A man comes in and asks the farmer, "Hey, why are you sitting here on this beautiful day getting drunk?"

Farmer: "Some things you just can't explain."

Man: "So what happened that's so horrible?"

Farmer: "Well, today I was sitting by my cow milking her. Just as I got the bucket about full, she took her left leg and kicked over the bucket."

Man: "OK, but that's not so bad."

Farmer: "Some things you just can't explain."

Man: "So what happened then?"

Farmer: "I took her left leg and tied it to the post on the left."

Man: "And then?"

Farmer: "Well, I sat back down and continued to milk her. Just as I got the bucket about full, she took her right leg and kicked over the bucket."

Man: "Again?"

Farmer: "Some things you just can't explain."

Man: "So, what did you do then?"

Farmer: "I took her right leg this time and tied it to the post on the right."

Man: "And then?"

Farmer: "Well, I sat back down and began milking her again. Just as I got the bucket about full, the stupid cow knocked over the bucket with her tail."

Man: "Hmmm..."

Farmer: "Some things you just can't explain."

Man: "So, what did you do?"

Farmer: "Well, I didn't have any more rope, so I took off my belt and tied her tail to the rafter. In that moment, my pants fell down and my wife walked in."

⸎

There's a guy who really takes care of his body: He lifts weights and jogs five miles every day.

One morning, he looks into the mirror and admires his body. He notices that he is really suntanned all over except one part and he decides to do something about it.

He goes to the beach, completely undresses and buries himself in the sand except for the one part sticking out.

Two little old ladies are strolling along the beach and one looks down and says, "There really is no justice in this world."

The other little old lady says, "What do you mean?"
The first little old lady says, "Look at that.
When I was 10 years old, I was afraid of it.
When I was 20 years old, I was curious about it.
When I was 30 years old, I enjoyed it.
When I was 40 years old, I asked for it.
When I was 50 years old, I paid for it.
When I was 60 years old, I prayed for it.
When I was 70 years old, I forgot about it.
And now that I'm 80, the damned things are growing wild!!"

Three bulls heard via the grapevine that the rancher was going to bring yet another bull onto the ranch, and the prospect raised a discussion among them.

First Bull: "Boys, we all know I've been here 5 years. Once we settled our differences, we agreed on which 100 of the cows would be mine. Now, I don't know where this newcomer is going to get HIS cows, but I'm not giving him any of mine."

Second Bull: "That pretty much says it for me, too. I've been here 3 years and have earned my right to the 50 cows we've agreed are mine. I'll fight him 'til I run him off or kill him, but I'm keeping all my cows."

Third Bull: "I've only been here a year, and so far you guys have only let me have 10 cows to 'take care of.' I may not be as big as you fellows yet, but I am young and virile, so I simply must keep all my cows."

They'd no sooner finished their big talk when an eighteen-wheeler pulls up in the middle of the pasture with only one animal in it—the biggest bull these guys had ever seen! At 4,700 pounds, each step he took toward the ground strained the steel ramp to breaking point.

First Bull: "You know, it's actually been some time since I really felt I was doing all my cows justice anyway. I think I can spare a few for our new friend."

Second Bull: "I'll have plenty of cows to take care of if I just stay on the opposite end of the pasture from him. I'm certainly not looking for an argument."

They look over at their young friend, the third bull, and find him pawing the dirt, shaking his horns and snorting.

First Bull: "Son, let me give you some advice real quick. Let him have some of your cows and live to tell about it."

Third Bull: "Hell, he can have all my cows. I'm just making sure he knows I'm a bull!"

An old maid wanted to travel by bus to the pet cemetery with the remains of her cat. As she boarded the bus, she whispered to the driver, "I have a dead pussy."

The driver pointed to the woman in the seat behind him and said, "Sit with my wife. You two have a lot in common."

Q. Did you hear about the new "morning after" pill for men?
A. It works by changing your blood type!!

After three years of marriage, Kim was still questioning her husband about his lurid past.

"C'mon, tell me," she asked for the thousandth time, "how many women have you slept with?"

"Baby," he protested, "if I told you, you'd throw a fit."

Kim promised she wouldn't get angry, and convinced her hubby to tell her.

"Okay," he said. "One, two, three, four, five, six, seven—then there's you—nine, ten, 11, 12, 13..."

What men would do if they had a vagina for a day:

Immediately go shopping for zucchini and cucumbers.

Squat over a handheld mirror for an hour and a half.

See if they could finally do the splits.

See if it's truly possible to launch a ping pong ball 20 feet.

Cross their legs without rearranging their crotch.

Get picked up in a bar in less than 10 minutes.

Have consecutive multiple orgasms and still be ready for more without sleeping first.

Go to the gynecologist for a pelvic examination and ask to have it recorded on video.

Sit on the edge of the bed and pray for breasts too.

Finally—find that damned G-spot.

One day a young girl wearing a skirt goes out to play with her friends. She goes to the park and meets a boy. They talk about climbing trees.

The boy says to the girl, "Go on, climb that tree."

The girl climbs up while the boy just stands there and looks up her skirt. After a while the girl goes home and tells her mom what happened.

Her mom says, "Oh my, stupid girl, he just wanted to stand there and look at your underpants."

The next day she goes out again with her skirt on and meets the same boy. He tells her to climb the tree again and she does.

When she gets home she tells her mom what happened and her mom says, "Oh, my, stupid girl, he just wanted to stand there and look at your underpants."

The girl replies, "No, actually I tricked him. This time I didn't wear any underpants!"

A little girl walks into her parents' bathroom and notices for the first time her father's nakedness. Immediately, she is curious: He has equipment that she doesn't have.

She asks, "What are those round things hanging there, daddy?"

Proudly, he replies, "Those, sweetheart, are God's Apples of Life. Without them we wouldn't be here."

Puzzled, she seeks her mommy out and tells her what daddy has said.

To which mommy asks, "Did he say anything about the dead branch they're hanging from?"

A man was walking one day when he came to a big house in a nice neighborhood.

Suddenly, he realized there was a couple making love out on the lawn. Then he noticed another couple over behind a tree, then another couple behind some bushes by the house.

He walked up to the door of the house and knocked. A well-dressed woman answered the door, and the man asked what kind of a place this was.

"This is a brothel," replied the madam.

"Well, what's all this out on the lawn?" queried the man.

"Oh, we're having a yard sale today."

A 16-year-old girl finally had the opportunity to go to a party by herself. Since she was very good-looking, she was a bit nervous about what to do if boys came on to her.

Her mother said, "It's very easy! Whenever a boy starts talking to you, you ask him, 'What will be the name of our baby?' That'll scare them off."

So off she went. After a little while at the party, a boy started dancing with her. Little by little he started kissing her and touching her.

She asked him, "What will our baby be called?"

The boy found some excuse and disappeared. Some time later, the same thing happened again: A boy started to kiss her neck and her shoulders. She stopped him and asked about the baby's name, and he ran off.

Later on, another boy invited her for a walk. After a few minutes, he started kissing her, and she asked him, "What will our baby be called?"

He continued, now slowly taking her clothes off. "What will our baby be called?" she asked once more. He began to have sex with her. "What will our baby be called?!" she asked again.

After he was done, he took off his full condom, tied it in a knot, and said, "If he gets out of this one... Houdini!"

A man from the armed services had just spent a year unaccompanied on an expedition to a remote part of the world. The first night he got home, he exclaimed to his wife, "Honey, I want you to know that I haven't wasted all this time alone. Instead, I've mastered the art of mind over matter. Just watch this!"

And with that he dropped his underwear and shorts and stood before her totally naked.

"Now watch," he said. Next he said, "Dick, ten-SHUN!"

And with that his dick sprang to full erection. Then he said, "Dick, at EASE!"

And his dick deflated again.

"Wow, that was amazing," said his wife. "Do you mind if I bring our next-door neighbor over to see this? It's really something else!"

The guy responded that he didn't mind at all, since he was proud of what he had accomplished. So the wife went next door and came back with a delicious-looking woman who got this guy's full attention! After a brief pause to take her in, he said, "Now watch this." Then he said, "Dick, ten-SHUN!"

And the dick sprang to life. Then it was, "Dick, at EASE!"

But nothing happened. So the guy again said, "Dick, at EASE!"

But still nothing happened. So the guy now says, "For the last time, I said AT EASE!!"

Still nothing. Well, the guy was embarrassed and ran off to the bathroom. His wife made excuses for him and then joined her husband in the bathroom, where she found him masturbating.

"What in the world are you doing?" she asked.

The guy said, "I'm giving this son-of-a-bitch a dishonorable discharge!"

Q. How do you get four old ladies to shout "Fuck"?
A. Get a fifth old lady to shout "Bingo!"

Three women were sitting around talking about their sex lives.

The first said, "I think my husband's like a championship golfer. He's spent the last ten years perfecting his stroke."

The second woman said, "My husband's like the winner of the Motor Racing Grand Prix. Every time we get into bed he gives me several hundred exciting laps."

The third woman was silent until she was asked, "Tell us about your husband."

She thought for a moment and said, "My husband's like an Olympic gold-medalist for the 400 meters."

"How so?"

"He's got his time down to under 45 seconds."

❖

The subway train was packed. It was rush hour, and many people were forced to stand. One particularly cramped woman turned to the man behind her and said, "Sir, if you don't stop poking me with your thing, I'm going to the police!"

"I don't know what you're talking about, Miss. That's just my pay check in my pocket."

"Oh really," she spat. "Then you must have some job, because that's the fifth raise you've had in the last half hour!"

Bad Bernie was in prison for seven years. The day he got out, his wife and son were there to pick him up. He came through the gates and got into the car.

The only thing he said was, "F.F."

His wife turned to him and answered, "E.F."

Out on the highway, he said, "F.F."

She responded simply, "E.F."

He repeated, "F.F."

She again replied, "E.F."

"Mom! Dad!" their son yelled. "What's going on?"

Bad Bernie answered, "Your mother wants to eat first!"

Making a cup of coffee is like making love to a beautiful woman. It's got to be hot. You've got to take your time. You've got to stir gently and firmly.

You've got to grind your beans until they squeak. And then you put in the milk.

Ways to say, "Excuse me, your fly is undone":

The cucumber has left the salad.

Someone tore down the wall, and your Pink Floyd is hanging out.

Your soldier isn't so unknown now.

Quasimodo needs to go back in the tower and tend to his bells.

Elvis Junior has LEFT the building!

Mini Me is making a break for the escape pod.

You've got your fly set for Monica instead of Hillary.

You've got a security breach at Los Pantaloons.

I'm talking about shaft; can you dig it?

Men are from Mars, women can see your penis.

A worried father confronted his daughter one night. "I don't like that new boyfriend; he's rough and common and incredibly stupid."

"Oh no, Daddy," the daughter replied, "Fred's ever so clever. We've only been going out nine weeks and he's cured me of that illness I used to get once a month."

At a local college dance, a guy from America asks a girl from Sweden to dance.

While they are dancing, he gives her a little squeeze, and says, "In America, we call this a hug."

She replies, "Yaah, in Sveden we call it a hug too."

A little later, he gives her a peck on the cheek, and says, "In America, we call this a kiss."

She replies, "Yaah, in Sveden we call it a kiss too."

Towards the end of the night, and a lot of drinks later, he takes her out on the campus lawn and proceeds to have sex with her, saying, "In America, we call this a grass sandwich."

She says, "Yaaah, in Sveden we call it a grass sandwich too, but we usually put more meat in it."

The young blonde bride made her first appointment with a gynecologist and told him that she and her husband wished to start a family.

"We've been trying for months now, Doctor, and I don't seem to be able to get pregnant," she confessed miserably.

"I'm sure we'll solve your problem," the doctor reassured her.

"If you'll just take off your clothes and get up on the examining table."

"Well, all right, Doctor," agreed the young woman, blushing, "but I'd rather have my husband's baby."

A small tourist hotel was all abuzz with an afternoon wedding in which the groom was 95 and the bride was 23.

The groom looked pretty feeble and the feeling was that the wedding night might kill him because his bride was a healthy, vivacious young woman.

But, lo and behold, the next morning the bride came down the main staircase slowly, step by step, hanging onto the banister for dear life.

She finally managed to get to the counter of the little shop in the hotel. The clerk looked really concerned, "Whatever happened to you, my dear? You look like you've been wrestling an alligator!"

The bride groaned, hung on to the counter and managed to speak, "Ohhh God! He told me he'd been saving up for 75 years and I thought he meant his money!!"

Q. What's the best form of birth control after 50?
A. Nudity.

This guy goes to a doctor and says he has a problem with sex.

"Doc, I think my dick is just too damn small," he says.

The doctor asks him which drink he prefers.

"Well, Japanese beer," he replies, quite bemused.

"Aaaahhh. There's your problem, they shrink things, those silly Japanese beers. You should try drinking Guinness. That makes things grow."

Two months later the guy returns to the doctor with a big smile on his face.

He shakes the doctor by the hand and thanks him.

"I take it you now drink Guinness?" asks the doctor.

"Oh no, Doc," replies the man, "but I've got the wife hooked on Japanese beer!"

Bedroom Golf

* Each player shall furnish his own equipment for play. Normally one club and two (2) balls.

* Play on a course must be approved by the owner of the holes.

* Owner of the course must approve the equipment before play may begin.

* For most effective play, the club must have a firm shaft. Course owners are permitted to check the shaft stiffness before play begins.

* Course owners reserve the right to restrict the shaft length to avoid any damage to the course.

* Unlike outdoor golf, the goal is to get the club into the hole, while keeping the balls out.

* The object of the game is to take as many strokes as deemed necessary until the course owner is satisfied that play is complete. Failure to do so may result in being denied permission to play the course in the future.

* It is considered bad form to begin playing the hole immediately upon arrival at the course. The experienced player will normally take time to admire the entire course with special attention being given to the well-formed bunkers.

* Players are cautioned not to mention other courses they may have played, or are currently playing, to the owner of the course being played. Upset course owners have been known to damage a player's equipment for this reason.

* Players should assure themselves that their match has been properly scheduled, particularly when a new course is being played for the first time. Previous players have been known to become irate if they discover someone else playing what they consider to be a private course.

* Players should not assume a course is in shape for play at all times. Some players may be embarrassed if they find the course to be temporarily under repair. Players are advised to be extremely tactful in this situation. More advanced players will find alternate means of play when this is the case. Players are encouraged to have proper rain gear, just in case.

* Players are advised to obtain the course owner's permission before attempting to play the back nine.

* Slow play is encouraged. However, players should be prepared to proceed at a quicker pace, at least temporarily, at the request of the course owner.

* It is considered outstanding performance, time permitting, to play the same hole several times in one match.

* The course owner will be the sole judge as to who is the best player.

* Players are advised to think twice before considering membership at a given course. Additional assessments may be levied by the course owner, and the rules are subject to change. For this reason many players prefer to continue to play several different courses.

Q. What have men and floor tiles got in common?

A. If you lay them properly the first time, you can walk all over them for life.

A man is talking to his best friend about married life.

"You know," he says, "I really trust my wife, and I think she has always been faithful to me. But there's always that doubt."

His friend says, "Yeah, I know what you mean."

A couple of weeks later, the man has to go out of town on business. Before he goes, he gets together with his friend.

"While I'm away, could you do me a favor? Could you watch my house and see if there is anything fishy going on? I mean, I trust my wife but there's always that doubt."

The friend agrees to help out, and the man leaves town.

Two weeks later, he comes back and meets his friend.

"So did anything happen?"

"I have some bad news for you," says the friend.

"The day after you left, I saw a strange car pull up in front of your house. The horn honked and your wife ran out and got into the car and they drove away. Later, after dark, the car came back. I saw your wife and a strange man get out. They went into the house and I saw a light go on, so I ran over and looked in the window. Your wife was kissing the man. Then he took off his shirt. Then she took off her blouse. Then they turned off the light."

"Then what happened?" says the man.

"I don't know. It was too dark to see."

"Damn, you see what I mean? There's always that doubt."

A young couple left the church and arrived at the hotel where they were spending the first night of their honeymoon. They opened the champagne and began undressing.

When the bridegroom removed his socks, his new wife asked, "Ewww—what's wrong with your feet? Your toes look all mangled and weird. Why are your feet so gross?"

"I had tolio as a child," he answered.

"You mean polio?" she asked.

"No, tolio. The disease only affected my toes."

The bride was satisfied with this explanation, and they continued undressing. When the groom took off his pants, his bride once again wrinkled up her nose.

"What's wrong with your knees?" she asked. "They're all lumpy and deformed!"

"As a child, I also had kneasles," he explained.

"You mean measles?" she asked.

"No, kneasles. It was a strange illness that only affected my knees."

The new bride had to be satisfied with this answer. As the undressing continued, her husband at last removed his underwear.

"Don't tell me," she said. "Let me guess…Smallcox?"

In a checkout line the other day a couple were arguing about whose turn it was to pay.

The checkout girl was listening when she heard the lady say to the guy, "Stop being a scrote."

With a furrowed brow the clerk asked, "What is a scrote?"

Without missing a beat the lady responded, "Short for scrotum. He is somewhere between a prick and an asshole."

The Dean of Women at an exclusive girls' school was lecturing her students on sexual morality.

"We live today in very difficult times for young people. In moments of temptation," she said, "ask yourself just one question: Is an hour of pleasure worth a lifetime of shame?"

A young woman rose in the back of the room and said, "Excuse me, but how do you make it last an hour?"

A man goes to his doctor and complains that his wife hasn't wanted to have sex with him for the past six months.

The doctor tells the man to bring his wife in so he can talk to her and hopefully determine what the problem is.

The following day, the wife goes to the doctor's office. The doctor asks her what's wrong, and why she doesn't want to have sex with her husband.

"Oh, that's easily explained. For the past six months," the wife says, "I've been taking a cab to work every morning. I don't have any money. The cab driver asks me, 'Are you going to pay today, or what?' So, I take an 'or what.'

"Then, when I get to work," she continues, "I'm late, so the boss asks me, 'Are we going to write this down in the book, or what?' So, I take an 'or what.'

I take a cab to go home after work and, as usual, I have no money. The cab driver asks me again, 'So, are you going to pay this time, or what?' Again, I take an 'or what.'

So you see, Doc, by the time I get home I'm all tired out and don't want it anymore."

"Yes, I see," replies the doctor. "So, are we going to tell your husband, or what?"

After a long night of making love, a young guy rolled over, pulled out a cigarette from his jeans and searched for his lighter.

Unable to find it, he asked the girl if she had one on hand.

"There might be some matches in the top drawer," she replied.

He opened the drawer of the nightstand and found a box of matches sitting neatly on top of a framed picture of another man.

Naturally, the guy began to worry.

"Is this your husband?" he inquired nervously.

"No, silly," she replied, snuggling up to him.

"Your boyfriend then?" he asked.

"No, not at all," she said, nibbling away at his ear.

"Well, who is he then?" demanded the bewildered guy.

Calmly, the girl replied, "That's me before the operation."

Two women friends had gone out for a girls' night out, and had been decidedly overenthusiastic on the cocktails. Incredibly drunk and walking home, they suddenly realized they both needed to pee. They were very near a graveyard and one of them suggested they do their business behind a headstone or something. The first woman had nothing to wipe with, so she took off her panties, used them and threw them away. Her friend, however, was wearing an expensive underwear set and didn't want to ruin hers, but was lucky enough to salvage a large ribbon from a wreath that was on a grave, and proceeded to wipe herself with it. After finishing, they made their way home.

The next day the first woman's husband called the other husband and said, "These damn girls' nights out have got to stop. My wife came home last night without her panties."

"That's nothing," said the other. "Mine came back with a sympathy card stuck between the cheeks of her butt that said, 'From all of us at the Fire Station; we'll never forget you!'"

A bride tells her husband, "You know I'm a virgin and I don't know anything about sex. Can you explain it to me first?"

"OK, sweetheart. Putting it simply, we will call your private place 'the prison' and call my private thing 'the prisoner.' So what we do is put the prisoner in the prison."

And then they make love for the first time.

Afterward, the guy is lying face up on the bed, smiling with satisfaction.

Nudging him, his bride giggles, "Darling, the prisoner seems to have escaped."

Turning on his side, he smiles. "Then we will have to re-imprison him."

After the second time, the guy reaches for his cigarettes but the girl, thoroughly enjoying the new experience of making love, gives him a suggestive smile, "Darling, the prisoner is out again!"

The man rises to the occasion, but with the unsteady legs of a recently born foal.

Afterward, he lies back on the bed, totally exhausted.

She nudges him and says, "The prisoner has escaped again."

Limply turning his head, he shouts at her, "It's not a life sentence, OK?!"

A guy walks into a bar holding three ducks. He sets them on the bar and orders a drink. After talking with the bartender for a while, the man excuses himself to use the restroom.

The bartender feels a tad awkward with just himself and three ducks at the bar, so he decides to make small talk with them.

He asks the first duck, "What's your name?"

"Huey," replies the duck.

"So, how's your day been?"

"Oh, I've had a great day," replies Huey. "I've been in and out of puddles all day."

The bartender asks the second duck, "What's your name?"

"Duey," replies the duck.

"So, how's your day been?"

"Oh, I've had a great day," replies Duey. "I've been in and out of puddles all day."

The witty bartender says to the third duck, "So I guess your name is Louie?"

The duck replies, "No, I'm Puddles."

Q. What do a Rubik's cube and a penis have in common?

A. The longer you play with them, the harder they get.

On returning from battle in the Falkland Islands, three soldiers are asked to report to their commander.

The commander states that because of services rendered the army will pay each soldier a sum of $100 per inch on their bodies, from one point to another of their choice.

The commander asks the first soldier, a Special Forces commando, how he can measure him up.

"I'll have the top of my head to the tips of my toes, Sir!" replies the man of war.

"Excellent," says the commander, "that's 70 inches, so here's $7,000."

Second up, a marine states that he will have the tip of one arm outstretched measured to the other outstretched.

"Excellent," replies the commander after measuring the marine, "75 inches, so that's $7,500."

Thirdly, he asks the explosives expert.

"I'll have the tip of my dick to the end of my balls measured, Sir!"

The commander is a little taken aback by this but agrees, and after several seconds down in the private's privates he snaps back up saying, "Where in Christ's name are your balls, soldier?"

The soldier smiles at him and says, "Falkland Islands, Sir!"

Laying a carpet is very much like making love to a beautiful woman. You check the dimensions, lay her out on the floor, pin her down, nail her, then walk all over her. If you're adventurous, you might like to try an underlay.

Q. What is the difference between a bachelor and a married man?
A. A bachelor comes home, sees what's in the refrigerator, then goes to bed. A married man comes home, sees what's in bed, then goes to the refrigerator.

Q. How do you know if a blonde likes you?
A. She screws you two nights in a row.

Old Mendel Rugelbaum was very old and suffering from a rare disease and could drink only human milk.
"How can I get human milk?" Mendel asked the doctor.
"Well, Ruby Finkelstein's just had a baby, maybe she'll help."
So every day Mendel went to Ruby's house for his daily feed. Ruby was a dark-eyed, big breasted lady who in spite of herself gradually became aroused as Mendel lapped at her ripe breasts.
One day as he quietly lay sucking, she whispered to him, "Tell me, Mr. Rugelbaum, do you like it?"
"Mmmm, wonderful," he sighed.

"Is there..." she hesitated, her lips parted, eyes aglow. "Is there anything else you'd like?"

"As a matter of fact there is," murmured Mendel.

"What?" Ruby asked breathlessly.

Mendel licked his lips. "Maybe a little cookie?"

"Doc," says Steve, "I want to be castrated."

"What on earth for?" asks the doctor in amazement.

"It's something I've been thinking about for a long time and I want to have it done," replies Steve.

"But have you thought it through properly?" asks the doctor. "It's a very serious operation and once it's done, there's no going back. It will change your life forever!"

"I'm aware of that and you're not going to change my mind. Either you book me in to be castrated or I'll simply go to another doctor."

"Well, OK," says the doctor, "but it's against my better judgment!"

So Steve has his operation, and the next day he is up and walking very slowly, legs apart, down the hospital corridor with his drip stand. Heading towards him is another patient, who is walking exactly the same way.

"Hi there," says Steve. "It looks as if you've just had the same operation as me."

"Well," said the patient, "I finally decided after 37 years of life that I would like to be circumcised."

Steve stared at him in horror and screamed, "Shit! THAT'S the word!"

Three women walk into a pet shop.

Suddenly the parrot yells out, "Yellow, pink, blue."

The first lady says, "That's funny, I'm wearing yellow underwear."

The second lady says, "Well, I'm wearing pink."

The third lady says, "No way, I'm wearing blue!"

To test the parrot, the next day all of them wear white and the parrot shouts, "White! White! White!"

The three women are amazed.

The final test is on the third day and just as they walk in the parrot yells, "Bald, curly and straight!"

They never went there again!!

Q. What does an old woman have between her breasts that a young woman doesn't?

A. A navel.

"Doc, I think my son has gonorrhea," a patient told his urologist on the phone. "The only woman he's screwed is our maid."

"OK, don't be hard on him. He's just a kid," the medic soothed. "Get him in here right away and I'll take care of him."

"But, Doc, I've been screwing the maid, too, and I've got the same symptoms he has."

"Then you come in with him and I'll fix you both up," replied the doctor.

"Well," the man admitted, "I think my wife now has it, too."

"Son of a bitch!" the physician roared. "That means we've all got it!"

A trucker had driven his fully-loaded rig to the top of a steep hill and was just starting down the equally steep other side when he noticed a man and a woman lying in the center of the road, making love.

He blew his horn several times as he was bearing down on them. Realizing that they were not about to get out of his way, he slammed on his brakes and stopped just inches from them.

Getting out of the truck, madder than hell, the trucker walked up to the two, still in the road, and yelled, "What the hell's the matter with you two? Didn't you hear me blowing the horn? You could've been killed!"

The man on the highway, obviously satisfied and not too concerned, looked up and said, "Look, I was coming, she was coming, and you were coming. You were the only one with brakes."

A man goes along to the Patent and Trademark Office with some of his new designs. He says to the clerk, "I'd like to register my new invention. It's a folding bottle."

"OK," says the clerk. "What do you call it?"

"A fottle," replies the inventor.

"A fottle? That's stupid! Can't you think of something else?"

"I can think about it. I've got something else though. It's a folding carton."

"And what do you call that?" asks the clerk.

"A farton," replies the inventor.

"That's obscene. You can't possibly call it that!"

"In that case," says the inventor, "you're really going to hate the name of my folding bucket."

Q. What is the difference between a woman and a washing machine?

A. You can toss your load in a washing machine and it won't call you a week later.

Roger is a hard worker and he spends most of his nights bowling or playing volleyball.

One weekend his wife decides that he needs to relax a little and take a break from sports, so she takes him to a strip club.

The doorman at the club spots them and says, "Hey, Roger! How are you tonight?"

His wife, surprised, asks her husband if he has been here before.

"No, no. He's just one of the guys I bowl with."

They are seated and the waitress approaches, sees Roger and says, "Nice to see you, Roger. A gin and tonic as usual?"

His wife's eyes widen. "You must come here a lot!"

"No, no," says Roger, "I just know her from volleyball."

Then a stripper walks up to the table. She throws her arms around Roger and says, "Roger! A table dance as usual?"

His wife, fuming, collects her things and storms out of the bar.

Roger follows her and spots her getting into a cab, so he jumps into the passenger seat. His wife looks at him, seething with fury and lets Roger have it.

At this, the cab driver leans over and says, "Sure looks like you picked up a bitch tonight, Roger!"

A guy wanted to buy a gift for his new girlfriend's birthday.

As they had only just started dating, after careful consideration he decided a pair of gloves would strike the right note: personal, but not too personal.

Accompanied by the girlfriend's younger sister, he went to Macy's and bought a pair of white gloves. The sister purchased a pair of panties for herself.

During the wrapping, however, the clerk got the items mixed up and the sister got the gloves and the girlfriend got the panties.

The guy sent the package to the girlfriend with the following note:

I chose these because I noticed that you don't wear any in the evening. If it had not been for your sister, I would have chosen the long ones with the buttons, but she wears the short ones that are easier to take off.

These are a delicate shade, but the sales clerk that helped me has a pair that she has been wearing for the past three weeks and they are hardly dirty. I had her try yours on for me and she looked really great.

I wish I was there to put them on for you the first time, as no doubt other hands will come into contact with them before I have a chance to see you again.

When you take them off, remember to blow in them before putting them away as they will naturally be a little damp from wearing.

Just think how many times I will kiss them during the coming year. I hope you will wear them for me Friday night.

All my love.

P.S. The latest style is to wear them folded down with a little fur showing.

A lady walked into a Lexus dealership just to browse. Suddenly, she spotted the most beautiful car that she had ever seen and walked over to inspect it. As she bent forward to feel the fine leather upholstery, an unexpected little fart escaped.

Embarrassed, she anxiously looked around to see if anyone had noticed and hoped a salesperson wouldn't pop up. But as she turned back, there standing next to her, was a salesman.

With a pleasant smile he greeted her, "Good day, Madam. How may we help you today?"

Trying to maintain an air of sophistication and acting as though nothing had happened, she smiled back and asked, "Sir, what is the price of this lovely vehicle?"

Still smiling pleasantly, he replied, "Madam, I'm very sorry to say that if you farted simply from touching it, you are going to shit when you hear the price."

A preacher wanted to raise money for his church and, being told there were fortunes in racehorses, he decided to purchase one and enter it in the races.

However, at the local auction, the going price for horses was so steep he ended up buying a donkey instead. He figured that since he had it, he might as well go ahead and enter it in the races, and to his surprise the donkey came in third.

The next day the racing sheets carried the headlines, "Preacher's ass shows."

The preacher was so pleased with the donkey that he entered it in the races again and this time he won! The papers said, "Preacher's ass out in front." The Bishop was so upset with this kind of publicity that he ordered the preacher not to enter the donkey in another race.

The newspaper printed this headline, "Bishop scratches preacher's ass." This was just too much for the Bishop and he ordered the preacher to get rid of the animal.

The preacher decided to give it to a nun in a nearby convent. The headlines the next day read, "Nun has the best ass in town."

The Bishop fainted.

He informed the nun that she would have to dispose of the donkey and she finally found a farmer who was willing to buy it for $10.

The paper states, "Nun peddles ass for ten bucks."

They buried the Bishop the next day.

A bus stops and two Italian men get on. They seat themselves and engage in animated conversation. The lady sitting behind them ignores their conversation at first, but her attention is galvanized when she hears one of the men say the following:

"Emma come first. Den I come. Two asses, they come together. I come again. Two asses, they come together again. I come again and pee twice. Then I come once-a-more."

"You foul-mouthed swine," retorted the lady indignantly. "In this country, we don't talk about our sex lives in public."

"Hey, coola down, lady," said the man. "Imma just tella my friend howa to spella Mississippi."

A husband and wife are sitting quietly in bed reading when the wife looks over at him and asks the question.

WIFE: "What would you do if I died? Would you get married again?"

HUSBAND: "Definitely not!"
WIFE: "Why not? Don't you like being married?"
HUSBAND: "Of course I do."
WIFE: "Then why wouldn't you remarry?"
HUSBAND: "Okay, okay, I'd get married again."
WIFE: "You would?" (with a hurt look)
HUSBAND: (makes audible groan)
WIFE: "Would you live in our house?"
HUSBAND: "Sure, it's a great house."
WIFE: "Would you sleep with her in our bed?"
HUSBAND: "Where else would we sleep?"
WIFE: "Would you let her drive my car?"
HUSBAND: "Probably, it is almost new."
WIFE: "Would you replace my pictures with hers?"
HUSBAND: "That would seem like the proper thing to do."
WIFE: "Would you give her my jewelry?"
HUSBAND: "No, I'm sure she'd want her own."
WIFE: "Would she use my golf clubs?"
HUSBAND: "No, she's left-handed."
WIFE: -- silence --
HUSBAND: "Shit."

This lady goes to a vet and learns that if you put a ribbon around a snoring dog's penis he'll roll over and stop snoring.

The next night her dog is snoring so she goes to the kitchen and gets a red ribbon and ties it around her dog's penis. His snoring stops.

Later on that night her husband is snoring and so she goes to the kitchen and gets a blue ribbon and ties it around her husband's penis, and he stops snoring.

The next morning her husband wakes up and looks at his dog, then looks down at himself.

"I don't know what happened last night, but it appears we came in first and second."

Guts: Arriving home late after a night out with the guys, being assaulted by your wife with a broom, and having the guts to ask, "Are you still cleaning, or are you flying somewhere?"

❖

Q. Why did God create Adam before he created Eve?
A. Because he didn't want anyone telling him how to make Adam.

Her diary:

Saturday night I thought he was acting weird. We had made plans to meet at a bar to have a drink. I was shopping with my friends all day long, so I thought he was upset at the fact that I was a bit late, but he made no comment. Conversation wasn't flowing so I suggested that we go somewhere quiet so we could talk. He agreed but he kept quiet and absent. I asked him what was wrong and he said nothing. I asked him if it was my fault that he was upset. He said it had nothing to do with me and not to worry. On the way home I told him that I loved him and he simply smiled and kept driving. I can't explain his behavior; I don't know why he didn't say I love you too. When we got home I felt as if I had lost him, as if he wanted nothing to do with me anymore. He just sat there and watched TV. He seemed distant and absent. Finally, I decided to go to bed. About 10 minutes later he came to bed and, to my surprise, he responded to my caress and we made love, but I still felt that he was distracted and his thoughts were somewhere else. I decided that I could not take it anymore so I decided to confront him with the situation but he had fallen asleep. I started crying and cried until I too fell asleep. I don't know what to do. I'm almost sure that his thoughts are with someone else. My life is a disaster.

His diary:

Today the Giants lost. At least I got laid.

Having balls: Coming home late after a night out with the guys smelling of perfume and beer and lipstick on your collar, slapping your wife on the ass, and having the balls to say, "You're next."

Once upon a time there was a woman who was about to have triplets.

In her womb the babies were talking to each other.

The first baby said, "I want to be a plumber, because there is so much water in here."

The second baby said, "I want to be an electrician because it is so dark in here."

And the last baby said, "I want to be a hunter, because if that damn snake comes back in here I'm going to cut off its head."

A man goes to the dentist to have a tooth pulled. The dentist gets the syringe ready to administer the anesthetic.

"No way! No needles! I hate needles!" the patient says.

The dentist starts to hook up the laughing gas and the man again objects.

"I can't do the gas thing—the thought of having the gas mask on is suffocating to me!"

The dentist then asks if the man has any objection to taking a pill.

"No," the patient says, "I am fine with pills."

The dentist then returns and says, "Here is a Viagra tablet."

The patient says, "Wow—I didn't know Viagra worked as a pain pill!"

"It doesn't," says the dentist, "but it will give you something to hold onto when I pull out your tooth."

Q. What do you call a woman who is paralyzed from the waist down?

A. Married.

Little Johnny watched his science teacher start an experiment with worms.

Four worms were placed into four separate jars.

The first worm was put into a jar of alcohol.

The second worm was put into a jar of cigarette smoke.

The third worm was put into a jar of sperm.

The fourth worm was put into a jar of soil.

After one day, these were the results:

The first worm in alcohol—dead.

The second worm in cigarette smoke—dead.

The third worm in sperm—dead.

The fourth worm in soil—alive.

So the science teacher asked the class, "What can you learn from this experiment?"

Little Johnny quickly raised his hand and said, "As long as you drink, smoke and have sex, you won't have worms."

For all those men who say, "Why buy the cow when you can get the milk for free." Here's an update for you:

Nowadays 80% of women are against marriage.

Why?

Because they realize it's not worth buying an entire pig just to get a little sausage!

A little boy goes to his dad and asks, "What is politics?"

Dad says, "Well, son, let me try to explain it this way: I'm the breadwinner of the family, so let's call me Capitalism. Your mom, she's the administrator of the money, so we'll call her the Government. We're here to take care of your needs, so we'll call you the People. The nanny, we'll consider her the Working Class. And your baby brother, we'll call him the Future. Now, think about that and see if that makes sense.

So the little boy goes off to bed thinking about what dad has said.

Later that night, he hears his baby brother crying, so he gets up to check on him. He finds that the baby has dirtied his diaper, so the little boy goes to his parents' room and finds his mother sound asleep.

Not wanting to wake her, he goes to the nanny's room. Finding the door locked, he peeks in the keyhole and sees his father in bed with the nanny. He gives up and goes back to bed.

The next morning, the little boy says to his father, "Dad, I think I understand the concept of politics now."

The father says, "Good, son, tell me in your own words what you think politics is all about."

The little boy replies, "Well, while Capitalism is screwing the Working Class, the Government is sound asleep, the People are being ignored, and the Future is in deep shit."

A chicken farmer goes to a local bar, sits next to a woman, and orders a glass of champagne.

The woman perks up and says, "How about that? I just ordered a glass of champagne, too!"

"What a coincidence," he says. "This is a special day for me. I'm celebrating."

"This is a special day for me, too, and I'm also celebrating!" says the woman.

"What a coincidence," says the man. As they clink glasses he asks, "What are you celebrating?"

"My husband and I have been trying to have a child, and today my gynecologist told me I'm pregnant!"

"What a coincidence," says the man. "I'm a chicken farmer. For years all my hens were infertile, but today they're finally laying fertilized eggs."

"That's great!" says the woman. "How did your chickens become fertile?"

"I switched cocks," he replies.

She smiles and says, "What a coincidence!"

An elderly gentleman went to the local drugstore and asked the pharmacist for the little blue Viagra pill.

The pharmacist asked, "How many?"

The man replied, "Just a few, maybe a half dozen. I cut each one into four pieces."

The pharmacist said, "That's too small a dose. That won't get you through sex."

The old fellow said, "Oh, I'm past eighty years old and I don't even think about sex much anymore. I just want it to stick out far enough so I don't pee on my new golf shoes."

A father put his three-year-old daughter to bed, told her a story and listened to her prayers which she ended by saying, "God bless Mommy, God bless Daddy, God bless Grandma and goodbye Grandpa."

The father asked, "Why did you say goodbye grandpa?"

The little girl said, "I don't know, daddy, it just seemed like the thing to do."

The next day grandpa died. The father thought it was a strange coincidence. A few months later the father put the girl to bed and listened to her prayers which went like this: "God bless Mommy, God Bless Daddy and goodbye Grandma."

The next day the grandmother died. Oh Christ, thought the father, this kid is in contact with the other side. Several weeks later when the girl was going to bed the dad heard her say, "God bless Mommy and goodbye Daddy."

He practically went into shock. He couldn't sleep all night and got up at the crack of dawn to go to his office. He was nervous all day, had lunch sent in and watched the clock. He figured if he could get by until midnight he would be okay.

He felt safe in the office, so instead of going home at the end of the day he stayed there, drinking coffee, looking at his watch and jumping at every sound. Finally, midnight arrived, he breathed a sigh of relief and went home.

When he got home his wife said, "I've never seen you work so late. What's the matter?"

He said, "I don't want to talk about it. I've just spent the worst day of my life."

She said, "You think you had a bad day. You'll never believe what happened to me. This morning the milkman dropped dead on our porch."

A man was concerned about his failing eyesight and went to an optician. The optician said the man should stop masturbating.

The man asked, "Will I go blind?'

The optician said, "No, but you are upsetting all the people in the waiting room."

Women are like apples on trees. The best ones are at the top of the tree.

Most men don't want to reach for the good ones because they are afraid of falling and getting hurt. Instead, they sometimes take the apples from the ground that aren't as good, but easy.

The apples at the top think something is wrong with them, when in reality, they're great. They just have to wait for the right man to come along, the one who's brave enough to climb all the way to the top of the tree.

Now men, men are like a fine wine. They begin as grapes, and it's up to women to stomp the shit out of them until they turn into something acceptable to have dinner with.

Little Johnny and his mother were out and about. Little Johnny, out of the blue, asked his mother, "Mommy, how old are you?"

The mother responded, "Women don't talk about their age. You'll learn this as you get older."

Little Johnny then asked, "Mommy, how much do you weigh?"

His mother responded again, "That's another thing women don't talk about. You'll learn this too, as you grow up."

Little Johnny, still wanting to know about his mother, then fired off another question, "Mommy, why did you and daddy get a divorce?"

The mother, a little annoyed by the questions, responded, "Johnny, that is a subject that hurts me very much, and I don't want to talk about it now."

Then Little Johnny, frustrated, sulks until he is dropped off at a friend's house to play. He consulted with his friend about his conversation with his mother.

His friend said, "All you have to do is sneak a look at your mother's driving license. It's just like a report card from school. It tells you everything."

Later, Little Johnny and his mother were out and about again. Little Johnny began with, "Mommy, mommy, I know how old you are. You're 32 years old."

The mother was very shocked. She asked, "Sweetheart, how do you know that?"

Little Johnny shrugged and said, "I just know. And I know how much you weigh. You weigh 130 pounds."

"Where did you learn that?" asked the mother again.

Little Johnny said, "I just know. And I know why you and daddy got a divorce. You got an 'F' in sex."

The other night I was invited out for a night with the boys. I promised my wife that I would be home by midnight!

Well, the hours passed and the beer was going down way too easy. At around 2:30 a.m., drunk as a skunk, I headed for home. Just as I got in the door, the cuckoo clock in the hall started up and cuckooed three times.

Quickly, I realized she'd probably wake up, so I cuckooed another nine times. I was really proud of myself for having a quick-witted solution, even when smashed, to escape a possible conflict.

The next morning my wife asked me what time I got in, and I told her twelve o'clock. She didn't seem disturbed at all. Whew! Got away with that one!

She then told me that we needed a new cuckoo clock. When I asked her why, she said, "Well, last night our clock cuckooed three times, then said 'oh shit,' cuckooed four more times, cleared its throat, cuckooed another three times, giggled, cuckooed twice more, and then farted."

A country doctor went to a very remote area to deliver a baby.

It was so far out, there was no electricity. When the doctor arrived, no one was home except for the mother in labor and her 5-year-old child. The doctor instructed the child to hold a lantern high so he could see, while he helped the woman deliver the baby.

The child did so, the mother pushed and after a little while, the doctor lifted the newborn baby by the feet and spanked him on the bottom to get him to take his first breath.

The doctor then asked the 5-year-old what he thought of the baby.

"Hit him again," the 5-year-old said. "He shouldn't have crawled up there in the first place!"

A young woman goes to church to confess her sins to the priest.

"Forgive me, Father, for I have sinned."

"Tell all of your sins, my daughter."

"Oh, Father, last night my boyfriend made hot, passionate love to me seven times," she says.

The priest thinks about this long and hard and says, "Take seven lemons and squeeze the juice into a tall glass and drink it."

"Will this cleanse my soul of my sins?"

"No," the priest says, "but it'll wipe that smile off your face!"

Q. Why do tits have nipples?
A. Because without them they would be pointless.

The rescue squad was called to the home of an elderly couple for an apparent heart attack the gentleman had. When the squad got there it was too late and the man had died.

While consoling the wife, one of the rescuers noticed that the bed was a mess. He asked the lady what symptoms the man had suffered and if anything had precipitated the heart attack.

The lady replied, "Well, we were in bed making love and he started moaning, groaning, thrashing about the bed, panting, and sweating. I thought he was coming, but I guess he was going."

A man walks into a pharmacy and tells the pharmacist, "I need some condoms with pesticide on them."

The pharmacist says, "They don't make them with pesticide on them. You mean spermicide."

The man says, "No, I need them with pesticide."

The pharmacist says, "Why do you need them with pesticide?"

The man says, "Well, my old lady's got a bug up her ass and I'm going in after it."

Q. Why were men given larger brains than dogs?
A. So they won't hump female legs at cocktail parties.

A businessman boards a flight and is seated next to a gorgeous woman. He notices that she is reading a manual about sexual statistics. He asks her about it and she replies, "This is a very interesting book! It says that American Indians have the longest penises and Italian men are the best in bed. By the way, my name is Jill. What's yours?"

"Tonto Tortolini, nice to meet you."

In a small town the patrolman was making his evening rounds.

As he was checking a used car lot, he came upon two little old ladies sitting in a used car. He stopped and asked them why they were sitting there in the car. Were they trying to steal it?

"Heavens no, we bought it," said the old ladies.

"Then why don't you drive it away?"

"We can't drive."

"Then why did you buy it?"

"We were told that if we bought a car here we'd get screwed, so we're just waiting."

The train was crowded and the U.S. Marine walked the entire length looking for a seat, but the only seat left was taken by a well-dressed middle-aged French woman's poodle.

The war-weary Marine asked, "Ma'am, may I have that seat?"

The French woman just sniffed and said to no one in particular, "Americans are so rude. My little Fifi is using that seat."

The Marine walked the entire train again, but the only seat left was under that dog. "Please, ma'am. May I sit down? I'm very tired."

She snorted, "Not only are you Americans rude, you are also arrogant."

This time the Marine didn't say a word, he just picked up the little dog, tossed it out the train window, and sat down.

The woman shrieked, "Someone must defend my honor! Put this American in his place."

An English gentleman sitting nearby spoke up, "Sir, you Americans often seem to have a penchant for doing the wrong thing. You hold the fork in the wrong hand. You drive your cars on the wrong side of the road. And now, sir, you've thrown the wrong bitch out the window."

A man and a woman meet at a bar one day and are getting along really well. They decide to go back to the woman's house where they engage in passionate lovemaking.

The woman suddenly cocks her ear and says, "Quick my husband just got home—go hide in the bathroom!"

So the man runs into the bathroom.

Her husband comes up into the bedroom and looks at her. "Why are you naked?" he asks.

"Well, I heard you pull up outside, so I thought I would come up here and get ready to receive you."

"Okay," the man replies, "I'll go get ready."

He goes into the bathroom before his wife can stop him and sees a naked man standing there clapping his hands.

"Who the fuck are you?" the man asks.

"I am from the exterminator company. Your wife called me in to get rid of the moths you are having problems with."

The husband exclaims, "But you are naked!"

The man then looks down and jumps back in surprise.

"Those little bastards!"

Q. What's the difference between your wife and your job?
A. After five years your job still sucks.

A man and a woman were driving down the road arguing about his deplorable infidelity when suddenly the woman reached over and sliced the man's penis off.

Angrily, she tossed it out the car window.

Driving behind the couple was a man and his six-year-old daughter. The little girl was chatting away to her father when all of a sudden the penis smacked their car windscreen, stuck for a moment, then flew off.

Surprised, the daughter asked her father, "Daddy, what the heck was that?"

Shocked, but not wanting to expose his little girl to anything sexual at such a young age, the father replied, "It... it was only a bug, honey."

The daughter sat with a confused look on her face, and after a moment said, "Sure had a big dick, didn't it?"

One day a scientist goes to a school where he is trying to do an experiment on children to see how good their taste buds are. He goes into a random classroom and explains to the class what he will be doing with them today. The class is excited and agrees to help him.

The scientist first blindfolds the children. Then he tells them that he will put a certain flavor of candy in front of them. He then tells them to eat it and tell him what flavor they think it is.

The first candy all the children get right: It is cherry. The second as well: It is orange. But the last one is the hardest. None of the children can get it, so the scientist gives them a clue. He says, "It's what your mom might call your dad."

A girl in surprise yells out, "I know, I know."

Then the scientist says, "Well, what is it?"

Then she says, "The flavor is asshole!"

The children in horror spit it out. The real flavor was honey!!

Marge was in bed with her lover. All of a sudden, they heard a noise downstairs.

"Oh my God, your husband is home!" the man said. "What am I going to do?"

"Just stay in bed with me. He's probably so drunk, he isn't going to notice you here with me."

The fear of getting caught trying to escape was more powerful than the thought of getting caught in bed with Marge, so he trusted her advice. Sure enough, Marge's husband came crawling into bed and as he pulled the covers over him, he pulled the blankets, exposing six feet.

"Honey!" he yelled. "What the hell is going on? I see six feet at the end of the bed!"

"Dear, you're so drunk, you can't count. If you don't believe me, count them again."

The husband got out of bed, and counted. "One, two, three, four... By God, you're right, dear!"

There was a church that had a very big-busted organist. Her breasts were so huge that they bounced and jiggled while she played. Unfortunately, she distracted the congregation considerably.

The very proper church ladies were appalled. They said something had to be done about this or they would have to get another organist.

One of the ladies approached her very discreetly and told her to mash up some green persimmons, (if you eat them they make you pucker, because they are so sour) and rub them on her breasts and maybe they would shrink in size. She agreed to try it.

The following Sunday morning the minister got up on the pulpit and said, "Dew to thircumsthanthis bewond my contwol we will not hath a thermon tewday."

A husband and wife are waiting at the bus stop. With them are their eight children. A blind man joins them after a few minutes. When the bus arrives, they find it overloaded and only the wife and her eight children are able to fit in the bus. So the husband and the blind man decide to walk. After a while the husband gets irritated by the ticking of the blind man's stick and says to him, "Why don't you put a piece of rubber at the end of your stick? That ticking sound is driving me crazy!!"

The blind man replies, "If you had put a rubber on the end of YOUR stick, we'd be sitting in the bus."

"Won't you kiss me, Doctor?" asks a beautiful woman.

"No, it would be against my code of ethics," says the doctor.

"Please, just one kiss," begs the woman.

"It's completely out of the question," he goes on. "I shouldn't even be having sex with you."

A mother cleaning her son's room finds an S&M magazine under the bed. Upset, she immediately shows the magazine to her husband.

"Well?" his wife asks. "What do you think we should do?"

"I'm not sure," the father replies. "But we certainly shouldn't spank him."

A young couple on their wedding night were in their honeymoon suite.

As they were undressing for bed, the husband, a big burly man, tossed his pants to his new bride and said, "Here, put these on."

She put them on and the waist was twice the size of her body.

"I can't wear your pants," she said.

"That's right," said the husband, "and don't you ever forget it. I'm the one who wears the pants in this relationship."

With that she flipped him her panties and said, "Try these on."

He tried them on and found he could only get them on as far as his kneecaps.

"Hell," he said, "I can't get into your panties!"

She replied, "That's right, and that's the way it is going to stay until your attitude changes."

A waitress walks up to one of her tables in a New York City restaurant and notices that the three Japanese businessmen seated there are furiously masturbating.

"What the hell do you think you are doing?" she asks.

One of the Japanese men replies, "We are all very hungry."

The waitress asks, "So how is jerking off in this restaurant going to help the situation?"

A second businessman replies, "Because menu says, FIRST COME, FIRST SERVED."

James Bond walks into a bar and takes a seat next to a very attractive woman. He gives the woman a quick glance and then casually takes a look at his watch. The woman notices this and asks, "Is your date running late?"

"No," he replies. "Q's just given me a state-of-the-art watch and I was testing it out."

Intrigued, the woman asks, "A state-of-the-art watch? What's so special about it?"

Bond coolly explains, "It uses alpha waves to talk telepathically."

The lady says, "So what's it telling you now?"

"Well, it says you're not wearing any panties," says Bond.

The woman giggles and replies, "Well, it must be broken because I am wearing panties!"

Bond shakes his head, taps his watch and says, "Damn thing's an hour fast."

Pinocchio bumps into his old pal Gepetto, the carpenter who made him.

Gepetto asks how he is doing with his girlfriend.

"Not bad," Pinocchio says, "but when we have sex she keeps complaining about the splinters."

"Don't worry," says Gepetto, "I'll give you a sheet of fine sandpaper. That should fix the problem."

A few weeks later, they meet again. "How are things with your girlfriend now?" asks Gepetto.

"Who needs a girlfriend?" Pinocchio replies.

Homer Simpson on getting women hot:

"Well, you know, boys, a nuclear reactor is a lot like women. You just have to read the manual and press the right button."

Two guys are camping. They are having a little conversation, when all of a sudden one guy yells, "I just got bitten by a snake on the tip of my penis."

The other guy says, "Don't worry, I'll go into town and ask a doctor what to do." So the guy goes to the nearest town and after 30 minutes he finds a doctor. He asks the doctor, "Doctor, my friend just got bitten by a snake. What can I do?"

The doctor says, "Calm down. All you have to do is suck the poison out."

So the friend goes back to the campsite where his friend is lying on the ground.

He asks, "So what did the doctor say?"

The friend says, "The doctor says you're going to die!"

A newlywed couple arrived back from their honeymoon to move into their tiny new flat.

"Care to go to bed?" the husband asked.

"Shh!" said his blushing bride. "These walls are paper thin. The neighbors will know what you mean! Next time, ask me in code—like, 'Have you left the washing machine door open'—instead."

So, the following night, the husband asks, "I don't suppose you left the washing machine door open, darling?"

"No," she snapped back, "I definitely shut it." Then she rolled over and fell asleep.

The next morning, she woke up feeling a little frisky herself, so she nudged her husband and said, "I think I did leave the washing machine door open after all."

"Don't worry," said the man. "It was only a small load so I did it by hand."

A hunter is stalking in the jungle when he finds a sexy woman naked on a blanket.

He stares at her intently then says, "Are you game?"

"I sure am," she purrs.

So he shoots her.

If you're in a long term relationship, try the following to spice up your sex life: Get your lover, blindfold them, get some ropes and chains and tie them very tightly to the bed. Then go and have sex with someone else.

A navy chief and an admiral are sitting in the barbershop.

They have both just finished shaving, and the barber reaches for some aftershave.

"Hey! Don't put that stuff on me!" the admiral shouts. "My wife will think I've been in a brothel!"

The chief turns to his barber and says, "Go ahead and put it on. My wife doesn't know what the inside of a brothel smells like."

A man is stranded on a desert island for 10 years.

One day a beautiful girl swims to shore in a wetsuit.

Man: "Hi! I am so happy to see you."

Girl: "Hi! It looks like you've been here a long time. How long has it been since you've had a cigarette?"

Man: "It's been 10 years!"

With this information the girl unzips a slot on the arm of her wet suit and gives the man a cigarette.

Man: "Thank you so much!"

Girl: "So tell me, how long has it been since you had a drink?"

Man: "It's been 10 years!"

The girl unzips another pocket on her wet suit and comes out with a flask of whiskey and gives the man a drink.

Man: "Thank you so much. You are like a miracle!"

Girl (starting to unzip the front of her wet suit): "So tell me then, how long has it been since you played around?"

Man: "Oh, my God, don't tell me you've got a set of golf clubs in there, too...!"

A young girl says to her boyfriend, "You're the first man I've ever been with. Am I your first?"

"Possibly," the boyfriend says. "Were you in Las Vegas in 2003?"

Q: What do you call a Norwegian prostitute?

A: A Fjord Escort.

A 16-year-old boy comes home and tells his father, "Dad, I had my first blow job today."

Dad is delighted. He thinks his son is going to be a world- class Casanova. "How did it feel?" asks Dad.

"Not too bad," replies the son, "but my jaw aches like hell, and it leaves a strange taste in your mouth."

Terry was talking to his friend at the bar, and said, "I don't know what to get my wife for her birthday—she has everything—and besides, she can afford to buy anything she wants, so I'm stuck."

His friend said, "I have an idea! Why don't you make up a certificate saying she can have 60 minutes of great sex, any way she wants it? She'll probably be thrilled."

Terry decided to take his friend's advice.

The next day at the bar his friend said, "Well? Did you take my suggestion?"

"Yes, I did," Terry replied.

"Did she like it?"

"Oh yes! She jumped up, thanked me, kissed me on the forehead and ran out the door, yelling, 'I'll be back in an hour!!'"

A man and a woman are having dinner in a restaurant. Their waitress, taking another order a few tables away, spots that the man is slowly sliding down his chair and under the table, with the woman acting unconcerned.

As the waitress watches, the man slides all the way under and out of sight. Still, the woman dining opposite him appears not to notice.

Finally, the waitress comes over to the table and whispers discreetly to the woman, "Pardon me, ma'am, but I think your husband just slid under the table."

"No, he didn't," the woman calmly replies. "He just walked in the door."

An old man, Mr. Goldstein, was living the last of his life in a nursing home. One day, he appeared to be very sad and depressed. Nurse Lisa asked if there was anything wrong.

"Yes, Nurse Lisa," said Mr. Goldstein. "My private parts died today and I am very sad."

Knowing her patients were forgetful and sometimes a little crazy, she replied, "Oh, I'm so sorry, Mr. Goldstein. Please accept my condolences."

The following day, Mr. Goldstein was walking down the hall with his private parts hanging out of his pajamas, when he met Nurse Lisa.

"Mr. Goldstein," she said, "you shouldn't be walking down the hall like that. Please put your private parts back inside your pajamas."

"But, Nurse Lisa," replied Mr. Goldstein, "I told you yesterday that my private parts died."

"Yes, you did tell me that, but why are they hanging out of your pajamas?" asked Nurse Lisa.

"Well," he replied. "Today's the viewing."

Kylie Minogue, Elton John and Robbie Williams are walking down the street. Kylie trips, jamming her head in some railings. Robbie pulls down her panties and takes her from behind!

He turns to Elton and says, "Your turn," but Elton starts crying. "What's wrong?" asks Robbie.

Elton sobs and says, "My head won't fit in the railings!"

An enraged woman says to her cheating boyfriend, "You just think with your penis."

"No, I don't," the boyfriend replies, "it does all the thinking for me."

An enraged woman says to her cheating boyfriend, "You just think with your penis."

A woman takes her 16-year-old daughter to the doctor. The doctor says, "Okay, Mrs. Jones, what's the problem?"

The mother says, "It's my daughter, Darla. She keeps getting these cravings, she's putting on weight, and she's sick most mornings."

The doctor gives Darla a good examination, then turns to the mother and says, "Well, I don't know how to tell you this, but your Darla is about four months pregnant."

The mother says, "Pregnant?! She can't be. She has never ever been left alone with a man! Have you, Darla?"

Darla says, "No, mother! I've never even kissed a man!"

The doctor walks over to the window and just stares out it. About five minutes pass and finally the mother says, "Is there something wrong out there, Doctor?"

The doctor replies, "No, not really. It's just that the last time anything like this happened, a star appeared in the east and three wise men came over the hill. I'll be damned if I'm going to miss it this time!"

Sometimes women are overly suspicious of their husbands. When Adam stayed out very late for a few nights, Eve became upset.

"You're running around with other women," she charged.

"You're being unreasonable," Adam responded. "You're the only woman on Earth." The quarrel continued until Adam fell asleep, only to be awakened by someone poking him in the chest. It was Eve.

"What do you think you're doing?" Adam demanded.

"Counting your ribs!"

A small boy is separated from his father at a football game, so he goes up to a policeman and says, "I've lost my dad!"

"What's he like?" the cop inquires.

"Beer and loose women..."

A woman is in bed with her lover, who also happens to be her husband's best friend. They have sex for hours, and afterward while they're just laying there, the phone rings.

Since it is the woman's house, she picks up the receiver. Her lover looks over at her and listens, only hearing her side of the conversation (she is speaking in a cheery voice).

"Hello? Oh, hi. I'm so glad that you called. Really? That's wonderful. I am so happy for you. That sounds terrific. Great! Thanks. Okay. Bye."

She hangs up the telephone and her lover asks, "Who was that?"

"Oh," she replies, "that was my husband telling me all about the wonderful time he's having on his fishing trip with you."

Two parents take their son on a vacation and go to a nude beach. The father goes for a walk on the beach and the son goes and plays in the water. The son comes running up to his mom and says, "Mommy, I saw ladies with boobies a lot bigger than yours!"

The mom says, "The bigger they are, the dumber they are."

So he goes back to play. Minutes later he runs back and says, "Mommy, I saw men with penises a lot bigger than Daddy's!"

The mom says, "The bigger they are, the dumber they are."

So he goes back to play. Several minutes later he comes running back and says, "Mommy, I just saw Daddy talking to the dumbest lady I've ever seen and the more he talked, the dumber he got!"

There was an artist who worked from a studio in his home. He specialized in nudes, and had been working on what he thought would be a masterpiece for several months now. As usual, his model reported, and after exchanging the usual greetings and small talk she began to undress for the day's work.

He told her not to bother because he felt pretty bad with a cold he had been fighting. He told her that he would pay her for the day, but that she could just go home—he only wanted some hot tea and then bed.

The model said, "Oh, please, let me fix it for you. It's the least I can do." He agreed and told her to fix herself a cup, too. They were sitting in the living room just exchanging small talk and enjoying their tea, when he heard the front door open and close, then some familiar footsteps.

"Oh my God!" he whispered loudly. "It's my wife. Quick, take all your clothes off."

Q. What's worse than getting raped by Jack the Ripper?
A. Getting fingered by Captain Hook.

A woman answers the door to a market researcher. "Good morning, madam, I'm doing some research for Vaseline. Do you use it at all in your household?"

"Oh yes, all the time. It's very good for cuts, scrapes and burns."

"Do you use it for anything else?"

"Like what?"

"Ahem.. err.. well.. during.. ahem.. sex."

"Oh, of course. Yes, I smear it on the bedroom doorknob to keep my husband out!"

This couple goes to an agricultural show way out in the countryside on a fine Sunday afternoon and are watching the bull auction. The guy selling the bulls announces the first bull to be auctioned off. "A fine specimen, this bull reproduced 60 times last year."

The wife nudges her husband in the ribs and comments, "See! That's more than five times a month!"

The second bull is to be sold. "Another fine specimen, this wonder reproduced 120 times last year."

Again the wife bugs her husband, "Hey, that's about 10 times a month. What do you say to that?" Her husband is getting really annoyed with this comparison.

The third bull is up for sale. "And this extraordinary specimen reproduced 365 times last year!"

The wife slaps her husband on the arm and yells, "That's once a day, every day of the year! How about you?"

The husband was pretty irritated by now and yells back, "Sure, once a day! Great! But you ask the auctioneer if they were all with the same cow!"

A man gets sent to prison and, as soon as he walks in, his huge, buff cellmate says to him, "We're going to play house. Do you want to be the mommy or the daddy?"

After thinking about it for a minute the man slowly answers, "Well, if I have to choose, I guess I'll be the daddy."

"OK," his cellmate says, "then get over here and suck mommy's dick."

After the baby was born, the panicked Japanese father went to see the obstetrician. "Doctor," he said, "I don't mind telling you, but I'm a little upset because my daughter has red hair. She can't possibly be mine."

"Nonsense," the doctor said. "Even though you and your wife both have black hair, one of your ancestors may have contributed red hair to the gene pool."

"It isn't possible," the man insisted. "We're pure Asian."

"Well," said the doctor, "let me ask you this. How often do you have sex?"

The man seemed ashamed. "I've been working very hard for the past year. We only made love once or twice a month."

"There you have it!" the doctor said confidently. "It's just rust."

A man has to attend a large convention in Chicago. On this particular trip he decides to bring his wife. When they arrive at their hotel and are shown to their room, the man says, "You rest here while I register—I'll be back within an hour."

The wife lies down on the bed, and just then, an elevated train passes by very close to the window and shakes the room so hard that she's thrown out of the bed. Thinking this must be a freak occurrence, she lies down once more. Again a train shakes the room so violently, she's pitched to the floor.

Exasperated, she calls the front desk and asks for the manager. The manager says he'll be right up. The manager (naturally) is skeptical but the wife insists the story is true. "Look, lie here on the bed—you'll be thrown right to the floor!"

So he lies down next to the wife. Just then, the husband walks in. "What," he says, "are you doing here?"

The manager replies, "Would you believe I'm waiting for a train?"

Shortly after being assigned to a new base, a lieutenant and his wife were invited to the colonel's home for an evening of bridge. The lieutenant was partnered with the colonel's wife and vice versa.

After many hands, the lieutenant excused himself to use the bathroom, but accidentally left the door ajar. When the sound of splashing echoed through the family room, his wife was greatly embarrassed and attempted to apologize.

The colonel's wife smiled demurely, "Don't worry about it—this is the first time all evening that I've been able to tell what he has in his hand."

❈

This guy in a bar noticed a woman, always alone, who came in on a fairly regular basis. After the second week, he made his move.

"No, thank you," she said politely. "This may sound rather odd in this day and age, but I'm keeping myself pure until I meet the man I love."

"That must be rather difficult," the man replied.

"Oh, I don't mind too much," she said. "But it has my husband pretty upset."

❈

A man decides to start a farm. So he walks into town to buy some animals. At the farmers' market he first asks for a rooster.

"We don't call them roosters here," the clerk says snootily. "We call 'em cocks."

So the man buys one cock, then points at another animal and asks, "What do you call that?"

The clerk replies, "That's a pullet."

The man agrees to buy one.

Finally, he asks for a donkey.

The clerk replies, "We don't call them donkeys, we call 'em asses, but we only have one left and it's very temperamental."

"What's wrong with it?" asks the man, who is determined to get a donkey.

"Once in a while it will stop walking and it won't budge unless you scratch it behind the ears," says the clerk.

The man decides to buy it anyway, and pays for all the animals before starting his walk home.

On the way, the donkey suddenly stops and doesn't move.

But the man has his arms full with the rooster and pullet, so has to stop a woman who is passing by to ask for help.

"Pardon me," he asks politely, "would you mind holding my cock and pullet, while I scratch my ass?"

A little boy and his grandfather are raking leaves in the yard. The little boy finds an earthworm trying to get back into its hole.

He says, "Grandpa, I bet I can put that worm back in that hole."

The grandfather replies, "I'll bet you five dollars you can't. It's too wiggly and limp to put back in that little hole." The little boy runs into the house and comes back out with a can of hairspray. He sprays the worm until it is straight and stiff as a board. Then he puts the worm back into the hole.

The grandfather hands the little boy five dollars, grabs the hairspray, and runs into the house. Thirty minutes later the grandfather comes back out and hands the little boy another five dollars.

The little boy says, "Grandpa, you already gave me five dollars."

The grandfather replies, "I know. That's from your grandma."

Hanging wallpaper is much like making love to a beautiful woman.

Clean all the relevant surfaces, spread her out on the table, cover her with paste, and stick her up. Then you clean your brush, light your pipe, stand back and admire your handiwork.

A husband and wife are staying in a hotel, and after a romantic evening wining and dining they go off to bed. However, as soon as they settle down, the man (not quite ready for slumber) leans over and whispers softly, "Hey, snuggle boopy boops, your lickle hubby wubby isn't quite ready for bye-byes yet."

The wife takes the hint and says, "OK, but I have to use the bathroom first." So off she goes, but on her way back she trips over a piece of carpet and lands flat on her face.

Her husband jumps up and exclaims in a concerned tone, "Oh, my little honey bunny, is your nosey-wosey all right?"

No harm is done, so she jumps into bed and they have mad passionate sex for three hours. Afterward, the wife goes off to the bathroom again, but on her way she trips over the same piece of carpet and again lands flat on her face on the floor.

Her husband looks over and grunts, "Clumsy bitch."

One day a construction worker left the job a little early, and when he got home he found his wife in bed with another man. Purple with rage, he hauled the man down the stairs and into the garage where he proceeded to secure the man's dick in a vice.

Utterly terrified, the man screamed, "Stop, stop! You're not going to cut it off, are you? ARE YOU?"

"Nope," replied the construction worker. "You are—I'm going to set the garage on fire."

Q. How did Pinocchio find out he was made of wood?
A. When his hand caught on fire.

A man with a bad stomach ache goes to the doctor where he is told the illness is quite serious but can be cured by a small dose of two suppositories inserted deep up his anal passage.

The doctor then tells the man to bend over while he shoves the first one all the way up. The doc then tells the man to repeat in six hours time.

At home six hours later, he can't do it himself so asks his wife to help. After telling her what to do, she nods and puts one hand on his shoulder and shoves really hard. The man screams in disgust.

"What's the matter?" asks the wife. "Did I hurt you?"

"No," replies the man, "but I just realized that when the doctor did that he had both hands on my shoulders."

One night a wife found her husband standing over their baby's crib. Silently, she watched him. As he stood looking down at the sleeping infant, she saw on his face a mixture of emotions: disbelief, doubt, delight, amazement, enchantment, scepticism.

Touched by this unusual display and the deep emotions it aroused, with eyes glistening she slipped her arm around her husband.

"A penny for your thoughts," she said.

"It's amazing!" he replied. "I just can't see how anybody can make a crib like that for only $49.99."

One day on the way home from work, I stopped at the local pharmacy and, while I was checking out, I picked up some candy to take home for me and my 7-year-old son.

It was a bag of gold coins (gold foil-covered chocolate candy coins). There were many sizes, from dime to dollar. I took the bag home, and me and my son opened the bag and ate all of the coins, my son taking the bigger dollar-sized ones and me taking the smaller ones.

The next day, my wife, my son and I stopped at the pharmacy again to pick up a few things. While my wife and I were shopping, we noticed that my son had picked up a gold coin condom. Before we could catch him, he took it up to the counter and asked the pharmacist, "What's this?"

The woman, looking very serious, said, "That's a condom, son."

To which my son replied, "My daddy bought me some of these yesterday!"

With a disgusted look on her face, the pharmacist replied, "Those are NOT for children, young man."

And finally, my son replied, "Then I'll buy this one for my daddy. He likes the LITTLE ones!"

Men are like parking spots: The good ones are taken, and the rest are too small.

Men are like copy machines: You need them for reproduction, but that's about it.

Men are like high heels: They're easy to walk on once you get the hang of it.

215

Men are like miniskirts: If you're not careful, they'll creep up your legs.

Men are like bananas: The older they get, the less firm they are.

A tired doctor was awakened by a phone call in the middle of the night.

"Please, you have to come right over," pleaded the distraught young mother, "my child has swallowed a contraceptive."

The doctor dressed quickly, but before he could get out the door, the phone rang again.

"You don't have to come over after all," the woman said with a sigh of relief. "My husband just found another one."

There are four kinds of sex:

HOUSE SEX—When you are newly married and have sex all over the house in every room.

BEDROOM SEX—After you have been married for a while, you only have sex in the bedroom.

HALL SEX—After you've been married for many, many years you just pass each other in the hall and say, "FUCK YOU."

COURTROOM SEX—When your wife and her lawyer fuck you in the divorce court in front of many people for every penny you've got.

This beautiful woman one day walks into a doctor's office and the doctor is bowled over by how stunningly beautiful she is. All his professionalism goes right out the window.

He tells her to take off her pants. She does, and he starts rubbing her thighs.

"Do you know what I am doing?" asks the doctor.

"Yes, checking for abnormalities," she replies.

He tells her to take off her shirt and bra. She takes them off. The doctor begins rubbing her breasts and asks, "Do you know what I am doing now?"

She replies, "Yes, checking for cancer."

Finally, he tells her to take off her panties, lays her on the table, gets on top of her and starts having sex with her. He says to her, "Do you know what I am doing now?"

She replies, "Yes, getting HIV—that's why I am here!"

A dog, a cat, and a penis are sitting around a campfire one night. The dog says, "My life sucks—my master makes me do my business on a fire hydrant!"

The cat says, "I don't think so—my master makes me do my business in a box of cat litter."

The penis, outraged, says, "At least your master doesn't put a bag over your head and make you do push ups until you throw up!"

A man and a woman start to have sex in the middle of a dark forest. After about 15 minutes of it, the man finally gets up and says, "Damn, I wish I had a flashlight!"

The woman says, "Me too, you've been eating grass for the past ten minutes!"

A couple just got married, and on the night of their honeymoon before passionate love, the wife tells the husband, "Please be gentle, I'm still a virgin."

The husband, being shocked, replies, "How's this possible? You've been married three times before."

The wife responds, "Well, my first husband was a gynecologist and all he wanted to do was look at it. My second husband was a psychiatrist and all he wanted to do was talk about it. Finally, my third husband was a stamp collector and all he wanted to do was... Oh, do I miss him!"

John has just graduated from clinical psychology and opens his first office. After some successful advertising he is astounded to have nearly 300 people wanting to be in group therapy. John decides to rent a big hall and invite the entire group. To break the ice, and to get the therapy started, John decides to ask for a show of hands as to how often the attendees have sex. He first asks for a show of hands of all the people who have sex almost every night. A modest number of hands are raised. He then asks, how many have sex once a week. This time a larger number of hands are raised. John then asks how many have sex once or twice a month. Again a few hands are raised. After John polls his group several more times, he notices one guy sitting off to the side with this huge beaming grin on his face. John notices that the guy has never raised his hand, so he asks him how often he has sex. The guy says, "Once a year!"

John responds, "Why are you so happy getting sex only once a year?" The grinning guy responds, "Tonight's the night!"

Three guys go to a ski lodge, but there aren't enough rooms so they have to share a bed. In the middle of the night, the guy on the right wakes up and says, "I had this wild, vivid dream of getting a hand job!"

The guy on the left wakes up, and, unbelievably, he's had the same dream, too.

Then the guy in the middle wakes up and says, "That's funny, I dreamt I was skiing!"

A kindergarten teacher one day is trying to explain to her class the definition of the word "definitely." To make sure the students have a good understanding of the word, she asks them to use it in a sentence. The first student raises his hand and says, "The sky is definitely blue."

The teacher says, "Well, that isn't entirely correct, because sometimes it's gray and cloudy."

Another student says, "Grass is definitely green."

The teacher again replies, "If grass doesn't get enough water, it turns brown, so that isn't really correct either."

Another student raises his hand and asks the teacher, "Do farts have lumps?"

The teacher looks at him and says, "No, but that isn't really a question you want to ask in class discussion."

So the student replies, "Then I've definitely shit in my pants."

Q. What's better than a rose on your piano?
A. Tulips on your organ.

A man decides to have a facelift for his birthday. He spends $5,000 and feels really good about the result. On his way home he stops at a newsstand and buys a paper.

Before leaving he says to the sales clerk, "I hope you don't mind me asking, but how old do you think I am?"

"About 35," is the reply.

"I'm actually 47," the man says happily.

A little while later he goes to McDonald's for lunch and asks the cashier the same question, to which the reply is, "I'd guess that you're 29?"

"No, I am actually 47." He's starting to feel really good about himself.

While standing at the bus stop he asks an old woman the same question.

She replies, "I am 85 years old and my eyesight is going. But when I was young there was a sure way of telling a man's age. If I put my hand down your pants and play with your penis for ten minutes I will be able to tell your exact age."

As there was no one else around the man thought what the hell and let her slip her hand down his pants.

Ten minutes later the old lady says, "OK, it's done. You are 47."
Stunned the man says, "That was great! How did you do that?"
The old lady replies, "I was behind you in line at McDonald's."

Q. Why is being in the military like a blow job?
A. The closer you get to discharge, the better you feel.

A woman and her little boy are walking through Central Park and they pass two squirrels having sex. The little boy asks his mom, "Mommy, mommy, what are they doing?"

The lady responds, "They're making a sandwich." Then they pass two dogs having sex and the little boy again asks what they were doing. His mother again replies that they are making a sandwich.

A couple of days later the little boy walks in on his mother and father and says, "Mommy, daddy, you must be making a sandwich because mommy has mayonnaise all over her mouth!!!"

Two five-year-old boys are standing at the toilet to pee. One says, "Your thing doesn't have any skin on it!"

"I've been circumcised," the other replies.

"What's that mean?"

"It means they cut the skin off the end."

"How old were you when it was cut off?"

"My mom said I was two days old."

"Did it hurt?" the kid asked inquiringly.

"You bet it hurt—I didn't walk for a year!"

A guy is driving his girlfriend home when she decides she wants to go to her friend's instead. Her friend lives out of the way so she tells her boyfriend that she would get naked for him if he drove her. The guy says OK and the girl takes off all her clothes. The boyfriend is so busy looking at her that he crashes the car and gets stuck between the steering wheel and the seat. He tells her to go get help and she replies that she can't because she doesn't have any clothes on.

He replies, "Take my shoe and cover your crotch with it, and go for help!"

She takes the shoe and runs to the closest gas station. She finds the clerk and says, "Help, my boyfriend is stuck! Can you help us?"

The clerk replies, "I'm sorry, I think he's too far in."

A woman is in the delivery room giving birth. The doctor tells her to push. She does and the baby's head pops out. The doctor says, "Oh! Your baby has slanted eyes."

To which she replies, "Yeah, I heard those Chinese men were pretty good, so I decided to give them a try."

The doctor shrugs it off and tells her to push again. This time the baby's body comes out. "Holy shit, your baby has a white body," the doctor says.

"Yeah, I heard those white men were pretty good, so I decided to give them a try," she says.

The doctor shrugs it off again and tells her to push one more time and that will be it. So she does and the legs come out. "Holy shit! Your baby has black legs," the doctor says.

"Yeah, I heard those black men were pretty good, so I decided to give them a try," she says.

So the doctor shrugs it off once more, ties the umbilical cord and slaps the baby on the ass so it starts to cry. The doctor turns to the woman and asks, "How are you going to deal with a baby who has slanted eyes, a white body, and black legs?"

The woman replies, "I'm just glad it didn't bark!"

Bill Clinton dies and of course goes straight to hell. When he gets there the Devil greets him and offers him three ways to spend eternity. They go to the first door and the Devil shows him Newt Gingrich hanging from the ceiling with fire under him. Bill says, "Oh no! That's not how I want to spend all eternity."

They go to the second door. The Devil shows him Rush Limbaugh chained to the wall being tortured. Bill says, "Oh no! Not for me!"

They go to the third door. Behind it is Ken Starr chained to the wall with Monica Lewinsky on her knees giving him a blow job. Bill thinks and decides, "Hmmm, looks okay to me. I'll take it."

The Devil then says, "Good. Hey, Monica, you've been replaced."

This little girl walks over to her grandmother and asks, "Granny, can you show me a magic trick?"

"No, dear, but I think your grandfather knows one."

So the little girl walks over to her grandpa and asks, "Grandpa, granny says you know some magic tricks. Could you show me one?"

The grandfather looks at her, "Sure, just hop on my lap!" So the little girl jumps on his lap. "Now, can you feel a finger poking up your ass?" asks the grandpa.

"Yeah," replies the girl.

"Well, look, no hands!"

A young boy and his father were in a store when they walked past a rack of condoms. Being a curious young lad, the boy asked his father, "What are these things, daddy?"

His dad said, "Condoms, son."

The boy asked, "Why do they come in packs of 1, 3, and 12?"

The dad replied, "The packs with one are for the high school boys on Saturday night; the ones with three are for the college boys for Friday, Saturday and Sunday, and the ones with twelve in them are for the married men, for January, February, March..."

The seven most important men in a woman's life:

1. The Doctor, who tells her to "take off all her clothes."

2. The Dentist, who tells her to "open wide."

3. The Milkman, who asks her "do you want it in the front or the back?"

4. The Hairdresser, who asks her "do you want it teased or blown?"

5. The Interior Designer, who assures her "once it's inside, you'll LOVE it!"

6. The Banker, who insists to her "if you take it out too soon, you'll lose interest!"

7. The Primal Hunter, who always goes deep into the bush, always shoots twice, always eats what he shoots, but keeps telling her to, "Keep quiet and lie still!"

Two gay male lovers are talking, and Bob says to Jon, "I wish I had chest hair like you."

So the next day Bob goes to the doctor and asks for something to grow chest hair. The doctor gives him something and he says, "It will work in about two months."

Two months later Bob still has no hair on his chest and back to the doctor he goes.

The Doctor says, "Rub some Vaseline on your chest, and in a week you will be growing hair."

Jon comes home that day and sees Bob rubbing Vaseline, and asks, "Why?"

Bob says, "To grow chest hair."

Jon says, "If Vaseline made your hair grow, you would have a ponytail coming out of your ass!"

A man is driving out in the middle of the country, very lost. Finally, he spots two farmhouses. He goes up to the first house and looks in the doorway. He sees an old lady yanking on her boobs and an old man jerking off. He is so freaked out that he goes to the next house and says, "What's up with your neighbors?"

And the owner of the house says, "Oh, that's the Robinson's—they're both deaf. She's telling him to go milk the cow and he's telling her to go fuck herself!"

One day a girl decided to buy some crotchless panties to surprise her boyfriend. She went and bought them, got home, put them on and waited. When the boyfriend got home, there she was spread-eagle on the bed with only her panties and bra on. "Come over here, baby," she said, smiling.

The boyfriend backed off, "If your pussy can do that to your panties, I'm not going anywhere near it!"

As a painless way to save money, a young couple arrange that every time they have sex the husband puts his pocket change into a china piggy bank on the bedside table. One night while being unusually athletic, he accidentally knocks the piggy bank onto the floor where it smashes.

To his surprise, among the masses of coins there are handfuls of five- and ten-dollar bills. He asks his wife, "What's up with all the bills?"

To which his wife replies, "Well, not everyone is as cheap as you are."

A guy comes home from work, walks into his bedroom, and finds a stranger fucking his wife. He says, "What the hell are you two doing?"

His wife turns to the stranger and says, "I told you he was stupid."

Q. What doesn't belong in this list: meat, eggs, wife, blow job?

A. Blow job: You can beat your meat, eggs or wife, but you can't beat a blow job.

A police officer was patrolling the highway when he saw a guy tied up to a tree, crying. The officer stopped and approached the guy. "What's going on here?" he asked.

The guy sobbed, "I was driving and picked up a hitchhiker. He pulled a gun on me, robbed me, took all my money, my clothes, my car and then tied me up."

The cop studied the guy for a moment, and then pulled down his pants and whipped out his dick. "I guess this isn't your lucky day, pal!"

"I've got some good news and some bad news," the doctor says.

"What's the bad news?" asks the patient.

"The bad news is that, unfortunately, you've only got three months to live."

The patient is taken back, "What's the good news then, Doctor?"

The doctor points over to the secretary at the front desk, "You see that blonde with the big breasts, tight ass and legs that go all the way up to heaven?"

The patient nods his head and the doctor replies, "I'm fucking her."

A guy goes up to a girl in a bar and says, "You want to play 'Magic?'"
She says, "What's that?"
He says, "We go to my house and fuck, and then you disappear."

A woman, pregnant with her first child, paid a visit to her obstetrician's office. After the examination, she shyly said, "My husband wants me to ask you..."

To which the doctor replies, "I know...I know..." placing a reassuring hand on her shoulder. "I get asked that all the time. Sex is fine until late in the pregnancy."

"No, that's not it," the woman confessed. "He wants to know if I can still mow the lawn."

An old man and an old lady are getting ready for bed one night when all of a sudden the woman bursts out of the bathroom, flings open her robe and yells, "Super pussy!"

The old man says, "I'll have the soup."

Three people—two men and one woman—and their dogs are in the vet's waiting room. The first man's dog asks the second man's dog what he's there for.

"They are putting me down."

"Oh no," says the first dog, "why?"

The second dog says, "Well, you see... I've been chasing the postman for years. Yesterday, I finally caught him, and bit him. So, I'm going to be put to sleep."

The second dog says, "Well, my master just completely remodelled the inside of his house. I didn't like it because my scent wasn't anywhere anymore. So, when he went to bed last night I pissed on everything I could find to get my scent back. This morning, my master found out what I had done, so he is putting me to sleep also."

The third dog says, "This is my master's new girlfriend. She runs around the house all the time with no clothes on. This makes me very horny. So, this morning, as she was getting out of the shower, she bent over to wipe up the water on the floor. I couldn't stand it anymore, so I jumped on her and gave it to her good!"

The other dogs say, "So that's why they are putting you to sleep?"

"No," says the dog, "she is bringing me here to get my toenails clipped!"

A doctor and his wife were having a big argument at breakfast. "You aren't so good in bed, either!" he shouted and stormed off to work. By mid morning, he decided he'd better make amends and called home.

"What took you so long to answer?"

"I was in bed."

"What were you doing in bed this late?"

"Getting a second opinion."

An American businessman was in Japan. He hired a local hooker and was going at it all night with her. She kept screaming, "Fujifoo, Fujifoo!!!" which the guy took to be pleasurable. The next day he was golfing with his Japanese counterparts and he got a hole-in-one. Wanting to impress the clients, he said, "Fujifoo."

The Japanese clients looked confused and said, "No, you got the right hole."

A man and a woman were waiting at the hospital donation center.

Man: "What are you doing here today?"

Woman: "Oh, I'm here to donate some blood. They're going to give me $5 for it."

Man: "Hmm, that's interesting. I'm here to donate sperm, myself. But they pay me $25."

The woman looked thoughtful for a moment and they chatted some more before going their separate ways.

A couple months later, the same man and woman meet again in the donation center.

Man: "Oh, hi there! Here to donate blood again?"

Woman: [shaking her head with mouth closed] "Unh-unh."

A man from the Internal Revenue Service knocks on a door and it is opened by a little boy.

The man asks the boy, "Where is your mother?"

The boy states, "She's in the backyard, screwing the goat."

The man exclaims, "Son, it's not nice to make up stories like that!"

The boy says, "Come on in and I'll show you."

So the taxman follows the little boy to the back of the house and looks out the window into the backyard. There, he sees a woman screwing a goat.

Disgusted, he turns to the boy and says, "That is gross! Doesn't it bother you?"

The little boy answers, "Naaaaaaaaaah!"

An old man went into confession and told the priest, "Father, I'm 81 and married with six children and 13 grandchildren. Last night I had an affair and made love to two 18-year-old girls. Twice."

"I see," said the priest. "When was the last time you were in confession?"

"Never, Father," replied the old man. "I'm Jewish."

"So why are you telling me?"

"I'm telling everybody!"

Q. What has lots of balls and fucks rabbits?
A. A 12-gauge shotgun.

A guy is walking down the street and enters a clock and watch shop. While looking around, he notices a drop-dead gorgeous female clerk behind the counter. He walks up to the counter where she is standing, unzips his pants, flops his cock out and places it on the counter. "What are you doing, sir?" she asks. "This is a clock shop!!"

He replies, "I know it is, and I would like two hands and a face put on this!"

A guy can't get an erection so he goes to the doctor. The doctor tells him the muscles at the base of his penis have broken down and there's nothing he can do unless he's willing to try an experimental surgery. The guy asks what the surgery is. The doctor tells him they take the muscles from the base of a baby elephant's trunk, insert them in the base of his penis, and hope for the best. The guy thinks that sounds pretty scary, but the thought of never having sex again is even scarier so he tells the doctor to go ahead.

The doctor goes ahead and performs the surgery and about six weeks later gives him the go-ahead to "try out his new equipment." The guy takes his girlfriend out to dinner. While at dinner he starts feeling an incredible pressure in his pants. It gets incredibly unbearable and he figures no one can see him so he undoes his pants. No sooner does he do this than his penis pops out of his pants, rolls across the table, grabs a dinner roll, and disappears back into his pants. His girlfriend sits in shock for a few moments, then gets a sly look on her face.

She says, "That was pretty cool! Can you do that again?"

With his eyes watering and a painful expression on his face, he says, "Probably, but I don't know if I can fit another dinner roll up my ass!"

In a tiny village lived an old maid. In spite of her old age, she was still a virgin. She was very proud of it. She knew her last days were getting closer, so she told the local undertaker that she wanted the following inscription on her tombstone:

"Born as a virgin, lived as a virgin, died as a virgin."

Not long after, the old maid died peacefully and the undertaker told his men what the lady had said. The men went to carve it in, but as the lazy no-goods they were, they thought the inscription to be unnecessarily long. They simply wrote: "Returned unopened."

Q. Have you heard about the new super-sensitive condoms?
A. They hang around after the man leaves and talk to the woman.

Q. Why don't Ken and Barbie have any kids?
A. Ken comes in a different box.

A teenager is walking down a street in Soho, New York, and a girl whispers to him, "Blow job, five dollars." He gives her a strange look and keeps walking.

Soon, another girl does the same thing. Confused, he keeps walking. The first thing out of his mouth when he returns home is, "Mom, what's a blow job?"

His mom replies, "Five dollars, just like Soho!

A blind man was walking down the street with his dog. They stopped at the corner to wait for the passing traffic. The dog, at this point, started pissing on the man's leg. As the dog finished, the man reached into his coat pocket and pulled out a doggie treat and started waving it at the dog. A passerby saw all the events happening and was shocked. He approached the blind man and asked how he could possibly reward the dog for such a nasty deed.

The blind man replied, "Oh, I'm not rewarding him—I'm just trying to find his head so I can kick his fucking ass."

As an ultimate test of his will power, a man decided to give up sex for Lent. Although not thrilled with the idea, his wife agreed to support him in this effort. The first few weeks weren't too difficult. Things got tougher during the next couple of weeks, so the wife wore her dowdiest nightclothes and chewed on garlic before going to bed. The last couple of weeks were extremely tough on the husband, so the wife took to locking the bedroom door and forcing the husband to sleep on the couch.

Easter morning finally came. A knock came on the wife's bedroom door.

KNOCK!!! KNOCK!!! KNOCK!!!

Husband: "Guess who?"

Wife: "I know who it is!"

Husband: "Guess what I want?"

Wife: "I know what you want!"

Husband: "Guess what I'm knocking with?"

A guy has been asking the prettiest girl in town for a date and finally she agrees to go out with him. He takes her to a nice restaurant and buys her a gourmet dinner with expensive wine. On the way home, he pulls over to the side of the road in a secluded spot. They start necking and he's getting pretty excited. He starts to reach under her skirt and she stops him, saying she's a virgin and wants to stay that way.

"Well, okay," he says, "how about a blow job?"

"Yuck!" she screams. "I'm not putting that thing in my mouth!"

He says, "Well, then, how about a hand job?"

"I've never done that," she says. "What do I have to do?"

"Well," he answers, "remember when you were a kid and you used to shake up a Coke bottle and spray your brother with it?" She nods. "Well, it's just like that."

So, he pulls it out and she grabs hold of it and starts shaking it. A few seconds later, his head flops back on the headrest, his eyes close, snot starts to run out of his nose, wax blows out of his ear and he screams out in pain.

"What's wrong?!" she cries out.

"Take your thumb off the end!!"

Q. What do a walrus and Tupperware have in common?

A. They both like a tight seal.

An angry wife met her husband at the door. There was alcohol on his breath and lipstick on his collar.

"I assume," she snarled, "that there is a very good reason for you to come waltzing in here at six o'clock in the morning?"

"There is," he replied. "Breakfast."

A husband and wife want to take golf lessons from a pro at a local country club. The man and woman meet the pro and head onto the driving range. The man goes up to hit first. He swings and hits the ball 100 yards.

The golf pro says, "Not bad. Now hold the club as firm as you hold your wife's breasts."

The man follows instructions and hits the ball 300 yards. The golf pro says, "Excellent!"

Now the woman takes her turn. Her ball goes 30 yards. The golf pro says, "Not bad, but try holding the club like you hold your husband's dick." She swings and the ball goes 10 yards.

"Not bad, but now try taking the club out of your mouth to hit the ball."

Two dwarfs decide to treat themselves to a vacation in Las Vegas. At the hotel bar they're dazzled by two women and wind up taking them to their separate rooms.

The first dwarf is disappointed, however, as he's unable to reach a certain physical state that would enable him to join with his date. His depression is enhanced by the fact that, from the next room, he hears cries of ONE, TWO, THREE...HUH! all night long.

In the morning, the second dwarf asks the first, "How did it go?"

The first whispers back, "It was so embarrassing. I simply couldn't get an erection."

The second dwarf shook his head. "You think that's embarrassing? I couldn't even get on the bed!"

A man and woman were dating and he asked her to marry him. She told him that to prove his love to her she wanted him to get her name,

Wendy, tattooed on his penis. When it was erect it said Wendy and when it was limp if said Wy.

They got married and went to Jamaica to a nude beach for their honeymoon. Wendy asked her husband to get them a drink, so he went to a stand on the beach and noticed the man who was waiting on him also had a Wy on his penis.

He said, "Oh, you must have a wife named Wendy, too."

And the waiter said, "No, my tattoo says 'Welcome to Jamaica, man, have a nice day!!!'"

A woman walked into a very busy butcher's shop. Looking at the meats and poultry on display, she suddenly grabbed hold of a dressed chicken. She picked up one wing, sniffed it, picked up the other wing and sniffed it, picked up one leg, sniffed it, picked up the other leg, sniffed it.

Just as she finished sniffing the second leg, the butcher walked up to her and said, "Madam, could you pass such a test?"

A man and a woman were having drinks when they got into an argument about who enjoyed sex more. The man said, "Men obviously enjoy sex more than women. Why do you think we're so obsessed with getting laid?"

"That doesn't prove anything," the woman countered. "Think about this: When your ear itches and you put your finger in it and wiggle it around, then pull it out, which feels better, your ear or your finger?"

Three explorers are captured by a tribe in the Amazon jungle. The chief is going to punish the intruders. He calls the first explorer to the front of the tribe and asks, "Death or Booka?!"

Well, the explorer doesn't want to die, so he opts for booka. The tribe starts screaming BOOKA! and dancing around. The chief then rips the explorer's pants off and fucks him in the ass.

The chief calls the second explorer to the front and asks, "Death or Booka?!"

Well, not wanting to die either, he also opts for booka. The tribe again starts screaming BOOKA! and dancing around. The chief rips the second man's pants off and fucks him in the ass.

The chief calls the third explorer to the front and asks, "Death or Booka?!"

Well, the third guy has a little more self-respect and thinks death would be better than being violated in front of hundreds of tribesman, so he opts for death.

The chief turns to the whole tribe and screams, "DEATH BY BOOKA!"

Q. What's the difference between a wife and a trash can?
A. You only have to take out a trash can once a week.

This lady goes to the gynecologist but won't tell the receptionist what's wrong with her, just that she must see a doctor. After hours of waiting, the doctor sees her in. "OK, my good woman, what is your problem?" the doctor asks.

"Well," she says, "my husband is a very compulsive gambler, and every nickel he can get his hands on he gambles. So I had five hundred dollars and I stuffed it in my vagina, but now I can't get it out."

The doctor says, "Don't be nervous, I see this happen all the time." He asks her to pull down her underwear, sits her down with her legs wide open puts his gloves on and says, "I only have one question. What am I looking for? Bills or loose change?"

The latest supermarket parking lot scam is becoming widespread and I suggest that everyone takes great care. The scam goes like this:

Two good-looking women in their late teens or early 20s approach you as you are about to drive out of the parking lot. One starts wiping your windscreen with a wet towel while the other—who seems to be wearing the lowest-cut T-shirt imaginable—comes to your window, leans down and says "Hello." Male instinct being what it is, one tends to get a little distracted.

When you thank them and offer them a tip for the windshield washing, they say "No" and ask instead for a lift to the nearest train station. They both get into the back of your car and, within a few minutes, they're having sex with each other right there on the back seat. One of the girls (in my case it was the blonde with the low-cut T-shirt and very substantial breasts) then jumps into the front seat and insists on giving you oral sex. But while this is going on, the other girl—still in the back seat—steals your wallet.

I fell for this vicious, nasty-minded scam last Monday, also Tuesday, Wednesday, Thursday and Friday, but I couldn't find them Saturday or Sunday…

Q. Why is the penis so depressed?
A. His closest friends are two nuts who live next to an asshole.

A nun was going to Chicago. She went to the airport and sat down waiting for her flight. When she looked over in the corner and saw one of those weight machines that tells your fortune, she thought to herself I'll give it a try just to see what it tells me. So she went over to the machine, put her nickel in and a card came out. It read, "You're a nun, you weigh 128 lbs. and you're going to Chicago, Illinois." So she sat back down and thought about it. She thought to herself that it probably told everyone the same thing and went to try it again.

So she went over to the machine again and put her nickel in it, and a card came out that read, "You're a nun, you weigh 128 lbs., you're going to Chicago, Illinois, and you're going to play a fiddle."

She said to herself, I know that's wrong. I have never played a musical instrument in my life. She sat back down and this cowboy came over and set his fiddle case down. She picked up the fiddle and just started playing beautiful music. She looked back at the machine and said, "This is incredible. I've got to try it again."

So she went back to the machine, put her nickel in and another card came out that read, "You're a nun, you weigh 128 lbs., you're going to Chicago, Illinois, and you're going to break wind."

She thought, I know it's wrong now. I've never broken wind in public in my life. Well, she tripped and fell down the stairs and farted like a donkey. So she sat back down and looked at the machine once again. She said to herself, "This is truly unbelievable—I've got to try it one more time."

She went back to the machine, put her nickel in and a card came out that read, "You're a nun, you weigh 128 lbs., you're going to Chicago, Illinois, and you're going to have sex." She thought, Ah-hah that does it—I know for sure it's wrong now. I'm a nun, I have never had sex, and am not ever going to have sex.

Well, a huge electrical storm came through and the electricity went off, and during the black-out she got raped.She sat back down and thought about it for few minutes and then said, "This is truly, truly, incredible. But one thing is for certain—I've got to try it one last time just to see what is going to happen to me before I leave this airport."

She went over to the machine, put her nickel in and a card came out that read, "You're a nun, you weigh 128 lbs., you have fiddled, farted and fucked around and missed your flight to Chicago!!!"

Mr. Perkins, the biology teacher at a girl's prep school, said during class, "Miss Smith, would you please name the organ of the human body that, under the appropriate conditions, expands to six times its normal size, and define the conditions."

Miss Smith gasped, then said coldly, "Mr. Perkins, I don't think that is a proper question to ask me. I assure you my parents will hear of this."

With that she sat down red-faced. Unperturbed, Mr. Perkins called on Miss Johnson and asked the same question. Miss Johnson, with composure, replied, "The pupil of the eye, in dim light."

"Correct," said Mr. Perkins. "And now, Miss Smith, I have three things to say to you. One, you have not studied your homework. Two, you have a dirty mind. And three, you will some day be faced with a dreadful disappointment."

A knockout young lady decided she wanted to get rich quick, so she proceeded to find herself a rich 75-year-old man, and planned to screw him to death on their wedding night.

The courtship and wedding went off without any problem, in spite of the half-century age difference. The first night of her honeymoon, she got undressed and waited for him to come out of the bathroom to come to bed.

When he emerged, however, he had nothing on except a condom to cover a twelve-inch erection, and was carrying a pair of earplugs and a pair of nose plugs.

Fearing her plan had gone desperately amiss, she asked, "What are those for?"

The elderly groom replied, "There are two things I can't stand: the sound of a woman screaming and the smell of burning rubber."

Q. Why do women have two sets of lips?

A. So they can piss and moan at the same time.

There is a white Superman, a black Superman and a Chinese Superman on top of a skyscraper. They are all having a contest to see who has the longest dick.

The white Superman pulls down his tights and BLUM, BLUM, BLUM, his cock unrolls down the side of the building and across the street.

The black Superman says, "That's shit—watch this," and pulls down his tights. BLUM, BLUM, BLUM, BLUM, CRASH!!! His cock unrolls down the side of the building, across the street and up the next building, then smashes through a window.

Now, the white Superman and the black Superman are looking at the Chinese Superman, who by this time is laughing his ass off! So, the black and white Supermen say, "What's so funny? Show us your cock!" So the Chinese Superman pulls out his dick and it's only three inches long, but he's still laughing.

Puzzled, the black and white Supermen ask, "What the fuck is so funny?!"

The Chinese Superman says, "There is steamroller coming down street!"

Definition:

Self deception: masturbating and then faking an orgasm.

Mistress: something between mister and mattress.

Lesbian: another woman trying to do a man's job.

I, the penis, hereby request a raise in salary for the following reasons:
1. I do physical labor.
2. I work at great depths.
3. I plunge head first into everything I do.
4. I do not get weekends off or public holidays.
5. I work in a damp environment.
6. I don't get paid overtime.
7. I work in a dark workplace that has poor ventilation.
8. I work in high temperatures.
9. My work exposes me to contagious diseases.

Q. Why does it take 1 million sperm to fertilize 1 egg?
A. They don't stop to ask for directions.

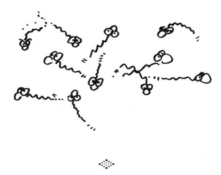

Thor, the god of thunder, assumes mortal form, comes down to earth on a Friday night and goes to a singles bar.

He ends up going home with a beautiful woman. They spend the weekend in her place making passionate love, over and over again.

Come Monday morning, Thor decides to reveal his true identity, saying, "I am Thor!"

The woman looks at him and replies, "You're thor! I'm tho thor I can hardly pith!"

Dear Penis,

After assessing your request and considering the arguments you have raised, the administration rejects your request for the following reasons:

1. You do not work 8 hours straight.
2. You fall asleep on the job after brief work periods.
3. You do not always follow the orders of the management team.
4. You do not stay in your allocated position and often visit other areas.
5. You do not take initiative—you need to be pressured and stimulated in order to start working.
6. You leave the workplace messy at the end of your shift.
7. You don't always observe necessary safety regulations, such as wearing the correct protective clothing.
8. You'll retire well before reaching 65.
9. You're unable to work double shifts.
10. You sometimes leave your allocated position before you have completed the day's work.
11. And if that were not enough, you have been seen constantly entering and leaving the workplace carrying two suspicious looking bags.

Sincerely,
The Management

Q. What's a wife?
A. An attachment you screw on the bed to get the housework done.

A man was sitting at a bar enjoying an after-work cocktail when an exceptionally gorgeous and sexy young woman entered. She was so striking that the man could not take his eyes away from her. The young woman noticed his overly attentive stare and walked directly towards him.

Before he could offer his apologies for being so rude, the young woman said to him, "I'll do anything, absolutely anything that you want me to do, no matter how kinky, for $100, on one condition."

Flabbergasted, the man asked what the condition was.

The young woman replied, "You have to tell me what you want me to do in just three words."

The man considered her proposition for a moment, withdrew his wallet from his pocket and slowly counted out five $20 bills, which he pressed into the young woman's hand. He looked into her eyes and slowly, meaningfully, said, "Paint my house."

Three priests were taking a shower together in the church. They ran out of soap. Thinking the church was empty, one walked naked down the hall to the supply closet.

Half way back, the naked priest saw three nuns walking towards him. He immediately froze and pretended to be a statue.

The first nun took one look and said, "What a realistic looking statue!"

The second nun reached and felt the priest's dick, and he dropped the bar of soap. "Wow a dispenser!" she exclaimed.

The third nun reached over, pulled on his dick and said, "Hand cream too!"

Q. Did you hear about the guy who entered his dog in the show?
A. He got 16 months.

Two guys had been having a few beers at the bar together, recounting old times, when the call of nature caused them to line up at the urinal together at the same time, still deep in conversation. But Fred could hardly ignore the fact that Chas was very well-endowed.

"Goodness, that's a remarkable schlong you have there, buddy," Fred was prompted to remark.

"Wasn't always that way," replied Chas. "Medical science can do wonders with transplants these days," he said. "I got this done over in Beverly Hills. Cost a thousand bucks, but as you can see, it's well worth every cent."

Fred was very envious. In fact, he packed his bag that night and flew off to Beverly Hills first thing.

It was a good six months later before he ran into his old buddy once again and Fred could hardly wait to tell him that he had taken his advice and was really pleased with the result.

"But, Chas, I will tell you something else," said Fred. "You were cheated; I got mine for $500, not a thousand."

Chas could hardly believe it. Same address in Beverly Hills, same doctor. Complaining that he had been ripped off, he asked Fred if he could take a look.

Once more they lined up at the urinal and when Chas took a peek over the partition the worried frown which had creased his face disappeared. "No wonder," he laughed. "That's my old one!"

A stranded Martian came upon two beautiful damsels in a nudist camp. He looked them over with obvious approval, then said, "Take me to your tailor!"

A date was arranged for an old fashioned visitor from America with a lively Irish girl. They strolled in the park under the moonlight until they came to a secluded spot where he kissed her several times lightly on the cheek.

"That, my dear," he said, "is called spooning."

"Spooning may be all right for you," she replied, "but I would rather shovel!"

I said to my coworker one day, "Man, your new girlfriend sure is big and ugly."

And he said, "So is my dick, but that doesn't stop me from having a good time with it."

A woman went to see her psychiatrist. "I'm really concerned," she said. "The other day I found my daughter and the little boy next door together naked and examining each other's bodies and giggling."

The psychiatrist smiled. "That's nothing to worry about—it's pretty normal."

"Well, I don't know," said the woman. "It worries me. It worries my daughter's husband too."

Two Arabs boarded a shuttle out of Washington for New York. One sat in the window seat, the other in the middle seat. Just before take off, a fat little Israeli guy got on and took the aisle seat next to the Arabs. He kicked off his shoes, wiggled his toes and was settling in when the Arab in the window seat said, "I think I'll go up and get a Coke."

"No problem," said the Israeli. "I'll get it for you."

While he was gone, the Arab picked up the Israeli's shoe and spat in it.

When the Israeli returned with the Coke, the other Arab said, "That looks good. I think I'll have one too." Again, the Israeli obligingly went to fetch it, and while he was gone the second Arab picked up the other shoe and spat in it.

The Israeli returned with the Coke, and they all sat back and enjoyed the short flight to New York. As the plane was landing the Israeli slipped his feet into his shoes and knew immediately what had happened.

"How long must this go on?" he asked. "This animosity between our peoples, this hatred, this hostility, this spitting in shoes—and peeing in Cokes?"

The other day, my friends and had a girls' night out. One of the girls wanted to impress the rest of us, so she pulled out a $10 bill. When the male dancer came over to us, my friend licked the $10 bill and stuck it to his right buttock!

Not to be outdone, another friend pulled out a $20 bill. She called the guy back over, licked the $20 bill, and stuck it to his left buttock.

In another attempt to impress the rest of us, my third friend pulled out a $50 bill and called the guy over. I was worried about the way things were going, but she licked the bill and just stuck it to one of his buttocks as well.

Seeing the way things were going, the guy gyrated over to me! Now everyone's attention was focused on me, and the guy was egging me on to try and top the $50. My brain was churning as I reached for my wallet. What could I do? I got out my ATM card, swiped it down the crack of his ass, grabbed the $80, and went home.

Naomi Campbell, Claudia Schiffer and Cindy Crawford are flying to a super models' conference in Paris, when the captain of the plane announces, "We have just lost power to the engines and are going to make an emergency crash landing. Assume the brace position immediately!"

Immediately, the three models start preparing for the worst. Claudia pulls out lipstick and makeup and starts fixing her face. Bewildered, Naomi and Cindy ask, "What the hell are you doing fixing your makeup when we are about to fucking crash?!"

Claudia responds, "I know for a fact the rescue workers will search for and save first the ones who have the best looking faces, which is why I am putting on my makeup."

Cindy Crawford rips open her blouse to expose two beautiful mounds of flesh which inexplicably defy the laws of gravity. Totally confused, Naomi and Claudia shout, "Cindy, have you lost your senses? Why are you baring your breasts for everyone to see when we are about to die!"

Cindy responds, "I have heard that in plane crashes, the rescue workers look to save the women with big beautiful breasts first, which is why I am exposing my tits!"

Not hesitating, Naomi Campbell pulls down her skirt and panties to expose her love triangle. Freaking out, Claudia and Cindy yell, "Naomi, are you crazy?? Why are you exposing your crotch for everyone to see?"

Calmly, Naomi responds, "Bitches, please! I know for a fact that the first thing rescue workers look for in plane crashes is a black box!"

A young man is starting his first ever job at a morgue. The boss of the morgue thinks, I'll throw him in at the deep end on his first day, give him a real challenge. So he takes the young man to a door and he tells the young man, "Behind this door is a room with nothing in it apart from a dead old woman lying completely naked on a slab. You have to go in and inspect her body."

"Inspect her body?" the young man asks.

"Yes," replies the boss. "Check if everything's OK."

So the young man goes through the door into the room, and the boss waits outside. After what seems like a very long time, the young man comes out of the room.

"Everything OK?" asks the boss.

"Yes," answers the young man, "except one thing. She's got a prawn stuck up her pussy."

"She's got a prawn stuck up her pussy!!?" exclaims the boss, astonished.

"Yes," replies the young man.

The boss decides he has to go and check this. So he goes into the room and the young man waits outside. The boss quickly returns, and the young man says, "See, I told you."

"That's not a prawn, that's her clitoris!" explains the boss.

"Well, it tasted like a prawn," answers the young man.

A man was in a long line at the supermarket. As he got to the checkout he realized he had forgotten to get condoms.

So he asked the checkout girl if she could have some condoms brought up to register.

She asked, "What size condoms?" The customer replied that he didn't know. She asked him to drop his pants. He did, and she reached over the counter, grabbed hold of him, then picked up the store intercom and said,

"One box of large condoms to register 5."

The next man in line thought this was interesting and, like most of us, was up for a cheap thrill. When he got to the register, he told the checkout girl that he too had forgotten to get condoms, and asked if she could have some brought up to the register. She asked him what size, and he stated that he didn't know. She asked him to drop his pants. He did, and she gave him a quick feel, picked up the store intercom and said,

"One box of medium-sized condoms to register 5."

A few customers back there was a teenage boy. He thought what he had witnessed was way too cool. He had never had any type of sexual contact with a live female, so he thought this was his chance. When he got up to the register, he told the girl he needed some condoms. She asked him what size, and he said he didn't know. She asked him to drop his pants and he did. She reached over the counter, gave him one quick squeeze, then picked up the intercom and said,

"Clean up at register 5!"

A guy was on his honeymoon near his favorite fishing lake, and he would fish from dawn to dark with his favorite fishing guide. One day the guide, a friend of many years, mentioned that the honeymoon seemed to be spent fishing.

"Yes, but you know how I love to fish."

"But aren't you newlyweds supposed to be into something else?"

"Yes, but she's got gonorrhea, and you know how I love to fish."

A few hours later the guide said, "I understand, but that's not the only way to have sex."

"I know, but she's got diarrhea, and you know how I love to fish."

The following day the guide said, "Sure, but that's still not the only way to have sex."

"Yeah, but she's got chlamydia, and you know how I love to fish."

Late that afternoon, thoroughly frustrated, the guide said, "I guess I'm not sure why you'd marry someone with health problems like that."

"It's 'cause she's also got worms, and you know I just love to fish."

Q. How do you make your wife scream for an hour after sex?
A. Wipe your dick on the curtains.

Q. What's the difference between a new husband and a new dog?
A. After a year the dog is still excited to see you.

I was walking in the park one bright, sunny Sunday afternoon, when I noticed a cute little girl out walking her dog. As she approached me on the path, I could see that she looked about nine years old. She was all dressed up in her Sunday best, with her freshly scrubbed face—just as cute as could be. Tugging on the leash was a well groomed terrier.

As we met on the path, I greeted her, "Hi there. My, aren't you pretty today and what a fine-looking dog you have."

"Thank you, sir," she said. "And what a nice day this is, isn't it?"

"Yes, it is," I answered. "My, what a polite little girl you are, and what a pretty dress you're wearing."

"Oh, thank you, sir. My mother taught me to always be polite and she made this dress for me. Isn't it lovely?" she asked with a beaming smile.

"Yes, very lovely," I answered. "By the way, what's your dog's name?"

"Oh, sir, my dog's name is 'Porky.' Isn't that cute?"

"Well, it certainly is an unusual name for a dog. Why do you call him 'Porky?'"

"Because he fucks pigs!"

An Israeli doctor said, "Medicine in my country is so advanced, we can take a kidney out of one person, put it in another, and have him looking for work in six weeks."

A German doctor said, "That's nothing! In Germany, we can take a lung out of one person, put it in another, and have him looking for work in four weeks."

A Russian doctor said, "In my country medicine is so advanced, we can take half a heart from one person, put it in another, and have them both looking for work in two weeks."

The American doctor, not to be outdone, said "Ha! We took an asshole out of Texas, put him in the White House and half the country will be looking for work tomorrow."

A physically large guy meets a woman at a bar and after a number of drinks they agree to go back to his place.

As they are making out in the bedroom, ready for the act, he stands up and starts to undress. After he takes his shirt off, he flexes his muscular arms and says, "See there, baby? That's 1,000 pounds of dynamite!"

She begins to drool. The man drops his pants, strikes a bodybuilder's pose, and says, referring to his bulging legs, "See those, baby? That's 1,000 pounds of dynamite!" She is aching for action at this point.

Finally, he drops his underpants, and she grabs her purse and runs screaming to the front door.

He catches her before she is able to run out the door and asks, "Why are you in such a hurry to leave?"

She replies, "With 2,000 pounds of dynamite and such a short fuse, I was afraid you were about to blow!"

Q. What's the ultimate rejection?
A. When you're masturbating and your hand falls asleep.

Q. How do you make five pounds of fat look good?
A. Give it a nipple.

Two gay guys are driving down the street when they see a dog on the side of the road licking its prick. "I sure wish I could do that," said one of them.

To which the other replied,

"Don't you think you ought to pet him first??"

Three guys are discussing women. "I like to watch a woman's tits best," the first guy says.

The second says, "I like to look at a woman's ass." He asks the third guy, "What about you?"

"Me? I prefer to see the top of her head."

When Mrs. Ghandi went to Moscow, Khrushchev took her for a tour of the city in his limo. Recalling his visit to India, he started giving her a hard time about the sanitary conditions there.

"When I was in Delhi, I saw human excrement lying everywhere."

Poor Mrs. Ghandi was terribly embarrassed, but only for a moment, because just ahead was a man sitting on his heels, shitting on the side of the road. She pointed this out.

Khrushchev was livid and didn't hesitate. "Driver, get out immediately and shoot that man!"

The driver got out, walked up to the man with his gun drawn, spoke briefly, and then returned to the car.

"Sir, I can't shoot that man. He's the Indian ambassador."

Joe: I got a problem.

Ed: What's the matter?

Joe: Women. I just don't understand them.

Ed: Do you understand your TV?

Joe: No.

Ed: So what's the problem?

Your basic virgin female was all set to get married to a virile man, when her mother took her aside for a little pre-nuptial advice.

"Dear, I know you love this man," the mother began, "and we've tried to welcome him into our family. But there is something you must know. Men like to make love in a disgusting way, so if he ever asks you to turn over before making love, DON'T do it. It's degrading and painful, and it will ruin your marriage."

So the wedding was fine. The happy couple enjoyed their first month of marital bliss, and then one night, the man said to his wife, "Honey, let's try making love a little differently tonight. Why don't you roll over?"

The woman lost it. "You brute," she sobbed. "My mother warned me about you men. I can't believe you would do this to me."

"But, honey," the startled man replied, "I just thought you might want to have children."

A guy decides to join the navy. On his first day of service, he gets aquatinted with all the facilities around the ship he will be serving on. The guy asks the sailor showing him around, "What do you guys do around here when you get really horny after months of being out at sea?"

To which the other replies,

"Well, there is a barrel on the upper deck—just pump your cock in the side with the hole."

Weeks pass, and the new guy is getting real horny and remembers the barrel. He climbs to the upper deck and sees it. He flings his shlong out and starts fucking the barrel. It's simply the best feeling he has ever experienced—truly a success!

After he's done, zipped up and merrily walking along, the guy who originally told him about the barrel walks by. "That barrel really was great! I could do it every day!"

To which the other crew member replies, "Yeah, you can do it every day except Thursday."

Confused, the new guy asks, "Why?"

The other guy replies, "Because its your turn in the barrel on Thursday."

A very good-looking man walks into a singles bar, gets a drink and takes a seat. During the course of the evening, he tries to chat with every single woman who walks into the bar, with no luck. Suddenly a really ugly man—and I mean a REALLY ugly man—walks into the bar. He sits at the bar, and within seconds he is surrounded by women. Very soon he walks out of the bar with two of the most beautiful women you've ever seen.

Disheartened by all this, the good-looking man asks the barman, "Excuse me, but that really ugly man just came in here and left with those two stunning women—what's his secret? He's as ugly as sin and I'm everything a girl could want, but I have not been able to hook-up all night. What's going on?"

"Well," says the barman, "I don't know how he does it, but he does the same thing every night. He walks in, orders a drink, and just sits there licking his eyebrows..."

A man comes home from work and finds his daughter in bed with a vibrator.

"What are you doing?" he asks.

"This has been my husband for the last four years," she replies.

The next day, the daughter finds her father in bed with her vibrator stuffed up his butt. He's drinking a pint of Guinness.

"What the hell are you doing?" she cries.

He replies, "I'm just having a beer with my son-in-law."

A lady goes to the doctor's office and tells the doctor that she can't get her husband to have sex with her anymore. So, the doctor gives her some pills and says to give her husband one each night in his dinner whenever she wants to have sex.

That night she gave him one and they had a decent night of sex. The next night she decided to try four pills and she had even better sex. Well, the next night she tried eight pills and the sex was wonderful. So the next night she decided to dump the whole bottle in his dinner.

The next day her son showed up at the doctor's office and and said, "Doctor, Doctor, what did you do to my Daddy? My mom's dead, my sister's pregnant, my butt hurts, and my dad's going around saying, 'Here, kitty, kitty, kitty!'"

There was a papa mole, a mamma mole and a baby mole. They lived in a hole out in the country near a farmhouse. Papa mole poked his head out of the hole and said, "Mmmm, I smell sausage!"

Mamma mole poked her head outside the hole and said, "Mmmm, I smell pancakes!"

Baby mole tried to stick his head outside but couldn't because of the two bigger moles. Baby mole said, "The only thing I smell is molasses."

Once there were twin brothers by the name of Jones. John Jones was married, and Joe Jones was single. The single brother Joe was the proud owner of a dilapidated row boat. It happened that John Jones's wife died the same day that Joe's rowboat filled with water and sank.

A few days later, a kind old lady met Joe and, mistaking him for John, said, "Oh, Mr. Jones, I am sorry to hear of your great loss. You must feel terrible."

Joe smiled and said, "Well, I am not a bit sorry—she was rather old from the start. Her bottom was all chewed up and she smelled of dead fish. Even the first time I got into her, she leaked water faster than anything I ever saw. She had a bad crack and a pretty big hole in her front, and that hole got bigger every time I used her. It got so bad I could barely handle her, but if anyone else used her she leaked like a faucet. The thing that finished her was four guys from the other side of town. They came down looking for a good time and asked if I could lend her to them. I warned them that she wasn't so hot, but they could take a crack at her if they liked. Well, the result was that the crazy fools tried to get inside her all at once, and it was too much for her! She cracked right up the middle."

Before he could finish, the old lady fainted!

The kindergarten class had a homework assignment to find out about something exciting and relate it to the class the next day. When the time came for the little kids to give their reports, the teacher was calling on them one at a time. She was reluctant to call upon little Johnny, knowing that he sometimes could be a bit crude. But eventually, his turn came.

Little Johnny walked up to the front of the class and, with a piece of chalk, made a small white dot on the blackboard, then sat back down.

Well, the teacher couldn't figure out what Johnny had in mind for his report, so she asked him just what that was.

"It's a period," reported Johnny.

"Well, I can see that," she said. "But what is so exciting about a period?"

"Damned if I know," said Johnny. "But this morning my sister said she missed one. Then daddy had a heart attack, mommy fainted and the man next door shot himself."

Q. What do you call two lesbians in a canoe?
A. Fur traders.

A guy was playing golf and a golf ball hit him in the balls and he passed out. His friends took him to the doctor.

The man asked him, "Well, what do you think, Doc?"

The doctor replied, "We're going to have to put in a support for about a week." He then took four tongue depressors and tied them all together with string.

The man's face looked disappointed. He told the doctor, "But tonight my girlfriend and I are going to have sex for the first time."

The doctor replied, "You're going to have to bear with it."

Later that night, the man and his girlfriend were alone. She took off her shirt and grabbed her breasts, "No one has ever seen these before."

The man pulled out his cock and said, "Well, mine's still in the crate!"

A married couple have been stranded on a deserted island for many years. One day, a second man washes up on shore. He and the wife become attracted to each other right away, but realize they must be creative if they are to engage in any hanky-panky. The husband, however, is very glad to see the second man there. "Now we will be able to have three people doing eight-hour shifts in the watchtower, rather than two people doing 12-hour shifts."

The newcomer is only too happy to help, and in fact, volunteers to do the first shift. He climbs up the tower to stand watch. Soon the couple on the ground are placing stones in a circle to make a fire to cook supper.

The second man yells down, "Hey, no screwing!"

They yell back, "We're not screwing!"

A few minutes later they start to put driftwood into the stone circle. Again the second man yells down, "Hey, no screwing!"

Again they yell back, "We're not screwing!"

Later, they are putting palm leaves on the roof of their shack to patch leaks. Once again, the second man yells down, "Hey, I said no screwing!"

They yell back, "We're not screwing!"

Eventually, the shift is over and the second man climbs down from the tower to be replaced by the husband. He's not even halfway up before the wife and her new friend are hard at it. The husband looks out from the tower and says, "Son-of-a-gun. From up here it DOES look like they're screwing."

⁘

A guy was rescued from a desert island after he'd spent six months there after a shipwreck. Later his friend asked, "What was it like?"

He smiled ruefully, "Well, it was pretty bad—only pineapples and coconuts to eat, and soon the pineapples ran out."

"Bet you missed sex?"

"Well, there was an ostrich there, and if I could catch it with its head in the sand I could go up behind and give it one."

"What was it like?"

"Well, it was OK for the first fifty yards. Then I fell out of step."

⁘

A blind man walks into a restaurant and sits down. The waiter, who is also the owner, walks up to the blind man and hands him a menu. "I'm sorry, sir, but I am blind and can't read the menu. Just bring me a dirty fork from the previous customer. I'll smell it and order from there."

A little confused, the owner walks over to the dirty dish pile and picks up a greasy fork. He returns to the blind man's table and hands it to him. The blind man puts the fork to his nose and takes in a deep breath.

"Ah, yes, that's what I'll have. Meatloaf and mashed potatoes."

Unbelievable, the owner says to himself as he walks towards the kitchen. The cook happens to be the owner's wife and he tells her what had just happened. The blind man eats his meal and leaves. Several days later the blind man returns and the owner mistakenly brings him a menu again.

"Sir, remember me? I'm the blind man."

"I'm sorry, I didn't recognize you. I'll go get you a dirty fork." The owner again retrieves a dirty fork and brings it to the blind man.

After another deep breath, the blind man says, "That smells great. I'll take the Macaroni and cheese with broccoli." Once again walking away in disbelief, the owner thinks the blind man is fooling him and tells his wife that the next time the blind man comes in he's going to test him.

The blind man eats and leaves.

He returns the following week, but this time the owner sees him coming and runs to the kitchen. He tells his wife, "Mary, rub this fork around your vagina before I take it to the blind man." Mary complies and hands her husband the fork back.

As the blind man walks in and sits down, the owner is ready and waiting. "Good afternoon, sir, this time I remembered you and I already have the fork ready for you."

The blind man puts the fork to his nose, takes a deep whiff and says, "Hey, I didn't know that Mary worked here!"

A young teenage girl was a prostitute and, for obvious reasons, kept it a secret from her grandma. One day, the police raided a brothel and arrested a group of prostitutes, including the young girl. The prostitutes were instructed to line up in a straight line on the sidewalk. Well, who should be walking by, but little old grandma. The young girl was frantic.

Sure enough, grandma noticed her young granddaughter and asked curiously, "What are you lining up for, dear?" Not willing to let grandma in on her little secret, the young girl told her that some people were passing out free oranges and that she was lining up for some.

"Mmm, sounds lovely," said grandma. "I think I'll have some myself," she continued as she made her way to the back of the line.

A police officer made his way down the line, questioning all of the prostitutes. When he got to Grandma at the end of the line, he was bewildered. "But you're so old. How do you do it?"

Grandma replied, "Oh, it's really easy, sonny. I just remove my dentures and suck 'em dry!"

A man entered a restaurant and sat at the only open table. As he sat down, he knocked the spoon off the table with his elbow. A nearby waiter reached into his shirt pocket, pulled out a clean spoon, and set it on the table. The diner was impressed. "Do all the waiters here carry spoons in their pockets?"

The waiter replied, "Yes, ever since an efficiency expert visited our restaurant. He determined that 17.8% of our diners knock the spoon off the table. By carrying clean spoons with us, we save trips to the kitchen."

The diner ate his meal. As he was paying the waiter, he commented, "Forgive the intrusion, but do you know that you have a string hanging from your fly?"

The waiter replied, "Yes, we all do. Seems that the same efficiency expert determined that we spend too much time washing our hands after using the men's room. So, the other end of that string is tied to my penis. When I need to go, I simply pull the string, do my thing, and then return to work. Having never touched myself, there really is no need to wash my hands. Saves a lot of time."

"Wait a minute," said the diner, "how do you get your penis back in your pants?"

"Well, I don't know about the other guys, but I use the spoon."

A couple were married and, following the wedding, the husband laid down some rules. "I'll be home when I want, if I want, and at what time I want," he insisted. "And I don't expect any hassle from you. Also, I expect a decent meal to be on the table every evening, unless I tell you otherwise. I'll go hunting, fishing, boozing, and card-playing with my buddies whenever I want. Those are my rules," he said. "Any comments?"

His new bride replied, "No, that's fine with me. But, just understand that there'll be sex here at seven o'clock every night, whether you're here or not."

Farmer Brown goes out one day and buys a brand new stud rooster for his chicken. The cocky young rooster walks over to the old rooster and says, "OK, old fellow, time to retire."

The old rooster says, "You can't handle all these chickens. Look what it did to me!"

The young rooster replies, "Now, don't give me a hassle about this old man. It's time for the old to step aside and the young take over, so take a hike!"

The old rooster says, "Aw, c'mon, just let me have those two old hens over there in the corner. I won't bother you."

The young rooster snarls, "Scram! Beat it! You're washed up! I'm taking over!"

The old rooster thinks for a minute and then says to the young rooster, "I'll tell you what, young fellow. I'll have a race around the farmhouse with you. Whoever wins the race gets full reign over the chicken coop."

The young rooster smiles, "You know I'm going to beat you, old man. So just to be fair, I'm even going to give you a head start."

The two roosters line up in back of the farm house; a hen clucks "Go!" and the old rooster takes off running. About five seconds later the young rooster takes off after him. They round the front of the farm house and the young rooster is inches behind the old rooster and gaining fast. Farmer Brown, sitting on the porch, hearing the commotion looks up and sees what's going on. Quickly, he grabs his shotgun and BOOM! The young rooster is blown to smithereens!

Farmer Brown sadly shakes his head in disgust, "Damn! That makes the third gay rooster I bought this week."

Q. What did the two lesbian frogs say to each other?
A. We do taste like chicken!

The weather was very hot and a man wanted desperately to take a dive in a nearby lake. He didn't bring his swimming trunks, but who cared? He was all alone. So he undressed and got into the water.

After some delightful minutes of cool swimming, he got out of the water and noticed two old ladies walking along the shore in his direction. He panicked and grabbed a bucket lying in the sand nearby. He held the bucket in front of his private parts and sighed with relief.

The ladies got closer and looked at him. He felt awkward and wanted to move. Then one of the ladies said, "You know, I have a special gift. I can read minds."

"Impossible," said the embarrassed man. "You really know what I think?"

"Yes," the lady replied. "Right now, I bet you think that the bucket you're holding has a bottom."

A woman in her 30s was taking her mother to the gynecologist. After dropping her mother off, she and her 10-year-old daughter ran a few errands, then returned to the doctor's office to get the older woman. When her daughter picked her up, she was quite upset. The following conversation ensued:

Mother: "Do you know what that doctor said to me? He said, 'Don't we look pretty today,' while he was looking between my legs! I was quite shocked. Do you think that he was inappropriate?"

Daughter: "Are you sure he wasn't referring to your hairstyle or something?"

Mother: "Well, it still wasn't appropriate or professional. I wonder if it could be considered sexual harassment. What do you think?"

Daughter: "I don't know. Were you embarrassed?"

Mother: "I was very embarrassed. I used some of your vaginal deodorant spray this morning, and he may have smelled that, but I still don't think he should have commented!"

Daughter: "I don't have any spray like that."

Mother: "Why, sure you do! In the blue can that was on back of the toilet. I used some before the appointment."

Granddaughter: "That's my Barbie Golden Glitter Hair Spray!"

A boy was walking down the street when he noticed his grandpa sitting on the porch in the rocking chair with nothing on from the waist down. "Grandpa, what are you doing?" he asked.

The old man looked off in the distance and did not answer him. "Grandpa, what are you doing sitting out here with nothing on below the waist?" he asked again.

The old man slowly looked at him and said, "Well, last week I sat out here with no shirt on, and I got a stiff neck. This is your grandma's idea."

A wife went in to see a therapist and said, "I've got a big problem, Doctor. Every time we're in bed and my husband climaxes, he lets out this earsplitting yell."

"My dear," the shrink said, "that's completely natural. I don't see what the problem is."

"The problem," she complained, "is that it wakes me up."

You may have heard about a new bride who was a bit embarrassed to be known as a honeymooner. So when she and her husband pulled up to the hotel, she asked him if there was any way that they could make it appear that they had been married a long time.

He responded, "Sure. You carry the suitcases!"

There is this guy who has a 25-inch dick. He goes to a witch in the woods and asks her if she can make his dick smaller because he just can't please the ladies with it being so big. He hasn't found a lady yet who likes it and he can't get any pleasure.

She tells him to go into the woods and he will find a frog. When he finds the frog, he is to ask it to marry him. If the frog says "no," his cock will shrink five inches.

He goes into the woods and finds this frog. He asks, "Frog, will you marry me?"

The frog says, "No." And his prick shrinks five inches.

The guy thinks to himself, Wow, that was pretty cool. But, it's still too big. So he goes back to the frog and again asks the frog, "Frog, will you marry me?"

Frog: "No, I won't marry you."

The guy's dick shrinks another five inches. But that's still 15 inches and he thinks it is still just a little bit too big. He thinks that 10 inches would be just great. He goes back to the frog and asks, "Frog, will you marry me?"

Frog: "How many times do I have to tell you? No, no, NO!!!"

A sixteen-year-old boy goes to the drugstore one day and asks for some condoms. The clerk says he looks very young for that kind of thing and asks what on earth he would want with such things. The boy replies that he has been seeing a girl for a few weeks and things are starting to heat up. That night he is going to her parents' house for dinner, and after dinner they are going up to her room where he is going to screw her every style from missionary to doggy and back again. The clerk sells the boy the condoms and off he goes.

That night he rings the doorbell at his girlfriend's house. She answers, and brings him into the dining room where her parents are sitting at the table. Immediately, the boy buries his face in his hands and starts saying grace. A minute passes, then two, and finally, after five minutes, the girlfriend leans over and whispers in his ear, "I didn't know you were so religious."

The boy replies, "I didn't know your father was a clerk."

Q. What's the difference between your wages and a penis?
A. You don't have to beg your girlfriend to blow your wages.

Two sweethearts had been together for a few years during high school and were devoted to each other. When they left school, they both wanted to go to the same university, but the girl was accepted to a university on the East Coast and the guy to one on the West Coast. They agreed to be faithful to each other and spend anytime they could together.

As time went on, the guy would call the girl and she would never be home, and when he wrote, she would take weeks to reply to the letters. Even when he emailed her, she took days to respond to his messages.

Finally, she confessed to him she wanted to date around. He didn't take this very well and increased his calls, letters and emails trying to win back her love. Because she became annoyed, and now had a new boyfriend, she wanted to get him off her back.

So, what she did is this: She took a Polaroid picture of her sucking her new boyfriend's cock and sent it to her old boyfriend with a note reading, "I've found a new boyfriend—leave me alone." Well, needless to say, this guy was heartbroken but also totally pissed off. So, he decided to take revenge.

He wrote on the back of the photo the following: "Dear Mom and Dad, having a great time at college, please send more money!" and sent the picture to her parents.

On the first day of university, the Dean addressed the students, pointing out some of the rules:

"The female dormitory will be out-of-bounds for all male students, and the male dormitory to the female students. Anybody caught breaking this rule will be fined $20 the first time." He continued, "Anybody caught breaking this rule the second time will be fined $60. Being caught a third time will cost you $180. Are there any questions?"

At this point, a male student in the crowd inquired:

"How much for a season ticket?"

Bob joins a very exclusive nudist colony. On his first day, he takes off his clothes and starts wandering around. A gorgeous petite blonde walks by him and the man immediately gets an erection. The woman notices his erection, comes over to him grinning sweetly and says, "Sir, did you call for me?"

Bob replies, "No, what do you mean?"

She says, "You must be new here; let me explain. It's a rule here that if I give you an erection, it implies you called for me." Smiling, she then leads him to the side of a pool, lies down on a towel, eagerly pulls him to her and happily lets him have his way with her.

Bob continues exploring the facilities. He enters a sauna, sits down and farts. Within a few seconds a huge, horribly corpulent, hairy man with a firm erection lumbers out of the steam towards him. The huge man says, "Sir, did you call for me?"

Bob replies, "No, what do you mean?"

The huge man says, "You must be new here; it is a rule that when you fart, it implies you called for me." The huge man then easily spins Bob around, bends him over the bench and has his way with him.

Bob rushes back to the colony office. He is greeted by the smiling, naked, receptionist. "May I help you?"

Bob says, "Here is your card and key back. You can keep the $500 joining fee."

The amazed receptionist says, "But, sir, you've only been here a couple of hours. You have only seen a small fraction of our facilities."

Bob replies, "Listen, lady, I am 58 years old. I get a hard-on twice a month, but I fart 15 times a day. No thanks."

The lion gathers all animals to a meeting and tells them that no one is allowed to use condoms anymore because the jungle needs to increase its population. One day, the fox sees that the donkey is wearing a condom and is ready to have sex. The fox runs to the lion and tells him about the donkey wearing a condom.

When the lion confronts the donkey, the donkey says, "That's not a condom—it's a snake giving me a blow job!"

There was a virgin who was going out on a date for the first time and she told her grandmother about it. So, the grandmother says, "Sit here and let me tell you about those young boys. He is going to try to kiss you. You are going to like that but don't let him do it. He is going to try to feel your breast and you are going to like it, but don't let him do it.

He is going to try to put his hand between your legs. You are going to like that but don't let him do it. But most important, he is going to try to get on top of you and have his way with you. You are going to like that but don't let him do it—it will disgrace the family."

With that bit of advice, the granddaughter went on her date and could not wait to tell her grandmother about it.

So the next day, she told her grandmother that her date went just like she said. But she said, "Grandmother, I didn't let him disgrace the family. When he tried I turned over, got on top of him and disgraced his family."

A man goes to the doctor after feeling ill. The doctor says, "You know, you should have come to see me sooner. Unfortunately, you have waited too long and you are going to die this evening."

The man is distraught and wonders how he is going to tell his wife. Well, he tells her and she takes it pretty well. "Honey, this is going to be a night that you will always remember," she says. "I am going to treat you like a king." She prepares a scrumptious gourmet dinner with wine, candles, the works.

After dinner she slips away and returns in the most incredible negligee the man has ever seen. She leads him to the bedroom. They make the most passionate love they have ever made. The man is beside himself. Once done, the wife rolls over to go to sleep knowing she kept her promise. Well, the husband is wide awake watching the clock.

He knows that he is doomed. He taps her. "Honey?" he whispers. She turns back to him and again they proceed to make love. After fninishing, she rolls over, but he taps her for more attention. She is getting cranky, but under the circumstances she grants her husband's dying wishes. Finally, the wife rolls over and begins to snore. Well, the man decides to tap her again. "Honey?" he whispers.

She rolls over and yells, "Oh sure! You don't have to get up in the morning!!!"

Young Johnny and Susie were playing doctor on the back porch when Susie's mom popped in on them. "You're going to get a good licking when daddy gets home," she said.

Susie replied, "Johnny's been doing that all afternoon."

Q. What did the banana say to the vibrator?
A. Why are you shaking? She's going to eat me.

A wife arrived home after a long shopping trip, and was horrified to find her husband in bed with a beautiful young woman. Just as she was about to storm out of the house, her husband stopped her with these words:

"Before you leave, I want you to hear how this all came about. Driving home, I saw this young girl looking poor and tired. I offered her a ride. She was hungry, so I brought her home and fed her some of the roast you had forgotten about in the refrigerator. Her shoes were worn out so I gave her a pair of your shoes you didn't wear because they were out of style. She was cold so I gave her that new birthday sweater you never wore even once because the color didn't suit you. Her pants were worn out so I gave her a pair of yours that you don't fit into anymore. Then as she was about to leave the house, she paused and asked, 'Is there anything else that your wife doesn't use anymore?' And so, here we are!"

A husband and wife are getting all snugly in bed. The passion is heating up. But then the wife stops and says, "I don't feel like it. I just want you to hold me."

The husband says, "WHAT??"

The wife explains that he must not be in tune with her emotional needs as a woman. The husband realizes that nothing is going to happen tonight and he might as well deal with it. So the next day, the husband takes her shopping at a big department store. He walks around and has her try on three very expensive outfits. And then tells his wife, "We'll take all three of them." Then he goes over and gets matching shoes worth $200 each. And then he goes to the jewelry department and gets a set of diamond earrings.

The wife is so excited, she thinks her husband has flipped out, but she does not care. She is jumping up and down, so excited she cannot even believe what is going on.

She says, "I am ready to go. Let's go pay."

The husband says, "No, no, no, honey, we're not going to buy all this stuff."

The wife's face goes blank.

"No, honey, I just want you to HOLD this stuff for a while."

Her face gets really red and she is about to explode and then the husband says, "You must not be in tune with my financial needs as a man!!!"

One day a pregnant wife announced to her husband that she was going to start looking for names for their unborn child. When the father got home from work the mother held up a baby book and said that if the baby was a girl the name was going to be Ophelia. The husband didn't like the name. But he said, "That's a good name—it reminds me of a girl I dated in college."

The next day the mother had changed the name to Sarah.

Once there was a little boy who was curious about what a strip club was like, so one day he decided to sneak into one. Once inside, he watched as the strippers danced. He watched until they started taking of their clothing. That's when he bolted out the door and started running down the street and into a man.

The man asked the boy, "What's wrong, young man? You look like you just saw a ghost!"

The little boy replied, "My mommy and daddy told me that if I ever watched anybody undress, I'd turn to stone, and all of a sudden I felt something go hard!"

A married man keeps telling his wife, "Darling, you have such a beautiful butt." Every person in the town agrees that she does have a very beautiful butt.

The man's birthday is coming up, so the wife decides to get the words Beautiful Butt tattooed on her ass.

She walks in and tells the tattoo artist that her husband thinks she has a beautiful butt.

He looks and says, "Yes, you do have a beautiful butt."

She then tells the man she wants "Beautiful Butt" tattooed on her ass.

The man tells her, "I can't fit that on your ass—it takes up too much space. But I tell you what, I will tattoo the letters BB on each cheek and that can stand for beautiful butt."

She agrees and gets it done.

On the man's birthday she hears him come home and she's only wearing a robe. She then stands at the top of the stairs.

He opens the door and she says, "Look, dear." She then takes off the robe she is wearing, bends over and the man yells, "Who the fuck is Bob?!"

A woman says to her husband that she wants to have plastic surgery to enlarge her breasts.

Her husband tells her, "Hey, you don't need surgery to do that. I know how to do it without surgery."

His wife asks, "How can I do it without surgery?"

"Just rub toilet paper between them."

Startled, the lady asks, "How does that make them bigger?"

"I don't know, but it worked for your ass."

A cop saw a car weaving all over the road and pulled it over. He walked up to the car and saw a nice-looking woman behind the wheel. There was a strong smell liquor on her breath.

He said, "I'm going to give you a breathalyzer test to determine if you are under the influence of alcohol."

She blew up the balloon and he walked it back to the police car.

After a couple of minutes, he returned to her car and said, "It looks like you've had a couple of stiff ones."

She replied, "You mean it shows that, too?"

There is a man who wants a pure wife. So he starts to attend church to find a woman. He meets a young lady who seems nice so he takes her home. When they get there, he whips out his manhood and asks, "What's this?"

She replies, "A cock."

He thinks to himself that she is not pure enough.

A couple of weeks later he meets another young lady and soon takes her home. Again, he pulls out his manhood and asks the question.

She replies, "A cock."

He is pissed off because she seemed more pure than the first.

A couple of weeks later he meets a girl who seems really pure. She won't go home with him for a long time, but eventually he gets her to his house. He whips it out and asks, "What is this?"

She giggles and says, "A pee-pee."

He thinks to himself that he has finally found his woman.

They get married but after several months every time she sees his member she giggles and says, "That's your pee-pee."

He finally breaks down and says, "Look, this is not a pee-pee, it is a cock."

She laughs and says, "No it's not. A cock is ten inches long and black."

A woman goes into a dentist's office, and after he is through examining her he says, "I am sorry to tell you this, but I am going to have to drill a tooth."

The woman then says, "Ooooohhhh, the pain is so awful I'd rather have a baby!"

To which the dentist replies, "Make up your mind—I have to adjust the chair."

Once upon a time in a land far away, a beautiful, independent, self-assured princess happened upon a frog as she sat contemplating ecological issues on the shores of an unpolluted pond in a verdant meadow near her castle.

The frog hopped into the princess' lap and said, "Elegant lady, I was once a handsome prince until an evil witch cast a spell upon me. One kiss from you, however, and I will turn back into the dapper young prince that I am. Then, my sweet, we can marry and set up house in your castle with my mother, where you can prepare my meals, clean my clothes, bear my children, and feel forever grateful doing so."

That night, as the princess dined sumptuously on lightly sautéed frogs legs seasoned in a wine and onion cream sauce, she chuckled to herself and thought: I don't fucking think so.

A woman had been away for two days visiting a sick friend in another town. When she returned, her little boy greeted her by saying, "Mommy, guess what! Yesterday I was playing in the closet in your bedroom and daddy came into the room with the lady next door and they got undressed and got into your bed, and then daddy got on top of her..."

Sonny's mother held up her hand. "Not another word. Wait until your father comes home and then I want you to tell him exactly what you've just told me."

The father came home. As he walked into the house, his wife said, "I'm leaving you. I'm packing now and I'm leaving you."

"But why?" asked the startled father.

"Go ahead, Sonny. Tell daddy just what you told me."

"Well," Sonny said, "I was playing in your bedroom closet and daddy came upstairs with the lady next door and they got undressed and got into bed and daddy got on top of her, and then they did just what you did with uncle John when daddy was away last summer."

Dave walks into a bar and sees his buddy Jeff huddled near the bar, depressed. Dave walks over and asks Jeff what's wrong.

"Well," replies Jeff, "you know that beautiful girl at work that I wanted to ask out, but I got a hard-on every time I saw her?"

"Yes," replies Dave with a smile.

"Well," says Jeff, straightening up, "I finally plucked up the courage to ask her out, and she agreed."

"That's great!" says Dave. "When are you going out?"

"I went to meet her this evening," continues Jeff, "but I was worried I'd get a stiffy again. So I got some duct tape and taped my dick to my leg, so if I did, it wouldn't show."

"Sensible," says Dave.

"So I get to her door," says Jeff, "and I rang her doorbell. And she answered it in the shortest skirt you ever saw."

"And what happened then?"

Jeff huddles near the bar again. "I kicked her in the face."

A doctor recently had a patient drop in on him for an unscheduled appointment. "What can I do for you today?" the doctor asked.

The aged gentleman replied, "Doctor, you must help me. Every time I make love to my wife, my eyes get all bleary, my legs go weak, and I can hardly catch my breath. Doctor, I'm scared!"

The doctor, looking at his 86-year-old patient, said, "Mr. Smith, these sensations tend to happen over time, especially to a man of your advanced years. But tell me, how often do you notice these symptoms?"

The old gent's response was, "Well, three times last night, and twice again this morning!"

Q. How do you make your girlfriend scream while having sex?
A. Call her and tell her.

Little Johnny and Susie were only 10 years old, but they just knew that they were in love. One day they decided that they wanted to get married, so Johnny went to Susie's father to ask him for her hand. Johnny bravely walked up to him and said, "Mr. Smith, Susie and I are in love and I want to ask you for her hand in marriage."

Thinking that this was the cutest thing, Mr. Smith replied, "Well, Johnny, you are only 10. Where will you two live?"

Without even taking a moment to think about it, Johnny replied, "In Susie's room. It's bigger than mine and we can both fit there nicely."

Still thinking this was just adorable, Mr. Smith said with a huge grin, "Okay then, how will you live? You're not old enough to get a job. You'll need to support Susie."

Again, Johnny instantly replied, "Our allowance. Susie has $5 a week and I have $10 a week. That's about $60 a month, and that'll do us just fine."

By this time Mr. Smith was a little shocked that Johnny had put so much thought into this. So, he thought for a moment trying to come up with something that Johnny wouldn't have an answer for.

After a second, Mr. Smith said, "Well, Johnny, it seems like you have got everything all figured out. I just have one more question for you. What will you do if the two of you should have little ones of your own?"

Johnny just shrugged his shoulders and said, "Well, we've been lucky so far..."

The manager hired a new secretary. She was young, sweet and polite. One day while taking dictation, she noticed his fly was open. While leaving the room, she courteously said, "Oh, sir, did you know that your barracks door was open?" He did not understand her remark, but later on happened to look down and saw that his zipper was open. He decided to have some fun with his new employee.

Calling her in, he asked, "By the way, Miss Jones, when you saw my barracks door open this morning, did you also see a soldier standing to attention?"

The secretary, who was very witty, replied, "Why, no, sir, all I saw was a little disabled veteran sitting on two duffel bags!"

A 92-year-old man went to the doctor to get a physical examination. A few days later, the doctor saw the man walking down the street with a gorgeous young lady on his arm. At his follow up visit the doctor talked to the man and said, "You're really doing great, aren't you?"

The man replied, "Just doing what you said, Doctor: 'Get a hot mamma and be cheerful.'"

The doctor said, "I didn't say that. I said you've got a heart murmur. Be careful."

A guy is walking down the street with some chicken wire under his arm. His neighbor sees him and asks what he has. The guy replies, "It's chicken wire and I'm going to catch some chickens."

His neighbor says, "You fool, you can't catch chickens with chicken wire."

Later that night he sees the guy walking down the street dragging 12 chickens.

The next day he sees him walking down the street with some duct tape under his arm. Once again he asks what the guy is up to. The guy says he has some duct tape and he is going to catch some ducks.

The neighbor replies, "You fool, you can't catch ducks with duct tape."

Sure enough, later that night, he sees the guy walking down the street dragging 12 ducks behind him.

The next day, he sees the guy walking with something else under his arm. He asks what it is.

The guy replies, "It's pussy willow."

He says, "Hold on, let me get my hat."

The husband emerged from the bathroom naked and was climbing into bed, when his wife complained as usual, "I have a headache."

269

THE GINORMOUS BOOK OF DIRTY JOKES

"Perfect," her husband said. "I was just in the bathroom powdering my dick with aspirin. You can take it orally or up the ass—it's up to you!!!"

Four men got together at a reunion. Three of them had sons and they started bragging about them, while the fourth guy went to the bar to get some drinks. The first man said his son was doing so well he now owned a factory manufacturing furniture. Why, just the other day he gave his best friend a whole house full of brand new furniture.

The second man said his son was doing just as well. He was a manager at a car sales firm. Why, just the other day he gave his best friend a Ferrari. The third man said his was doing well too. He was a manager at a bank. Why, just the other day he gave his best friend the money to buy a house.

The fourth man came back and the other three told him they were just talking about how successful their sons were. He just shook his head and said his son was gay and hadn't amounted to much. But he must be doing something right because, just the other day, he was given a house, furniture and a Ferrari by his lovers!

News Flash: Today the world was stunned by the death of the Energizer Bunny. He was six years old. Authorities believe that the death occurred at approximately 8:42 p.m. last evening. Best known as the irritating pink bunny that kept going, and going and going, "Pinkie," as he was known to his friends and family, was alone at the time of his death. An emergency autopsy was performed early this morning. Chief Medical Examiner, Dura Cell, concluded that the cause of death was acute cardiac arrest induced by sexual overstimulation. Apparently, someone had put the bunny's batteries in backward and he kept coming, and coming, and coming...

A man calls home from his office and says to his wife, "I have the chance to go fishing for a week. It's the opportunity of a lifetime. I have to leave right away. Pack my clothes, my fishing equipment, and especially my blue silk pajamas. I'll be home in an hour to pick them up." The man rushes home to grab everything. He hugs his wife, apologizes for the short notice, and then hurries off.

A week later, the man returns and his wife asks, "Did you have a good trip, dear?"

The man replies, "Yep, the fishing was great—but you forgot to pack my blue silk pajamas."

His wife smiles and says, "Oh, no I didn't. I put them in your tackle box!"

One day, after striking gold in Alaska, a lonesome miner came down from the mountains and walked into a saloon in the nearest town. "I'm looking for the meanest, roughest and toughest whore in the Yukon!" he said to the bartender.

"We got her!" replied the barkeeper. "She's upstairs in the second room on the right." The miner handed the bartender a gold nugget to pay for the whore and two beers. He grabbed the beer bottles, stomped up the stairs, kicked open the second door on the right and yelled,

"I'm looking for the meanest, roughest and toughest whore in the Yukon!"

The woman inside the room looked at the miner and said, "You found her!" Then she stripped naked, bent over and grabbed her ankles.

"How do you know I want to do it in that position?" asked the miner.

"I don't," replied the whore, "but I thought you might like to open those beers before we get started."

Three boys received their grades from their female sex education instructor. One got a D+, the second a D- and the third an F.

"One day we should get her for this," said the first boy.

"I agree. We'll grab her..." said the second.

"Yeah," said the third. "And then we'll kick her in the nuts!"

There is a tour bus in Egypt that stops in the middle of a town square. The tourists are all shopping at the little stands surrounding the square. One tourist looks at his watch, but it is broken, so he leans over to a local who is squatting down next to his camel. "What time is it, sir?"

The local reaches out and softly cups the camel's genitals in his hand, and raises them up and down. "It's about 2:00," he says. The tourist can't believe what he just saw.

He runs back to the bus, and sure enough it is 2:00. He tells a few of the fellow tourists his story, "The man can tell the time by the weight of the camel's genitals!!" One of the doubting tourists walks back to the local and asks him the time, the same thing happens!! It is 2:05 p.m.

He runs back to tell the story. Finally, the bus driver wants to know how it is done. He walks over and asks the local how he knows the time from the camel's genitals.

The local says, "Sit down here and grab the camel's genitals. Now, lift them up in the air. Now, look underneath them to the other side of the courtyard where that clock is hanging on the wall."

There are three girls, and their boyfriends all have the same name. So in order to keep them from getting confused, they decide to give their boyfriends nicknames. They ask the first girl what she calls her boyfriend. She says, "I call my man 7-Up."

They ask her, "Why do you call your man that?"

And she says, "Because he's seven inches long and is always up."

They ask the second girl what she calls her man.

She says, "I call my man Mountain Dew."

They ask, "Why do you call your man that?"

And she says, "Because he likes to mount and do me."

They ask the third girl the same thing and she says, "I like to call my man Jack Daniels."

They look at her puzzled and say, "Why do you call your man that? Jack Daniels is a hard liquor!"

She says, "Exactly!"

A woman enrolls in nursing school and is attending an anatomy class. The subject of the day is involuntary muscles. The instructor, hoping to perk up the students a bit, asks her if she knows what her asshole does when she's having an orgasm.

"Sure," she says. "He's at home taking care of the kids."

A baby was just born. He had all his parts and looked quite normal, except that he was laughing like mad. All the doctors and nurses were examining the little thing in front of the worried parents but he kept on laughing, his tiny fists all closed and tears rolling from his eyes. One at a time, a pediatrician unfolded the tiny fingers to check if the hand was all right, and guess what he found?

The birth control pill!

A baby was just born. He had all his parts and looked quite normal,

Two married buddies are out drinking one night when one turns to the other and says, "You know, I don't know what else to do. Whenever I go home after we've been out drinking, I turn the headlights off before I get to the driveway; I shut off the engine and coast into the garage. I take my shoes off before I go into the house; I sneak up the stairs; I get undressed in the bathroom and I ease into bed, and my wife STILL wakes up and yells at me for staying out so late!"

His buddy looks at him and says, "Well, you're obviously taking the wrong approach. I screech into the driveway, slam the door, storm up the steps, throw my shoes into the closet, jump into bed, rub my hands on my wife's ass and say, 'How about a blow job?' and she's always sound asleep."

Q. How do men sort their laundry?
A. Filthy, and filthy but wearable.

Three old men were sitting around talking about who had the worst health problems.

The seventy-year-old said, "Have I got a problem? Every morning I get up at 7:30 and have to take a piss, but I have to stand at the toilet for an hour 'cause my pee barely trickles out."

"Heck, that's nothing," said the eighty-year-old. "Every morning at 8:30 I have to take a shit, but I have to sit on the pot for hours because of my constipation. It's terrible."

The ninety-year-old said, "You guys think you have problems! Every morning at 7:30 I piss like a racehorse, and at 8:30 I shit like a pig. The trouble with that is, I don't wake up until eleven!"

Little Johnny was sitting in Beginning Sex Education class one day when the teacher drew a picture of a penis on the board. "Does anyone know what this is?" she asked.

Little Johnny raised his hand and said, "Sure, my daddy has two of them!"

"Two of them?!" the teacher asked.

"Yeah. He has a little one that he uses to pee with and a big one that he uses to brush mommy's teeth!"

Going to the brink of death and back in a nine-car pile-up on a two-lane road is very much like making love to a beautiful woman.

First of all, brace yourself. Hold on tight—particularly if it's a rear-ender. And pray you make contact with her twin airbags as soon as possible.

Two gay guys are in a bar and a beautiful blonde walks in wearing a tight T-shirt with no bra.

"God, look at that," says one gay guy, "it's enough to make you want to be a lesbian."

Q. What's another name for pickled bread?
A. Dill dough.

Crazy Mike walks into the pharmacy and says to the pharmacist, "Look, I've got three girls coming over tonight. I've never had three girls at once, so what have you got to keep me horny and potent all night?"

The pharmacist reaches down, unlocks a bottom drawer and brings up a box labeled "Viagra Extra Strength" containing single wrapped packets. He says, "Take one of these and you'll go crazy for 12 hours."

Crazy Mike replies, "Hell, give me three."

The next day Mike returns to the same pharmacist, who smiles and asks, "Well, how'd it go?"

In answer, Mike pulls down his pants to display his penis that's black and blue and blistered, one of the sorriest sights the pharmacist had ever seen.

Crazy Mike says, "Give me a tube of Icy Hot."

The pharmacist replies in horror. "You're not going to put Icy Hot on that, are you?"

Mike replies, "Hell, no, it's for my arms. The girls didn't show up."

Three guys were on a trip to Saudi Arabia. One day, they stumbled into a harem tent filled with over 100 beautiful women. They started getting friendly with the women, when suddenly the sheik came in.

"I am the master of all these women. No one else can touch them except me. You three men must pay for what you have done today. You will be punished in a way corresponding to your profession." The sheik turns to the first man and asks him what he does for a living.

"I'm a cop," says the first man.

"Then we will shoot your penis off!" said the sheik. He then turned to the second man and asked him what he did for a living.

"I'm a fireman," said the second man.

"Then we will burn your penis off!" said the sheik.

Finally, he asked the last man, "And you, what do you do for a living?"

And the third man answered, with a sly grin, "I'm a lollipop salesman!"

A wealthy couple prepared to go out for the evening. The woman of the house gave their butler, Jervis, the night off. She said they would return home very late, and she hoped he would enjoy his evening. The wife wasn't having a good time at the party, so she came home early, alone. Her husband stayed there, socializing with important clients. As the woman walked into her house, she found Jervis by himself in the dining room. She called him to follow her, and led him into the master bedroom.

She turned to him and said, in a voice she knew he must obey, "Jervis, I want you to take off my dress."

This he did, hanging it carefully over a chair.

"Jervis," she continued, "now take off my stockings and garter belt."

Again, Jervis silently obeyed.

"Now, Jervis, I want you to remove my bra and panties."

Eyes downcast, Jervis obeyed. Both were breathing heavily, the tension mounting between them.

She looked sternly at him and said, "Jervis, if I ever catch you wearing my stuff again, you're fired!"

There once was a queer from Khartoum
Took a lesbian up to his room,
But they argued all night
Over who had the right
To do what and with which and to whom.

What am I? I am a common object enjoyed by both sexes, normally about 8 inches long, with little hairs on one end, and a hole in the other. For most of the day I am laying down, but I am ready for instant action. When in use, I move back and forth and in and out of a warm, moist hole. When the work is finally done, a white, slushy, sticky mush is left behind, and I return to my original position. Cleaning is usually done after I have finished. What am I?

Why, I am your very own—toothbrush! What were you thinking, you pervert?

A woman recently lost her husband. She had him cremated and brought his ashes home. Picking up the urn that he was in, she poured him out on the counter.

Then, while tracing her fingers in the ashes, she started talking to him. "Irving, you know that fur coat you promised me? I bought it with the insurance money!

Irving, remember that new car you promised me? Well, I also bought it with the insurance money!

Irving, that emerald necklace you promised me? I bought it, too, with the insurance money."

Still tracing her finger in the ashes, she said, "Irving, remember that blow job I promised you? Here it comes."

An officer shouted orders to a nearby soldier. With considerable bravery, the GI ran directly onto the field of battle, into the line of fire, to retrieve a dispatch case from a dead soldier. In a hail of bullets, he dived back to safety.

"Private," the officer said, "I'm recommending you for a medal. You risked your life to save the locations of our secret warehouses."

"Warehouses!?" the private shouted. "I thought you said whorehouses!"

A retired gentleman went into the social security office to apply for social security.

After waiting in line a long time he got to the counter. The woman behind the counter asked him for his driver's license to verify his age. He looked in his pockets and realized he didn't have it with him.

He told the woman that he was very sorry but he seemed to have left his wallet at home. "Will I have to go home and come back?" he asks.

The woman says, "Unbutton your shirt."

So he opens his shirt revealing lots of curly silver hair. She says, "That silver hair on your chest is proof enough for me," and she processes his social security application. When he gets home, the man excitedly tells his wife about his experience at the social security office.

She said, "You should have dropped your pants—you might have qualified for disability, too."

The word of the day is legs.
Spread the word.

Lori, a pert and pretty nurse, took her troubles to a resident psychiatrist in the hospital where she worked.

"Doctor, you must help me," she pleaded. "Every time I date one of the young doctors here I end up in bed with him. And then afterward I feel guilty and depressed for a week."

"I see," nodded the psychiatrist. "And you want me to strengthen your will power and resolve in this matter?"

"For God's sake, no!" exclaimed the nurse. "I want you to fix it so I won't feel guilty and depressed afterward."

Q. Why does the bride always wear white?
A. Well, aren't all kitchen appliances that color?

The pretty teacher was concerned with one of her young students so she took him aside after class one day. "Little Johnny, why has your school work been so poor lately?"

"I'm in love," replied Little Johnny.

Holding back an urge to smile, the teacher asked, "With whom?"

"With you!" he said.

"But, Little Johnny," said the teacher gently, "don't you see how silly that is? Sure, I'd like a husband of my own someday, but I don't want a child."

"Oh, don't worry," said Little Johnny reassuringly, "I'll use a condom!"

"That wife of mine is a liar," said the angry husband to a sympathetic pal seated next to him in the bar.

"How do you know?" the friend asked.

"She didn't come home last night, and when I asked her where she'd been she said she'd spent the night with her sister, Shirley."

"So?" the friend replied.

"So, she's a liar. I spent the night with her sister Shirley!"

In pharmacology, all drugs have a generic name: Tylenol is Acetaminophen, Advil is Ibuprofen, and so on. The FDA has been looking for a generic name for Viagra, and announced today that they have settled on Mycoxafloppin.

John woke up one morning with an enormous erection, so he turned over to his wife's side of the bed. His wife, Heather, had already awakened, and she was downstairs preparing breakfast in the kitchen. Afraid that he might spoil things by getting up, John called his little boy into the room and asked him to take a note to his wife. The note read:

The Tent Pole Is Up,
The Canvas Is Spread,
The Hell With Breakfast,
Come Back To Bed.

Heather answered the note and then asked her son to take it to her husband. The note read:

Take The Tent Pole Down,
Put The Canvas Away,
The Monkey Had A Hemorrhage,
No Circus Today.

John read the note and quickly scribbled a reply. Then, he asked his son to take it to his wife. The note read:

The Tent Pole's Still Up,
And The Canvas Still Spread,
So Drop What You're Doing,
And Come Give Me Some Head.

Heather answered the note and then asked her son to take it to her husband. The note read:

I'm Sure That Your Pole's
The Best In The Land.
But I'm Busy Right Now,
So Do It By Hand!

He who stands with hands in pockets feels foolish.
He who has holes in pockets feels nuts.

Two women were picking potatoes one autumn day. The first woman had two potatoes in her hands. She looked at the other woman and said, "These potatoes remind me of my husbands testicles."
And the other woman said,
"Are his testicles that big?"
"No," she commented, "they're that dirty."

Jon left for a two-day business trip, but he was only a few blocks away from his house when he realized he'd left his plane ticket on top of his dresser. He turned around and headed back to the house. He quietly entered the door and walked into the kitchen. He saw his wife washing the breakfast dishes, wearing her skimpiest negligee.

She looked so good that he tiptoed up behind her, reached out, and squeezed her left tit.

"Leave only one pint of milk," she said. "Jon won't be here for breakfast tomorrow."

In a second grade class, a little girl asks, "Teacher, can my mommy get pregnant?"

"How old is your mother, dear?" asks the teacher.

"Forty," she replies.

"Yes, dear, your mother could get pregnant."

The little girl then asks, "Can my big sister get pregnant?"

"Well, dear, how old is your sister?"

The little girl answers, "Nineteen."

"Oh yes, dear, your sister certainly could get pregnant."

The little girl then asks, "Can I get pregnant?"

"How old are you, dear?"

The little girl answers, "I'm seven years old."

"No, dear, you can't get pregnant."

Then, the little boy behind the little girl pokes her and says, "See, I told you we had nothing to worry about."

A woman asks her husband if he'd like some breakfast. "Bacon and eggs, perhaps a slice of toast? Maybe a nice, sliced grapefruit, and a cup of fresh coffee?"

He declines. "It's this Viagra," he says. "It's really taken the edge off my appetite."

At lunchtime, she asks if he would like something. "A bowl of homemade soup maybe, with a cheese sandwich? Or how about a plate of snacks and a glass of milk?"

Again he declines. "No, thanks. It's this Viagra," he says. "It's really taken the edge off my appetite."

At dinner time, she asks if he wants anything to eat, offering to send out for some curry. "Or would you rather I make you a pizza from scratch? Or how about a tasty stir fry? That'll only take a couple of minutes."

Once more, he declines. "Again, thanks, but it's this Viagra. It's really taken the edge off my appetite."

"Well, then," she says. "Would you mind getting off me? I'm fucking STARVING!"

One bright sunny morning, a husband turns to his lovely wife and says, "Wife, we're going fishing this weekend. You, me and the dog."

The wife grimaces, "But I don't like fishing!"

"Look! We're going fishing and that's final."

"Do I have to go fishing with you? I really don't want to go!"

"OK, I'll give you three choices: 1) You come fishing with me and the dog, 2) You give me a blow job, or 3) You take it up the ass!"

The wife grimaces again, "But I don't want to do any of those things!"

"Wife, I've given you three options. You'll have to do one of them! I'm going to the garage to sort out my fishing tackle and when I come back I expect you to have made up your mind!"

The wife sits and thinks about it.

Twenty minutes later her husband comes back.

"Well! What have you decided? Fishing with me, blow job, or ass?"

The wife complains some more and finally makes up her mind. "OK, I'll give you a blow job!"

"Great!" he says and drops his pants.

The wife is on her knees doing the business. Suddenly, she stops, looks up at her husband, "Oh! It tastes absolutely disgusting. It tastes like shit!"

"Yes!" says her husband. "The dog didn't want to go fishing either."

A major Hollywood star decided to do a charity dinner and invited hundreds of people to take part. To make it interesting, the host decided to make it a costume party with the theme of "emotions." So that night, the first couple came to the front door, dressed in all blue.

"You were supposed to dress up as an emotion," stated the doorman.

"We are dressed in all blue because we picked the sad emotion."

Thinking it over, the doorman decided that was good enough. The next couple came up to the door dressed in all red clothing.

"Sorry, you needed to dress up in a costume tonight!"

To which the couple replied, "We are. Our red clothes symbolize anger. Besides, you let the other couple in blue in."

Again, the doorman agreed to let them in.

Then along came a black guy, completely naked with the exception of a pear with the core cut out and his penis stuck into it.

The wide-eyed doorman looked at him, "I'm sorry, but I don't think you have been invited to this dinner."

To which the black man responded in a thick Jamaican accent, "Actually, I was invited!"

"Well, you were supposed to be dressed up in a costume that conveys a certain emotion."

The black guy said, "I am in a costume. I'm deep in despair!"

A woman goes to her doctor and says she wants an operation because her vaginal lips are much to large. She asks the doctor to keep the operation a secret because she's embarrassed and doesn't want anyone to find out. The doctor agrees.

She wakes up from her operation and finds three roses carefully placed beside her bed. Outraged, she immediately calls in the doctor and says, "I thought I asked you not to tell anyone about my operation!"

"Don't worry," he says, "I didn't tell anybody. The first rose is from me. I felt bad because you went through this all by yourself. The second one is from the nurse. She assisted me with the operation, and she had the operation done herself."

"Who is the third rose from?" she asked.

"Oh," says the doctor, "that rose is from the guy upstairs in the burns unit. He wanted to thank you for his new ears!"

One night, Joe brought home a dozen red roses to his wife.

"How lovely, dear," she said, "what's the occasion?"

"I want to make love to you," he said simply.

"Not tonight, dear. I have a headache."

The next night Joe came home with a big box of chocolates and explained that he wanted to make love to her.

"I'm awfully tired," said his wife. "Not tonight."

Every night for a week Joe brought home something, but each time his wife's answer was "no." Finally, he came home with six black kittens with little red bows around their necks and handed them to his wife.

"How adorable, Joe!" she cried. "But what are they for?"

"These are six little pallbearers for your dead pussy."

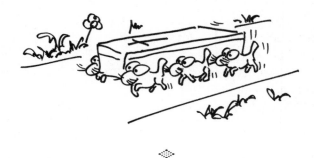

Q. What are those little bumps around women's nipples?
A. It's Braille for "suck here."

There once was a couple named Blairs,
Who liked to fuck on the stairs,
When the banister broke,
He quickened his stroke,
And finished her off in the air.

Cinderella wanted to go to the ball one night, but she was having her period and didn't have any tampons. Her Fairy Godmother came to the rescue and turned a pumpkin into a tampon. The Godmother says, "Now use the tampon, but be sure to get back home before midnight or it will turn back into a pumpkin, and that wouldn't be good."

Cinderella agrees and leaves the house.

Midnight comes along...no Cinderella! 1 a.m., 2 a.m. and 3 a.m., and still no Cinderella!

Finally, 5 a.m. rolls by and Cinderella waltzes through the door. The fairy godmother jumps up. "Where the hell have you been?!?"

To which Cinderella replies, "I met this amazing guy, and well, I went back to his place and I had a great time. His name was Peter, Peter, Pumpkin ..."

During his monthly visit to the corner barbershop, a guy asked his barber for any suggestions on how to treat his increasing baldness. After a brief pause, the barber leaned over and confided that the best thing he'd come across was, in fact, female juices.

"But you're balder than I am," protested the customer.

"True," admitted the barber. "But you've got to admit, I've got one hell of a moustache!"

Two deaf people got married. During the first week of marriage, they find they are unable to communicate in the bedroom when they turn the lights off because they can't see each other using sign language.

After several nights of fumbling around and misunderstandings, the wife decides to find a solution. "Honey," she signs, "Why don't we agree on some simple signals? For instance, at night, if you want to have sex with me, reach over and squeeze my right breast once. If you don't want to have sex, reach over and squeeze my left breast once."

The husband thinks this is a great idea and signs back to his wife, "Great idea. Now, if you want to have sex with me, reach over and pull on my penis once, and if you don't want to have sex, reach over and pull on my penis fifty times."

A young lady came home from a date feeling rather sad. She told her mother, "Anthony proposed to me an hour ago."

"Then why are you so sad?" her mother asked.

"Because he also told me he is an atheist. Mom, he doesn't even believe there's a hell."

Her mother replied, "Marry him anyway. Between the two of us, we'll show him how wrong he is."

Q. What did one lesbian vampire say to the other lesbian vampire?
A. "See you next month!"

A city boy wants to marry a country girl. She insists that he has to ask her father for her hand in marriage. So off he goes to their farm to ask her father. "I want to marry your daughter."

"Well, my boy, you will have to prove to me that you are a man worthy of my daughter."

"I'll do anything for my love," says the young man.

"You see that cow out in the pasture? Well, go screw it."

A little puzzled the boy says, "OK, anything for my love." On finishing the deed, he asks, "Now can I marry your daughter?"

"Nope," says the father. "See that goat over yonder? Go screw it."

Again the boy obliges and returns saying, "Now can I marry your daughter?"

"Nope. Not yet. One more thing. See that pig in the sty? Well, get to it."

Once again, he obliges and returns. This time the farmer is amazed at seeing this boy doing these deeds just to marry his daughter.

So the father finally tells the boy, "Now you can marry my daughter."

To which the boy replies, "Screw your daughter. How much do you want for that pig?"

Q. What do parsley and pubic hair have in common?
A. You push them both aside and keep on eating.

There was a construction worker on the third floor of an unfinished building. He needed a hand saw, but was too lazy to go down and get it himself. He tried to call his fellow worker on the ground to get it for him, but this guy could not hear a word he said. So he started to give a sign so the guy on the ground could understand him.

First he pointed at his eyes (meaning "I"), then pointed at his knees (meaning "need"), and moved his hand back and forth describing the movement of a hand saw.

Finally, the guy on the ground started nodding his head like he understood, and then dropped his pants and started to jerk off.

The guy on the third floor got pissed off and ran down to the ground and started yelling at this guy, "You idiot, I was trying to tell you I needed a hand saw."

The other guy replied, "I know. I was trying to tell you that I was coming."

One day a fireman was washing his fire engine and, conscious of someone behind him, turned around to see a little boy with a fireman's outfit sitting in a little cart he had painted red. He had a rope tied around a dog's neck and a rope tied around a cat's testicles. The fireman said to the boy that his cart would go faster if he tied the rope that was around the cat's testicles around the cat's neck instead. The little boy thought for a moment and told the fireman the cart would go faster, but then he wouldn't have a siren.

Important Press Release: The manufacturers of KY Jelly have announced that their product is now fully Year 2000 compliant. In light of this they have now renamed it as "Y2KY Jelly."

A spokesman said, "The main benefit of this revision to our product is that you can now insert four digits into your date instead of two."

An old man woke up in the middle of the night and found, to his utter astonishment, that his pecker was as hard as a rock for the first time in two years. He shook his wife by the shoulder until she woke up and showed her his enormous boner. "Check this out!" he happily exclaimed. "What do you think we should do with it?"

With one eye open, his wife replied, "Well, now that you've got all the wrinkles out, it would be a good time to wash it."

A businessman and his secretary, overcome by passion, go to his house for an early afternoon quickie. "Don't worry," he assures her, "my wife is out of town on a business trip, so there's no risk." As one thing leads to another, the woman reaches into her purse and suddenly gasps, "We have to stop! I forgot to bring my contraceptive!"

"No problem," he replies, "I'll get my wife's diaphragm."

After a few minutes of searching, he returns to the bedroom in a fury. "That witch!" he exclaims. "She took it with her! I always knew she didn't trust me!"

An escaped convict broke into a house and tied up a young couple who had been sleeping in the bedroom. As soon as he had the chance, the husband turned to his voluptuous young wife, bound up on the bed in a skimpy nightgown, and whispered, "Honey, this guy hasn't seen a woman in years. Just cooperate with anything he wants. If he wants to have sex with you, just go along with it and pretend you like it. Our lives depend on it!"

"Dear," the wife hissed, spitting out her gag, "I'm so relieved you feel that way, because he just told me he thinks you have a nice butt!"

When her husband passed away, the wife put the usual death notice in the newspaper, but added that he had died of gonorrhea. Once the daily newspapers had been delivered, a good friend of the family called and complained bitterly, "You know very well that he died of diarrhea, not gonorrhea."

The widow replied, "Yes, I know that he died of diarrhea, but I thought it would be better for posterity to remember him as a great lover rather than the big shit that he really was."

"Your Honor, I am 75 years old. So there I am, sitting on my porch on a warm spring evening, when a young man comes creeping up and sits beside me. He starts to rub my thigh, and it feels good, Your Honor. So I don't stop him, and he begins to rub my old breasts, Your Honor. Why, Your Honor, I haven't felt that good in years! So I just spread my old legs and say to him, 'Take me, young man, take me!' That's when he yelled, 'April Fool,' and that's when I shot the bastard!!"

Q. How do you teach a blonde math?
A. Subtract her clothes, divide her legs, and square root her.

An elderly couple came back from a wedding one afternoon and were in a pretty romantic mood. While sitting on their loveseat, the elderly woman looked at her companion and said, "I remember when you used to kiss me every chance you had."

The old man, feeling a bit obliged, leaned over and gave her a peck on the cheek.

Then she said, "I also remember when you used to hold my hand at every opportunity."

The old man again feeling obligated reached over and gently placed his hand on hers.

The elderly woman then stated, "I also remember when you used to nibble on my neck and send chills down my spine."

This time the old man had a blank stare on his face and started to get up off the couch. As he began to walk out of the living room, his wife asked, "Was it something I said? Where are you going?"

The old man looked at her and replied, "I'm going in the other room to get my teeth!"

There was a little boy who had just learned to count on his fingers. One day his uncle came to visit and the boy was anxious to show off his newly acquired skill. He told the uncle to ask him an addition question. So the uncle asked, "What is three plus four?"

The little boy counted it out on his fingers and said, "Seven."

The uncle said, "Listen, kid, you can't count it out on your hands because someday when you are in school a teacher will get mad at you for it. Now put your hands in your pockets."

So the little boy put his hands in his pockets and his uncle asked, "What is five plus five?"

The uncle saw movement in the boys pockets, then the boy said, "Eleven."

A man went to the police station wishing to speak with the burglar who had broken into his house the night before.

"You'll get your chance in court," said the desk sergeant.

"No, no, no!" insisted the man. "I want to know how he got into the house without waking my wife. I've been trying to do that for years!"

This guy is banging a girl and the girl asks, "You haven't got AIDS have you?"

He replies, "No."

She responds, "Oh, thank God for that! I don't want to get that again!"

One day an 85-year-old man is taking a stroll around his hometown, where he has lived his whole life. As he sees the landmarks, homes and streets from his youth, he starts reminiscing.

"I remember helping build that bridge when I was 25. I worked hard on that. But people won't call you 'the bridge builder' if you do that here. No, no, they don't!

I remember building that house over there when I was 30. But people won't call you 'the house builder' if you do that. No, no they don't!

I remember building that tavern where I still drink when I was 35. If you do that people won't call you 'the tavern builder' either. They sure won't!

But if you fuck one goat..."

Q. Why did Frosty the snowman pull down his pants?
A. He heard the snow-blower coming.

A man went into a pharmacy and asked to talk to a male pharmacist. The woman he was talking to said that she was the pharmacist and that she and her sister owned the store, so there were no males employed there. She then asked if there was something she could help the gentleman with.

The man said, "This is embarrassing for me, but I have a permanent erection which causes me a lot of problems and severe embarrassment. I was wondering what you could give me for it?"

The pharmacist said, "Just a minute, I'll go talk to my sister." When she returned, she said, "The best we can do is 1/3 ownership in the store and $3000 a month in living expenses."

Little Johnny was at school and his teacher was teaching the four basic food groups.

Johnny asks, "What food group do light bulbs fall into?"

His teacher replies, "Light bulbs are not edible and they don't fall into any food group."

Little Johnny insists that light bulbs are food because his dad eats light bulbs. The teacher tries to get Little Johnny to drop the subject, but he just would not let it go.

He says, "I know that light bulbs are edible because I heard my dad tell my mom that if she would turn off the light, he would eat it!"

Twelve monks were about to be ordained. The final test was for them to line up naked in a garden while a nude model danced before them. Each monk had a small bell attached to his privates, and they were told that anyone whose bell rang would not be ordained because he had not reached a state of spiritual purity.

The model danced before the first monk candidate, with no reaction. She proceeded down the line with the same response until she got to the final monk. As she danced, his bell rang so loudly it fell off and clattered to the ground. Embarrassed, he bent down to pick up the bell, and eleven other bells began to ring...

A local law enforcement officer stops a car for traveling faster than the speed limit. Since he was in a good mood that day, he decides to give the poor guy a break and give him a warning instead of a ticket. So, he asks the man his name.

"Fred," he replies.

"Fred what?" the officer asks.

"Just Fred," the man responds.

When the officer presses him for a last name, the man tells him that he used to have a last name but lost it. The officer thinks he has a nutcase on his hands but plays along with it.

"Tell me, Fred, how did you lose your last name?"

The man replies, "It's a long story so stay with me. I was born Fred Dingaling. I know, funny last name. The kids used to tease me all the time. So I kept to myself. I studied hard and got good grades. When I got older I realized that I wanted to be a doctor. I went through college, medical school, internship, residency and finally got my degree, so I was Fred Dingaling, MD. After a while I got bored being a doctor so I decided to go back to school. Dentistry was my dream. I got all the way through school and got my degree, so I was now Fred Dingaling, MD DDS. Got bored doing dentistry so I started fooling around with my assistant. She gave me VD. So, I was Fred Dingaling MD DDS with VD. Well, the ADA found out about the VD so they took away my DDS, so I was Fred Dingaling MD with VD. Then the AMA found out about the ADA taking away my DDS because of the VD, so they took away my MD leaving me as Fred Dingaling with VD. Then the VD took away my dingaling so now I'm just Fred."

The officer let him go without even a warning.

Three women were sitting around talking about their husbands' performance as a lover. The first woman says, "My husband works as a marriage counselor. He always buys me flowers and chocolate before we make love. I like that."

The second woman says, "My husband is a motorcycle mechanic. He likes to play rough and slaps me around sometimes. I kinda like that."

The third woman just shakes her head and says, "My husband works for Microsoft. He just sits on the edge of the bed and tells me how great it's going to be when I get it."

A farmer and his wife were lying in bed one evening. She was knitting and he was reading the latest issue of Animal Husbandry. He looked up from the page and said to her, "Did you know that humans are the only species in which the female achieves orgasm?"

She looked at him wistfully, smiled and replied, "Oh, yeah? Prove it."

He frowned for a moment, then said, "Okay." He got up and walked out, leaving his wife with a confused look on her face.

About a half hour later, he returned all tired and sweaty and proclaimed, "Well, I'm sure the cow and sheep didn't orgasm, but the way that pig is always squealing, how can I tell?"

Nina and Liz are having a conversation during their lunch break. Nina asks, "So, Liz, how's your sex life these days?"

Liz replies, "Oh, you know. It's the usual social security kind."

"Social security?" Nina asked quizzically.

"Yeah, you get a little each month, but it's not enough to live on."

It was the talk of the town when an 80-year-old man married a 20-year-old girl. After a year, she went to a hospital to give birth. The nurse came out to congratulate the guy. "This is amazing. How do you do it at your age?"

He answered, "You've got to keep that old motor running."

The following year she gave birth again. The same nurse said, "You really are amazing. How do you do it?"

He again said, "You've got to keep the old motor running."

The same thing happened the next year. The nurse said, "You must be quite a man."

He responded, "You've got to keep that old motor running."

The nurse then said, "Well, you had better change the oil—this one's black."

A nurse was on duty in the emergency department when a punk rocker entered. The patient had purple hair plus a variety of tattoos and strange clothing. It was quickly determined that the patient had acute appendicitis, so she scheduled for immediate surgery. When the patient was completely disrobed on the operating table, the surgeons noticed that her pubic hair had been dyed green, and just above it there was a tattoo that read, "Keep off the grass." After the surgical procedure was completed, the surgeon added a small note to the wound's dressing that said, "Sorry, had to mow the lawn."

Business was good at the local whorehouse and the madam decided to divide one of the larger rooms. After the work was complete the carpenter asked for payment but was put off. After several weeks he still hadn't been paid and he regularly threatened, "Pay me or I'll rip out the partition."

Finally, the madam offered to pay him in trade. "Take any girl in the house and have your pleasure with her."

"I'll take you."

"Me? I'm an old lady. Take one of those young, good-looking chicks."

"I want you."

So he took her upstairs and removed all her clothes, laid her on her back and put one finger in her pussy and one finger up her ass. "What are you doing?" she asked.

"I told you before. Pay me or I'll rip out the partition."

Annoyed by the professor of anatomy who liked to tell "naughty" stories during class, a group of female students decided that the next time he started to tell one, they would all rise and leave the room in protest. The professor, however, got wind of their scheme just before class the following day, so he bided his time.

Then, halfway through the lecture, he began. "They say there is quite a shortage of prostitutes in France."

The girls looked at one another, arose and started for the door.

"Young ladies," said the professor with a broad smile, "the next plane doesn't leave until tomorrow afternoon."

An 80-year-old man was having his annual checkup and the doctor asked him how he was feeling. "I've never been better!" he boasted. "I've got an eighteen–year-old bride who's pregnant and having my child! What do you think about that?"

The doctor considered this for a moment, then said, "Let me tell you a story. I knew a guy who was an avid hunter. He never missed a season. But one day he went out in a bit of a hurry, and he accidentally grabbed his umbrella instead of his gun." The doctor continued, "So he was in the woods, and suddenly a grizzly bear appeared in front of him! He raised up his umbrella, pointed it at the bear and squeezed the handle. And do you know what happened?" the doctor queried.

Dumbfounded, the old man replied, "No."

The doctor continued, "The bear dropped dead in front of him!"

"That's impossible!" exclaimed the old man. "Someone else must have shot that bear."

"That's kind of what I'm getting at," replied the doctor.

Q. How do you confuse a female archaeologist?
A. Give her a used tampon and ask her what period it's from.

A wife says to her friend, "Our sex life is great."

Her friend says, "Do you ever watch your husband's face when you're having sex?"

She says, "Once, and I saw rage."

Her friend says, "Why would he be angry during sex?"

The wife says, "Because he was looking through the window at us."

Q. What do you call a lesbian dinosaur?

A. Lickalotopuss.

Jack and Jill were twins who couldn't find dates to the graduation ball. So Jill asked Jack to go with her. Jack said, "No, you're my sister. That's gross."

Jill said, "Come on. Promise me if you can't find another date, you'll take me."

So Jack said, "OK." Well, Jack couldn't find a date so he went with Jill.

They were just standing by the bar, and Jill asked Jack to dance. Jack said, "No, you're my sister. That's gross."

Jill said, "Come on. It'll be fun."

So Jack said, "OK," and they had a great time.

After the dance, Jill asked Jack to take her to Lovers' Lane. Jack said, "No, you're my sister! It would be really gross."

Jill said, "We'll just talk. We don't talk anymore."

So Jack said, "OK."

They were at Lovers' Lane talking, when Jill moved to the back seat and said, "Come on, Jack, take me." Jack didn't argue. When Jack moved on top of Jill, Jill murmured, "You're a lot lighter than dad."

Jack said, "I know. Mom told me last night."

A couple drove down a country road not saying a word. An earlier discussion had led to an argument, and neither would concede their position. As they passed a barnyard of mules and pigs, the wife sarcastically asked, "Relatives of yours?"

"Yep," the husband replied. "In-laws."

Every night after dinner, Harry took off for the local watering hole. He would spend the whole evening there and always arrive home really inebriated around midnight. He usually had trouble getting his key to fit the keyhole and couldn't get the door open. And, every time this happened, his wife would go to the door and let him in. Then she would proceed to yell and scream at him for his constant nights out and coming home in a drunken state. But, Harry still continued his nightly routine.

One day, the distraught wife was talking to a friend about her husband's behavior. The friend listened and suggested, "Why don't you treat him a little differently when he comes home? Instead of berating him, why don't you give him some loving words and welcome him home with a kiss? Then, he might change his ways." The wife thought that this might be a good idea.

That night, Harry took off again after dinner. And, at about midnight, he arrived home in his usual condition.

His wife heard him at the door. She quickly opened it and let Harry in. Instead of berating him as she had always done, this time she took his arm and led him into the living room. She sat Harry down in an easy chair, put his feet up on the foot stool, and took his shoes off. Then, she went behind him and started to cuddle him a little. After a short while, she whispered to Harry, "It's pretty late, dear. I think we should go upstairs to bed now, don't you think?"

Harry replied in his inebriated state, "Heck, I guess we might as well. I'll get in trouble when I get home anyway!"

A guy visits the doctor and says, "Doc, I think I've got a sex problem. I can't get it up for my wife anymore."

The doctor says, "Come back tomorrow and bring her with you."

The next day, the guy shows up with his wife. The doctor says to the wife, "Take off your clothes and lie on the table."

She does it, and the doctor walks around the table a few times looking her up and down. He pulls the guy to the side and says, "You're fine. She doesn't give me a hard-on either."

297

A woman whose husband often came home drunk decided to cure him of the habit. One Halloween night, she put on a devil suit and hid behind a tree to intercept him on the way home. When her husband came by, she jumped out and stood before him with her red horns, long tail, and a pitchfork.

"Who are you?" he asked.

"I'm the Devil," she responded.

"Well, come on home with me," he said, "I married your sister."

A man is at work one day when he notices that his co-worker is wearing an earring. This man knows his co-worker to be a somewhat conservative fellow, so naturally he's curious about the sudden change in fashion sense. The man walks up to his co-worker and says, "I didn't know you were into earrings."

"Don't make such a big deal. It's only an earring," he replies sheepishly.

"Well, I'm curious," begs the man, "how long have you been wearing an earring?"

"Er, ever since my wife found it in our bed."

Q. What do you call a farmer with a sheep under each arm?
A. A pimp.

Two guys had just gotten divorced and they swore they would never have anything to do with women again. They were best friends and they decided to move up to Alaska—as far north as they could go— and never look at a woman again. They got up there and went into a trader's store and told him, "Give us enough supplies to last two men for one year."

The trader got the gear together and on top of each one's supplies he laid a board with a hole in it with fur around the hole.

The guys asked, "What's that board for?"

The trader said, "Well, where you're going there are no women and you might need this."

They said, "No way! We've sworn off women for life!"

The trader said, "Well, take the boards with you, and if you don't use them I'll refund your money next year."

"Okay," they said and left. The next year a guy came into the trader's store and said, "Give me enough supplies to last one man for one year."

The trader said, "Weren't you in here last year with a partner?"

"Yeah," said the guy.

"Where is he?" asked the trader.

"I killed him," said the guy.

Shocked, the trader asked, "Why?"

To which the guy replied, "I caught him in bed with my board!"

A man and his wife are on their honeymoon and they have been having sex for ages. The man's cock is burning so he runs for the Vaseline but can't find any. So he goes to the fridge and sees an ice cold glass of milk and puts his cock in it.

He turns around and his wife says, "Oh, that's how you refill it."

A man was complaining to a friend, "I had it all: money, a magnificent house, a fast car, the love of a beautiful woman—then, poof! It was all gone!"

"What happened?" asked the friend.

"My wife found out."

Little Johnny walked into his dad's bedroom one day only to catch him sitting on the side of his bed sliding on a condom. Johnny's father, in attempt to hide his full erection with a condom on it, bent over as if to look under the bed. Little Johnny asked curiously, "What are you doing, dad?"

His father quickly replied, "I thought I saw a rat go underneath the bed."

Little Johnny replied, "What are you going to do, fuck him?"

Three old guys are sitting around complaining. The first guy says, "My hands shake so bad that when I shaved this morning, I almost cut my ear off."

The second guy says, "My hands shake so bad that when I ate breakfast today, I spilled half my coffee on my toast."

The third guy says, "My hands shake so bad that the last time I went to pee I ejaculated just taking my cock out."

A young couple went to the doctor for their annual checkups. Afterward, the doctor called the young man into his office and told him that he had some good news and some bad news. "The good news," he explained, "is that your fiancée has a particular strain of gonorrhea that I have only heard of once before."

The guy paled. "If that's the good news, then what the hell is the bad news?"

"Well," the doctor elaborated, "the bad news is that I heard about this nasty strain just last week from my dog's vet."

A farmer takes her three sons to the doctor for a medical exam for the first time in their lives.

The doctor examines the boys and tells the woman that they are healthy but she needs to give them iron supplements. She goes home and wonders exactly what iron supplements are. Finally, she goes to the hardware store and buys iron ball bearings and mixes them into their food.

Several days later the youngest son comes to her and tells her that he is pissing ball bearings. She tells him that it is normal because she had put them in his food. Later, the middle son comes to her and says that he is crapping ball bearings. Again, she says that it is OK.

That evening the eldest son comes in very upset. He says, "Mom, you won't believe what happened."

She says, "I know, you're passing ball bearings."

"No," he says. "I was out behind the barn jerking off and I shot the dog."

A five-year-old boy was mowing his front lawn and drinking a beer. The preacher who lived across the street saw the beer and came over to harass the kid. "Aren't you a little young to be drinking, son?" he asked.

"That's nothing," the kid said after taking a swig of beer. "I got laid when I was three."

"What? How did that happen?"

"I don't remember. I was drunk."

Two soldiers were chatting during their free time.

First Soldier: "Why did you join the Army?"

Second Soldier: "I didn't have a wife and I loved war. So I joined. How about you? Why did you join the Army?"

First Soldier: "I had a wife and I loved peace. So I joined."

A handsome young lad went into the hospital for some minor surgery, and the day after the procedure, a friend stopped by to see how he was doing. The friend was amazed at the number of nurses who entered the room in short intervals with refreshments, offers to fluff his pillows, make the bed, give back rubs, etc. "Why all the attention?" the friend asked. "You look fine to me."

"I know!" grinned the patient. "But the nurses kind of formed a little fan club when they all heard that my circumcision required twenty-seven stitches."

Q. Why are women like tires?
A. There's always a spare.

A gentleman had called room service.

"And will there be anything else, sir?" the bellboy asked after setting out an elaborate dinner for two.

"No, thank you," the gentleman replied. "That will be all."

As the young man turned to leave, he noticed a beautiful satin negligee on the bed. "Anything for your wife?" he asked.

"Yeah! That's a good idea," the guy said. "Please bring up a postcard."

One day an old farmer fell asleep on the upper floor of his hay loft. When he woke up, he saw his son having sex with his girlfriend in the hay below. He decided he wouldn't disturb them, so he lay down and rested. After a while he heard his son say, "Father, father up above, give me strength for one last shove."

So the father, being witty, replied, "Son, son down below, get off and give your father a go."

Two women were having lunch together and discussing the merits of cosmetic surgery. The first woman says, "I need to be honest with you—I'm getting a boob job."

The second woman says, "Oh, that's nothing. I'm thinking of having my asshole bleached!"

To which the first replies, "Whoa, I just can't picture your husband as a blonde!"

David Copperfield has just finished his magic show. He decides to ask the audience if they have any tricks they would like to share.

Nobody puts their hand up except one man. David beckons him on to the stage and tells him to perform his trick. The man says, "For this trick, David, I will require the assistance of the lovely Claudia Schiffer, who I see is here tonight. I will also need a table."

He walks Claudia Schiffer over to the table and bends her over it. He then proceeds to lift up her skirt, pull down her panties and take her from behind.

David Copperfield is horrified and says, "That's not a trick!!"

The man replies, "Maybe not for you, but for me it's fucking magic."

A married man, unfortunately, had a very small dick, so every time he had sex with his wife he used a cucumber instead of his dick. For seven years he had been doing that. One night his wife suspected that something was wrong. So while they were having sex she quickly threw back the cover and turned on the lights!

The woman said, "What the hell is that? Are you using a cucumber on me? I am shocked! For seven years you have been doing that, you bastard!"

So the man said, "Shut up! It's been seven years and I never asked where the hell those kids came from!"

A doctor walked into a bank. Preparing to sign a check, he pulled a rectal thermometer out of his shirt pocket and tried to 'write' with it. Realizing his mistake, he looked at the thermometer with annoyance and said, "Well that's great, just great—some asshole's got my pen."

A gay guy walks into the doctor's office. He takes off his clothes for examination. When he takes his clothes off, the doctor sees a Nicoderm patch at the end of his penis. The doctor says, "Hmmm, that's interesting. Does it work?"

The man answers, "Sure does... I haven't had a butt in three weeks!"

A husband and wife were out playing golf. They tee off, and one drive goes to the right and one drive goes to the left. The wife finds her ball in a patch of buttercups. She grabs a club and takes a mighty swing at the ball. She hits a beautiful second shot, but in the process she hacks the hell out of the buttercups. Suddenly, a woman appears out of nowhere. She blocks her path to her golf bag, looks at her and says,

"I'm Mother Nature, and I don't like the way you treated my buttercups. From now on, you won't be able to stand the taste of butter. Each time you eat butter you will become physically ill to the point of total nausea."

The mystery woman then disappears as quickly as she appeared.

Shaken, the wife calls out to her husband, "Hey, where's your ball?"

"It's over here in the pussy willows."

The wife screams back, "DON'T HIT THE BALL!!! DON'T HIT THE BALL!!!"

There's a duck staying in a hotel and he's having a few drinks in the bar when he notices a woman sitting alone and starts chatting with her.

They hit it off, so the duck suggests going back to his room for a nightcap.

The woman agrees.

One thing leads to another and they end up on the bed.
This is all very unexpected for the duck, who's totally unprepared.
He calls room service and asks if they can supply him with a condom.
"Certainly, sir," a voice on the end of the phone replies. "Shall I put it on your bill?"
The duck yells back, "What do you think I am, some sort of pervert?"

Q. Why do men pay more for car insurance?
A. Women don't get blow jobs while they're driving.

John invited his mother over for dinner. During the meal, his mother couldn't help noticing how beautiful John's roommate was. She had long been suspicious of a relationship between John and his roommate and this only made her more curious. Over the course of the evening, while watching the two interact, she started to wonder if there was more between John and the roommate than met the eye. Reading his mother's thoughts, John volunteered, "I know what you must be thinking, but I assure you, Julie and I are just roommates."

About a week later, Julie came to John and said, "Ever since your mother came to dinner, I've been unable to find the beautiful silver gravy ladle. "You don't suppose she took it, do you?"

John said, "Well, I doubt it, but I'll write her a letter just to be sure."

So he sat down and wrote:

Dear Mother, I'm not saying you did take a gravy ladle from my house, and I'm not saying you did not take a gravy ladle. But the fact remains that one has been missing ever since you were here for dinner.

Several days later, John received a letter from his mother that read:

Dear Son, I'm not saying that you do sleep with Julie, and I'm not saying that you do not sleep with Julie. But the fact remains that if she was sleeping in her own bed, she would have found the gravy ladle by now.

Love, Mom.

In the days before birth control pills, a young bride-to-be asked her gynecologist to recommend some sort of contraceptive. He suggested she try either the withdrawal method, douches or condoms. Several years later, the woman was walking down the street with three children when she happened to run across her old doctor.

"I see you decided not to take my advice," he said, eyeing the young children.

"On the contrary, Doc," she exclaimed. "Davey here was a pullout, Darcy was a washout, and Delores was a blowout!"

Two women walked into a department store, stopped at the perfume counter and picked up a sample bottle. One sprayed the perfume on her wrist and smelled it.

"That's nice, isn't it?" Sharon said, waving her arm under her friend's nose.

"Yeah. What's it called?"

"Viens a moi."

"Viens a moi? What's that mean?"

A clerk offered some help. "Viens a moi, ladies, is French for 'come to me.'"

Sharon took another sniff. "That doesn't smell like come to me," she said, offering her arm to her friend again. "Does that smell like come to you?"

Morris wakes up in the morning. He has a massive hangover and can't remember anything he did last night. He picks up his bathrobe from the floor and puts it on. He notices there's something in one of the pockets and it turns out to be a bra. He thinks, what the hell happened last night?? He walks towards the bathroom and finds a pair of panties in the other pocket of his robe. Again he thinks, what happened last night—what have I done? Must have been a wild party. He opens the bathroom door, walks in and has a look in the mirror. He notices a little string hanging out of his mouth and his only thought is, please, if there's a God, let this be a teabag.

Two poor kids go to a birthday party at a rich kid's house. The kid is so rich that he has his own swimming pool and all the kids go in. As they're changing afterward, one of the poor kids says to the other one, "Did you notice how small the rich kid's penis was?"

"Yeah," says his friend, "it's probably because he's got toys to play with."

Q. Who's the world's greatest athlete?
A. The guy who finishes first and third in a masturbation contest.

Police officers George and Mary had been assigned to walk the beat. They had only been out a short while when Mary said, "Damn, I was running late this morning after my workout, and after I showered I forgot to put on my panties! We have to go back to the station to get them."

George replied, "We don't have to go back. Just give the K-9 unit, Fido, one sniff, and he will go fetch them for you."

It was a hot day and Mary didn't feel like heading back to the station, so she lifted her skirt for the dog. Fido's nose shot between her legs, sniffing and snorting. After 10 seconds of sniffing, Fido's ears pricked up, he sniffed the wind, and he was off in a flash towards the station house. Five minutes went by with no sign of Fido. Ten minutes passed, and the dog was nowhere to be seen. Fifteen minutes passed, and they were starting to worry.

Twenty minutes passed, and they heard sirens in the distance. The sirens got louder and louder. Suddenly, followed by a dozen police cars, Fido rounded the corner with the Desk Sergeant's balls in his mouth.

Two brothers from the Third World have a lifelong dream to emigrate to America. They work hard and save their money. After many years, they have saved enough money and finally emigrate to New York. Before they begin building their new lives in America, they decide to see some of the famous places they dreamed of for so long: the Statue of Liberty, the Empire State Building, and others. Eventually, they make their way to Coney Island. As they stroll down the beach, taking in all the newness of America, they see a very large billboard that reads: HOT DOGS, with a big arrow pointing down to a little hot dog stand. Being hungry and seeing that having an American hot dog would be something new, they decide to try one. So they order two hot dogs and sit on a nearby bench to enjoy another piece of Americana. The first brother sets his hot dog in his lap, unfolds the paper wrapper, looks at his hot dog for a moment, and suddenly wraps it back up. He then turns to his brother and says, "What part of the dog did you get?"

An elderly couple went to the clinic and asked to be tested for HIV. When the counselor asked why they felt that they should be tested at their age, the old man said, "Well, we heard on TV that people should be tested after annual sex!"

Bill pulled up a stool at his favorite bar and announced, "My wife Suzie must love me more than any woman has ever loved any man!"

"What makes you say that?" the bartender inquired.

"Last week," Bill explained, "I had to take a couple of sick days from work. Suzie was so thrilled to have me around that every time the milkman and the postman came by, she'd run down the driveway, waving her arms and hollering, 'My husband's home! My husband's home!'"

A college teacher reminded her class of tomorrow's final exam.

"Now, class," she said, "I won't tolerate any excuses for you not being here tomorrow. I might consider a nuclear attack, a serious personal injury or illness, or a death in your immediate family. But that's it—no other excuses whatsoever!"

A smart-ass guy in the back of the room raised his hand and asked, "What would you say if tomorrow I said I was suffering from complete and utter sexual exhaustion?"

The entire class was reduced to laughter and snickering. When silence was restored, the teacher smiled knowingly at the student, shook her head and sweetly said,

"Well, I guess you'd have to write the exam with your other hand."

A tourist arrived in Australia, hired a car and set off for the Outback. On his way he saw a guy having sex with a sheep. Deeply horrified, he pulled up at the nearest bar and ordered a straight Scotch. Just as he was about to throw it back, he saw a guy with one leg masturbating furiously at the bar.

"For fuck's sake!" the tourist cried, "what the hell's going on here? I've been here one hour and I've seen a guy fucking a sheep, and now some guy's jerking himself off in the bar!"

"Well, mate," the bartender told him, "you can't expect a man with only one leg to catch a sheep."

A salesman in a strange city was feeling horny and wanted release. He inquired for the address of a good "house of ill repute." He was told to go to 225 West 42nd St. By mistake, he went to 255 West 42nd St., the office of a chiropodist. Being met by a beautiful woman in a white uniform surprised but intrigued him. She directed him to an examining room and told him to get ready and someone would be with him soon.

He loved the thought of the table and the reclining chair and was really getting aroused because of the strange and different approach this house offered. Finally, the doctor's assistant, a really gorgeous redhead, entered and found him sitting in the chair with his generous member in his hand.

"My goodness," she exclaimed, "I was expecting to see a foot."

"Well," he said, "if you're going to complain about an inch then I'll take my business elsewhere."

Sitting at home one night with his wife, a man is casually tossing peanuts into the air and catching them in his mouth. As they take in the latest episode of their favorite program, the man loses concentration for a split second, and a peanut goes into his ear. He tries to get it out, but succeeds only in forcing the thing in deeper.

After a few hours of fruitless rooting they decide to go to the hospital, but on their way out of the front door they meet their daughter coming in with her boyfriend.

The boyfriend takes control of the situation; he tells them he's studying medicine and that they're not to worry about a thing. He then sticks two fingers up the man's nose and asks him to blow, and, low and behold, the nut shoots from the ear and out across the room.

As the daughter and her boyfriend go through to the kitchen to get drinks, the man and his wife sit down to discuss their luck. "So," the wife says, "what do you think he'll become after he finishes school? A GP or a surgeon?"

"Well," says the man, rubbing his nose, "from the smell of his fingers, I think he's likely to be our son-in-law."

A man stops by to visit his poor friend. They talk for a while and then the friend asks, "My feet are cold. Would you be so kind as to go get me my slippers please?"

The guest obliges and goes upstairs. There he sees his friend's daughters, both very good-looking. Being the adventurous and quick-thinking kind, he says, "Hi, ladies! Your daddy sent me here to have sex with you!"

They stare at him and say, "That can't be!"

He replies, "OK, let's check!" He shouts to his friend down the stairs, "Both of them?"

"Yes, both of them!"

Three women walking down the street are stopped by a man doing a survey. He asks, "Ladies, would you mind telling me how you know if you've had a good night out?"

The first replies, "I come home, get into bed and if I lay there and tingle all over, I know that I had a good night."

The second one replies, "I come home, have a shower and a glass of wine, get into bed, and if I tingle all over, I know it was a good night."

The third one turns around and says, "If I get home, rip off my panties, throw them against the wall and they stick, then I know it was a good night!"

There are a few guys who always get together on Fridays after work for a drink. One Friday, Jeff showed up late, sat down at the bar, and kicked back his entire first beer in one gulp. Then he turned to Bob and said, "Times are getting tough, my friend. I mean, just today my wife told me that she's going to cut me back to only two times a week. I can't believe it."

At which point Bob put his hand on Jeff's shoulder and said reassuringly, "You think you've got it bad—she's cut some guys out all together."

A guy went out hunting. He had all the gear: the jacket, the boots and the double-barrelled shotgun. As he was climbing over a fence, he dropped the gun and it went off, right on his penis. Obviously, he had to see a doctor. When he woke up from surgery, he found that the doctor had done a marvellous job repairing it. As he got ready to go home, the doctor gave him a business card. "This is my brother's card. I'll make an appointment for you to see him."

The guy says, "Is your brother a doctor?"

"No," doc replies, "he plays the flute. He'll show you where to put your fingers so you don't piss in your eye."

Q. What do you call kids born in whorehouses?
A. Brothel sprouts.

A man wanted to determine if both his wife and mistress were faithful to him. So he decided to send them on the same cruise, then later question each one on the other's behavior. When his wife returned, he asked her about the people on the trip in general, then casually asked her about the specific behavior of the passenger he knew to be his mistress.

"She slept with nearly every man on the ship," his wife reported.

The disheartened man then met with his cheating mistress to ask her the same questions about his wife.

"She was a real lady," his mistress said.

"How so?" the encouraged man asked.

"She came on board with her husband and never left his side."

A well-endowed young advertising secretary wore very tight clothes that showed off her figure, especially when she walked. Her young, aggressive boss called her into his office one afternoon and closed the door. Pointing to her tightly covered derriere, he asked, "Is that for sale?"

"Of course not!" she snapped angrily, blushing furiously.

He replied quietly, "Then, I suggest you stop advertising it."

A young man was lying on his back on a massage table, wearing only a towel over his groin. A young, very attractive Swedish girl was massaging his shoulders, then his chest, and gradually working her way down his torso. The man was getting sexually excited as the masseuse approached the towel. The towel began to lift and the Swedish girl arched her eyebrows. "You want to jerk off?" she asked.

"You bet," came the excited reply.

"OK," she said. "I'll come back in ten minutes."

A woman goes to her doctor complaining that her husband is 300% impotent. The doctor says, "I'm not sure I understand what you mean."

She says, "Well, the first 100% you can imagine. In addition, he burned his tongue and broke his finger!"

A woman came up behind her husband while he was enjoying his morning coffee and slapped him on the back of the head. "I found a piece of paper in the pocket of your pants with the name 'Marylou' written on it," she said, furious. "You had better have a good explanation."

"Calm down, honey," the man replied. "Remember last week when I was at the dog track? That was the name of the dog I bet on."

The next morning, his wife snuck up on him and smacked him again.

"What was that for?" he complained.

"Your dog called last night."

A man is lying in bed in a hospital with an oxygen mask over his mouth. A young student nurse appears to sponge his face and hands.

"Nurse," he mumbles from behind the mask, "are my testicles black?"

Embarrassed, the young nurse replies, "I don't know, I'm only here to wash your face and hands."

He struggles again to ask, "Nurse, are my testicles black?"

Again the nurse replies, "I can't tell. I'm only here to wash your face and hands."

The head nurse was passing by and saw the man getting a little distraught so she marched over to inquire what was wrong.

"Sister," he mumbled, "are my testicles black?"

Being a nurse of longstanding experience, she was undaunted. She whipped back the bedclothes, pulled down his pajama pants, moved his penis out of the way, had a good look, pulled up the pajamas, replaced the bedclothes and announced, "Nothing is wrong with them!!!"

At this point the man pulled off his oxygen mask and asked again, "That's very nice, but are my test results back???"

Ask any man what a woman's ultimate fantasy is and they will tell you: To have two men at once. According to a recent sociological study this is true; however, most men do not realize that in this fantasy, one man is cooking, and the other is cleaning.

Q. What is the lightest thing in the world?
A. A penis—even a thought can raise it.

Between the ages of 16 and 18 she is like Africa, virgin and unexplored. Between the ages of 19 and 35 she is like Asia, hot and exotic.

Between the ages of 36 and 45 she is like America, fully explored, breathtakingly beautiful, and free with her resources. Between the ages of 46 and 56 she is like Europe, exhausted but still has points of interest.

After 56 she is like Australia—everybody knows it's down there but no one gives a damn.

A huge guy marries a tiny girl and, at the wedding, one of his friends says to him, "How the hell do the two of you have sex?"

The big guy says, "I just sit there, naked, on a chair. She sits on top and I bob her up and down."

His friend says, "You know, that doesn't sound too bad."

The big guy says, "Well, it's kind of like jerking off, only I've got somebody to talk to."

Mom walked into the bathroom one day and found young Mickey furiously scrubbing his dick with a toothbrush and toothpaste. "What the hell do you think you're doing, young man?!" she exclaimed.

"Don't try to stop me!" Mickey warned. "I'm going to do this three times a day, because there's no way I'm going to get a cavity that looks and smells as bad as my sister's."

One night two aliens landed their spaceship next to a gas station. There was a smart alien and a hooligan alien. They both went up to the gas pump and the hooligan alien looked at the pump and said, "Take me to your leader!"

Of course the gas pump said nothing. The smart alien said, "I don't think that is a good idea."

The hooligan alien looked at the pump again and demanded to be taken to the leader.

The smart alien said, "Really, that's not a good idea."

Losing his patience, the hooligan alien pulled his death ray and blew the gas station to pieces. Burnt and bruised, the hooligan alien looked at the smart alien and asked, "How did you know that wasn't a good idea?"

The smart alien replied, "Anybody who can throw their dick over their shoulder has got to be a bastard!!!"

Matt's dad picked him up from school to take him to a dental appointment. Knowing the parts for the school play were supposed to be announced that day, he asked his son if he got a part.

Matt enthusiastically announced that he had. "I play a man who's been married for twenty years."

"That's great, son. Keep up the good work and before you know it they'll be giving you a speaking part."

A poor guy went to the hospital for a circumcision but, because of some mix up during the operation, he ended up having a complete sex change. All the doctors and nurses had gathered around his bed as he was waking up so they could give him the bad news. Naturally, the poor bloke went to pieces and started crying when they explained what had happened to him.

"Shit!" he moaned. "This means I'll never be able to experience an erection ever again!"

"Of course you will," one of the doctors soothed. "It'll just have to be someone else's, that's all."

Having determined that the husband was infertile, a childless couple decided to try artificial insemination. When the woman showed up at the clinic, she was told to undress, get up on the table and place her feet in the stirrups. She was feeling very uncomfortable about the whole situation and when the doctor started dropping his pants, she freaked.

"Wait a second! What the hell is going on here?" she yelled.

"Don't you want to get pregnant?" asked the doctor.

"Well, yes, but…" stammered the woman.

"Well, lie back and spread 'em," replied the doctor. "Were out of the bottled stuff, so you'll just have to settle for what's on tap."

Q. What did the Indian say when the white man tied his penis in a knot?

A. "How come?"

A truck driver pulled over to the side of the road and picked up two homosexuals who were hitchhiking. They climbed into the cab and the truck driver pulled back onto the road. A few minutes later, the first gay guy said, "Excuse me, but I have to fart." He held his breath, and the truck driver heard a low Hssssssss.

A few miles down the road, the second gay guy announced, "Excuse me, but I have to fart."

The announcement was followed by another low Hssssssss.

"Jesus fucking Christ!" the driver exclaimed. "You queers can't even fart like men. Listen to this." A moment later he emitted a deafening, staccato machine-gun burst from his ass.

"Ohhh!" one gay exclaimed, turning to the other. "You know what we have here, Bruce? A real virgin!"

Two brothers enlisting in the army were having their medical exams. During the inspection, the doctor was surprised to discover that both of them possessed incredibly long, oversized penises.

"How do you account for this?" he asked the brothers.

"It's hereditary, sir," the older one replied.

"I see," said the doctor, writing in his file. "Your father's the reason for your elongated penises?"

"No sir," said the younger brother, "our mother."

"Your mother?" the doctor asked. "You idiot, women don't have penises!"

"I know, sir," replied the recruit, "but she only had one arm, and when it came to getting us out of the bath, she had to manage as best as she could."

A newly married sailor was informed by the Navy that he was going to be stationed a long way from home on a remote island in the Pacific for a year. A few weeks after he got there he began to miss his new wife, so he wrote her a letter. "My love," he wrote, "we are going to be apart for a very long time. Already I'm starting to miss you and there's really not much to do here in the evenings. Besides that, we're constantly surrounded by attractive young native girls. Do you think if I had a hobby of some kind I would not be tempted?"

So his wife sent him back a harmonica saying, "Why don't you learn to play this?"

Eventually his tour of duty came to an end and he rushed back to his wife. "Darling," he said, "I can't wait to get you into bed so that we make passionate love!"

She kissed him and said, "First, let's see you play that harmonica."

A funeral service is being held for a woman who has just passed away. At the end of the service the pallbearers are carrying the casket out when they accidentally bump into a wall, jarring the casket. They hear a faint moan. They open the casket and find that the woman is actually alive. She lives for ten more years, and then dies. A ceremony is again held at the same place, and at the end of the ceremony the pallbearers are again carrying out the casket. As they are walking, the husband cries out, "Watch out for the wall!"

A patient awoke after a serious operation only to find herself in a room with all the blinds drawn.

"Why are all the blinds closed?" she asked her doctor.

"Well," the surgeon responded, "they're fighting a huge fire across the street, and we didn't want you to wake up and think the operation had failed."

Young Bill was courting Mabel, who lived on an adjoining farm way out in the sticks. One evening, as they were sitting on Bill's porch watching the sun go down over the hills, Bill spied his prize bull fucking one of his cows. He sighed in contentment at this idyllic rural scene and figured the omens were right for him to seduce Mabel. He leaned in close and whispered in her ear, "Mabel, I'd sure like to be doing what that bull is doing."

"Well then, why don't you?" Mabel whispered back. "It is YOUR cow."

A young man excitedly tells his mother he's fallen in love and is going to get married. He says, "Just for fun, Ma, I'm going to bring over three women and you try and guess which one I'm going to marry."

The mother agrees. The next day, he brings three beautiful women into the house and sits them down on the couch and they chat for a while. He then says, "Okay, Ma. Guess which one I'm going to marry."

She immediately replies, "The redhead in the middle."

Stunned, the young man says, "That's amazing, Ma. You're right. How did you know?"

"I don't like her," she says.

Q. Which sexual position produces the ugliest children?
A. Ask your Mom.

A young doctor had moved into town and was setting up a new practice. He had a new sign painted and hung it in front of his office, proclaiming his specialties: "Homosexuals & Hemorrhoids." The town fathers were upset with the sign and asked him please to change it. The doctor was eager to please, so he put up a new sign: "Queers & Rears." The town fathers were really fuming about that one, so they demanded that the doctor come up with a decent sign that would not offend the townspeople. So the doctor came up with an acceptable sign: "Odds & Ends."

A very elderly couple went to a see a sex therapist. The doctor asked, "What can I do for you?"

The man said, "Will you watch us have sexual intercourse?"

The doctor looked puzzled, but agreed. When the couple finished, the doctor said, "There's nothing wrong with the way you have intercourse," and charged them $50.

This happened several weeks in a row. The couple would make an appointment, have intercourse with no problems, pay the doctor, and then leave.

Finally, the doctor asked, "Just exactly what are you trying to find out?"

The old man said, "We're not trying to find out anything. She's married so we can't go to her house. I'm married so we can't go to my house, either. The Holiday Inn charges $90. The Hilton charges $108. We do it here for $50, and I get $43 back from my medical insurance."

There was a guy riding through the desert on his camel. He had been traveling so long that he felt the need to have sex. Obviously, there were no women in the desert so the man turned to his camel.

He tried to position himself to have sex with his camel but the camel ran away. The man ran to catch up to the camel and got back on and started to ride again. Soon he was feeling the urge to have sex again so once again he turned to his camel. The camel refused by running away. So he caught up to it again and got on it again.

Finally, after riding the camel through the whole desert the man came to a road. There was a broken-down car with three big-chested, beautiful blondes sitting in it.

He went up to them and asked the women if they needed any help.

The hottest girl said, "If you fix our car we will do anything you want."

The man luckily knew a thing or two about cars and fixed it in a flash.

When he finished the three girls asked, "How could we ever repay you, mister?"

After thinking for a short while he replied, "Could you hold my camel?"

A teacher asks her class, "If there are five birds sitting on a fence and you shoot one of them, how many will be left?"

She calls on Little Johnny to answer. He replies, "There are none left—they all fly away with the first gun shot."

The teacher replies, "The correct answer is four, but I like your thinking."

Then Little Johnny says, "I have a question for YOU. There are three women sitting on a bench having ice cream. One is delicately licking the sides of the triple scoop of ice cream. The second is gobbling down the top and sucking the cone. The third is biting off the top of the ice cream. Which one is married?"

The teacher, blushing a great deal, replies, "Well, I suppose the one that's gobbled down the top and sucked the cone."

To which Little Johnny replies, "The correct answer is the one with the wedding ring on, but I like your thinking."

A man was walking in the street when he heard a voice. "Stop! Stand still! If you take one more step, a brick will fall down on your head and kill you."

The man stopped and a big brick fell right in front of him. The man was astonished. He went on, and after a while he was going to cross the road. Once again the voice shouted:

"Stop! Stand still! If you take one more step a car will run over you and you will die."

The man did as he was instructed just as a car came careening around the corner, barely missing him.

"Where are you?" the man asked. "Who are you?"

"I am your guardian angel," the voice answered.

"Oh yeah?" the man asked. "And where the hell were you when I got married?"

A little old lady entered the sex shop and asked in a quivering voice, "Y-young man, d-do y-you sell dildos h-here?"

The salesman, somewhat taken aback by the little old lady in his shop, answered, "Uh, yes, ma'am. We do."

The little old lady, holding her quivering hands about 10 inches apart, asked, "D-do y-you ha-have any ab-bb-bout th-this l-long?"

"Well, yes, ma'am, we do. We have several that size."

Forming a 5-inch circle with her fingers, she then asked, "A-are an-nny of th-them about thi-is b-big ar-round-d?"

"Well, yes, a few of them are about that big."

"D-do aa-ny of th-them ha-ave a vv-ii-bra-a-ator?"

"Yes, ma'am, one of them does."

"W-Wel-ll, h-how d-do y-you t-turn it off?"

321

A guy goes to the post office to interview for a job.

The interviewer asks him, "Are you a veteran?"

The guy says, "Why yes, in fact, I served two tours in Vietnam."

"Good," says the interviewer. "That counts in your favor. Do you have any service-related disabilities?"

The guy says, "In fact, I am 100% disabled. During a battle an explosion removed my private parts so they declared me disabled. It doesn't affect my ability to work though."

"Sorry to hear about the damage, but I have some good news for you. I can hire you right now! Our working hours are 8 to 4. Come on in about 10, and we'll get you started."

The guy says, "If working hours are from 8 to 4, why do you want me to come at 10?"

"Well, here at the post office, we don't do anything but sit around and scratch our balls for the first two hours. Don't need you here for that!"

Q. What's red and blue with a long string?

A. A smurfette with her period.

Ten-year-old Johnny rushes home from school. He invades the fridge and is scooping out some cherry vanilla ice cream when his mother enters the kitchen. She says, "Put that away, Johnny. You can't have ice cream now. It's too close to supper time. Go outside and play."

Johnny whimpers and says, "There's no one to play with."

Trying to placate him, she says, "OK. I'll play with you. What do you want to play?"

He says, "I want to play Mommy and Daddy."

Trying not to register surprise, and to further appease him, she says, "Fine, I'll play. What do I do?"

Johnny says, "You go up to the bedroom and lie down." Figuring that she can easily control the situation, Mom goes upstairs. Johnny, feeling a bit cocky, swaggers down the hall and opens the utility closet. He dons his father's old fishing hat. As he starts up the stairs, he notices a cigarette butt in the ashtray on the table. He picks it up and slips it in the corner of his mouth. At the top of the stairs he moves to the bedroom doorway.

His mother raises her head and says, "What do I do now?"

In a gruff manner, Johnny says, "Get your ass downstairs and get that kid some ice cream!"

According to archaeologists, for millions of years Neanderthal man was not fully erect. That's pretty easy to understand considering how ugly Neanderthal women were.

Grandma and Grandpa were watching a healing service on television. The evangelist called to all who wanted to be healed to go to their television set, place one hand on the TV and the other hand on the body part where they wanted to be healed. Grandma got up and slowly hobbled to the television set, placed her right hand on the set and her left hand on her arthritic shoulder that was causing her to have great pain. Then Grandpa got up, went to the TV, placed his right hand on the set and his left hand on his crotch.

Grandma scowled at him and said, "I guess you just don't get it. The purpose of doing this is to heal the sick, not raise the dead."

After just a few years of marriage filled with constant arguments, a young man and his wife decided the only way to save their marriage was to try counseling. They had been at each other's throats for some time and felt that this was their last chance. When they arrived at the counselor's office, the counselor jumped right in and opened the floor for discussion.

"What seems to be the problem?"

Immediately, the husband held his long face down without anything to say. On the other hand, the wife began talking 100 miles an hour describing all the wrongs within their marriage. After five, then 10, then 15 minutes of listening to the wife, the counselor went over to her, picked her up by her shoulders, kissed her passionately for several minutes, and sat her back down.

The wife sat there—speechless. He looked over at the husband who was staring in disbelief at what had happened. The counselor spoke to the husband,

"Your wife NEEDS that at least twice a week!"

The husband scratched his head and replied, "I can have her here on Tuesdays and Thursdays."

Q. Did you hear about the guy who finally figured out women?

A. He died laughing before he could tell anybody.

Batman arranges a party and invites all the fashionable superheroes. He is particularly good friends with Superman, who, as the party reaches its peak, hasn't turned up. The night goes on and Superman turns up as the last of the guests are leaving.

"So what happened, Superman?" asks Batman, upset that his closest acquaintance has missed the party.

"I was on my way," starts Superman in a fluster, "when I saw Wonderwoman lying naked in her backyard with her legs wide apart. I've always liked her and guessed that she was expecting me. I dived down as fast as I could from 30,000 feet to give her a good fuck there and then."

"I bet she was surprised," says Batman.

"Not half as surprised as the Invisible Man," replies Superman.

An elderly man goes into a brothel and tells the madam he would like a young girl for the night. Surprised, she looks at the ancient man and asks how old he is. "I'm 90 years old," he says.

"90!" replies the woman. "Don't you realize you've had it?"

"Oh, sorry," says the old man, "how much do I owe you?"

After 40 years as a gynecologist, John decided he had enough money to retire and take up his real love—car mechanics. He left his practice, enrolled in a car mechanics class and studied hard. The day of the final exam came and John worried if he would be able to complete the test with the same proficiency as his younger classmates. Most of the students completed their exam in two hours. John, on the other hand, took the entire four hours allotted. The following day, John was delighted and surprised to see a score of 150% for his exam. John spoke to his teacher after class.

"I never dreamed I could do this well on the exam. How did I earn a score of 150%?"

The teacher replied, "I gave you 50% for perfectly disassembling the car engine. I awarded another 50% for perfectly reassembling the engine. I gave you an additional 50% for having done all of it through the exhaust pipe."

A young playboy took a blind date to an amusement park. They went for a ride on the Ferris wheel. When the ride was over, she seemed bored.

"What would you like to do next?" he asked.

"I want to be weighed," she said.

So the young man took her over to the weight guesser.

"112," said the man at the scale, and he was absolutely right. Next they rode the roller coaster. After that, he bought her some popcorn and cotton candy, then asked what else she would like to do.

"I want to be weighed," she said.

I really latched onto an odd one tonight, thought the young man, and using the excuse that he had developed a headache, he took the girl home. The girl's mother was surprised to see her home so early, and asked,

"What's wrong, dear, didn't you have a nice time tonight?"
"Wousy," said the girl.

The ambitious coach of a girls' track team gives the squad steroids. The team's performance soars. They win all the events they are entered for and they are favored to easily win the nationals.

Penelope, a 16-year-old hurdler, visits her coach and says, "Coach, I have a problem. Hair is starting to grow on my chest."

"What?" the coach says in a panic. "How far down does it go?"

She replies, "Down to my testicles. That's something else I want to talk to you about."

An artist tried to concentrate on his work, but the attraction he felt for his model finally became irresistible. He threw down his palette, took her in his arms and kissed her. She pushed him away.

"Maybe your other models let you kiss them," she said, "but I'm not that kind!"

"Actually, I've never tried to kiss a model before," he protested.

"Really?" she said, softening. "Well, how many models have there been?"

"Four so far," he replied, thinking back. "A jug, two apples and a vase."

Q. What did Cinderella do when she got to the ball?
A. Gagged.

A man returned home from the night shift and went straight up to the bedroom. He found his wife with the sheet pulled over her head, fast asleep. Not to be denied his marital rights, the horny husband crawled under the sheet and proceeded to make love to her. Afterward, he hurried downstairs for something to eat and was startled to find breakfast on the table and his wife pouring coffee.

"How'd you get down here so fast?" he asked. "We were just making love!"

"Oh my God," his wife gasped. "That's my mother up there! She came over and complained of having a headache. I told her to lie down for awhile." Rushing upstairs, the wife ran to the bedroom. "Mother, I can't believe this happened. Why didn't you say something?"

The mother-in-law huffed, "I haven't spoken to that bastard for 15 years and I wasn't about to start now!"

A limousine was taking the beautiful, raven-haired model to the airport. Halfway there, the front tire went flat. The model said, "Driver, I don't have time to wait for road service. Can you change it yourself?"

The driver said, "Sure." He got out of the car and proceeded to change the tire, but couldn't get the wheel cover off.

The model saw him struggling and asked, "Do you want a screwdriver?"

He said "Sure! But first I have to change this tire."

Q. Why is a woman's pussy like a warm toilet seat?
A. They both feel good, but you wonder who was there before you.

One day, Elephant and Camel get talking. During the conversation Elephant says, "Camel, if you don't mind me asking, how does it feel to spend your life walking around with a huge set of tits on your back?"

Camel replies, "No, I don't mind at all, but it is a silly question coming from someone with a huge dick on his face!"

A man and a woman are at a bar having a few beers. They start talking and soon realize they're both doctors. After an hour the man says, "Hey, how about if we sleep together tonight? No strings attached."

The woman doctor agrees to it. They go back to her place and he goes into the bedroom. She goes into the bathroom and starts scrubbing up like she's about to go into the operating room. She scrubs for a good ten minutes. At last, she goes into the bedroom and they have sex.

Afterward, the man says, "You're a surgeon, aren't you?"

"Yes," says the woman, "how did you know?"

"I could tell by the way you scrubbed up before we started," he says.

"That makes sense," says the woman. "You're an anesthetist, aren't you?"

"Yeah, how did you know?" asks the man.

The woman replies, "Because I didn't feel a thing."

"Mom, may I take the dog for a walk around the block?" a little girl asked.

"No, I don't think so. Fifi is in heat," replied the mother.

"What does that mean?" asked the child.

Embarrassed and not wanting to get into a biological discussion with her young daughter, the Mother said, "Oh, just go ask your father. I think he is in the garage."

The little girl goes to the garage and says, "Dad, may I take Fifi for a walk around the block? I asked Mom, but she said that Fifi was in heat, and that I had to come talk to you."

Not wanting to have the biological discussion either, the father said, "Bring Fifi over here." He took a rag, soaked it with gasoline, and scrubbed the dog's rear end with it. "Okay, now you can go for a walk but keep Fifi on the leash and you can only go around the block once."

The little girl left, and returned a few minutes later with no dog.

"Where is Fifi?" her father asked.

"She should be here in a minute," advised the daughter. "She ran out of gas about halfway down the block and another dog is pushing her home."

A couple is lying in bed. The man says, "I am going to make you the happiest woman in the world."

The woman says, "I'll miss you."

A young, attractive woman thought she might have some fun with a stiff-looking military man at a cocktail party, so she walked over and asked him, "Major, when was the last time you had sex?"

"1956," was his reply.

"No wonder you look so uptight!" she exclaimed. "Major, you need to get out more!"

"I'm not sure I understand you," he answered, glancing at his watch. "It's only 20:14 now."

A gay man, finally deciding he could no longer hide his sexuality from his parents, went over to their house and found his mother in the kitchen cooking dinner. He sat down at the kitchen table, let out a big sigh, and said, "Mom, I have something to tell you. I'm gay."

His mother made no reply nor gave any response, and the guy was about to repeat it to make sure she'd heard him when she turned away from the pot she was stirring and said calmly, "You're gay. Doesn't that mean you put other men's penises in your mouth?"

The guy said nervously, "Uh, yeah, Mom, that's right."

His mother went back to stirring the pot, then suddenly whirled around, whacked him over the head with her spoon and said,

"Don't you EVER complain about my cooking again!!!"

Once there was a sperm named Bob. When all the other sperm were just swimming around, Bob was doing sprints and lifting weights. One day, the other sperm gathered around and asked him, "Why don't you just swim around like us?"

Bob replied with a smirk, "Well, when the time comes, I'm going to be the first one there."

The others told him it was just destiny, but he said it wasn't. It was, according to Bob, survival of the fittest.

So the day finally came when they were called upon. They were swimming along with Bob pulling way ahead of the rest. Suddenly he stopped, turned around and headed back.

"What's up, Bob?" the others asked.

To which Bob replied, "False alarm. Back up, boys, it's a BLOW JOB!"

The pretty student nervously asked the doctor to perform an unusual operation: the removal of a large chunk of green wax from her navel.

Looking up from the ticklish task, the physician asked, "How did this happen?"

"Let me put it this way, Doc," the girl began. "My boyfriend likes to eat by candlelight."

One day Little Susie got her first period ever. Having failed to understand what was going on, and being really frightened, she decided to share her trouble with little Johnny. Having found Johnny, she told and showed him what her problem was.

Johnny's face grew serious and he said, "You know, I'm not a doctor but it looks like someone just ripped your balls off!"

A woman with really hairy underarms boards a crowded bus. Unable to find a seat, she settles for hanging onto one of the poles. A drunk man next to her stares at her for three minutes, then tells her, "I love a woman who does aerobics."

The woman replies angrily, "I don't DO aerobics!"

The drunk man then looks at the woman and says, "Then how did you get your leg up so high?"

A guy meets this girl in a bar and asks, "May I buy you a drink?"

Looking unimpressed at the man she replies, "Okay, but it won't do you any good."

A little later, he asks, "May I buy you another drink?"

"Okay, but it still won't do you any good."

He invites her up to his apartment and she replies, "Okay, but it won't do you any good."

They get to his apartment and he says, "You are the most beautiful thing I have ever seen. I want you for my wife."

She says, "Oh, that's different. Send her in."

A group of first-year medical students is gathered around an operating table for their first anatomy lesson with a dead body.

"As a doctor, you'll need to develop two key skills," the professor begins. "The first is stoicism. You can't be disgusted by anything involving the human body."

The professor then rolls the body over, sticks his finger into the corpse's ass, withdraws it and sticks his finger in his mouth.

"Now do the same," he instructs.

The horrified students hesitate, but eventually take turns dipping a finger into the cadaver's anus and then sucking on it.

When everyone has finished, the professor continues, "The second skill is observation. I stuck in my middle finger and then I sucked on my index finger. Pay attention."

A woman sought the advice of a sex therapist, confiding that she found it increasingly difficult to find a man who could satisfy her, and that it was very wearisome getting in and out of short-term relationships. "Isn't there some way to judge the size of a man's equipment from the outside?" she asked earnestly.

"The only foolproof way is by the size of his feet," counseled the therapist.

So the woman went into town and proceeded to cruise the streets until she came across a young man standing in an unemployment line with the biggest feet she had ever laid her eyes on. She took him out to dinner, wined and dined him, and then took him back to her apartment for an evening of wild sex.

When the man woke up the next morning, the woman had already gone but by the bedside table was $40 and a note that read, "With my compliments, take this money and go out and buy a pair of shoes that fit you."

Q. What is the first sign of AIDS?
A. A pounding sensation in the ass.

A bride who got a little too drunk at her wedding reception was still determined to say a few words of thanks to the guests for all their presents. She stumbled through a short speech and then slowly turned to point to the presents on display, which included a coffee percolator. "And finally," she said, "I do thank my new parents-in-law for their present—such a beautiful perky copulator."

The undertaker calls Mrs. Banley and says "Excuse me, Mrs. Banley, but I can't seem to close the lid to your husband's coffin because he has a huge erection."

To which she replies, "Why don't you cut it off and stick it up his ass? That's the only hole in town it hasn't been in."

I've never gone to bed with an ugly man, but I've woken up with a few.

A truck driver goes into a brothel and hands the Madam five hundred dollars. He says, "I want your ugliest woman and a cheese sandwich."

The Madam says, "For that kind of money, you could have one of my finest girls and steak and fries."

The driver says, "I'm not horny, I'm homesick!"

A guy walks into a bar, orders a scotch and soda and puts a frog on the bar. The bartender gives him the drink and asks what the frog is for.

The guy snaps his fingers and the frog jumps down and gives the man a blow job.

The bartender is amazed, and asks to see that again.

So the guy snaps his fingers a second time, the frog jumps down, gives the man a blow job and then hops back on the bar. The bartender is astounded and offers the guy $3000 for the frog.

The man of course accepts, and gives the frog to the bartender.

The bartender goes home after his shift. He sits in his kitchen, calls his wife over and says he has something to show her.

His wife walks in and the bartender takes the frog out of his pocket, puts it on the table and snaps his fingers, and the frog jumps down, gives the bartender a blow job and hops back on the kitchen table.

The wife asks, "Why the hell are you showing me this?"

The bartender says, "Because you're going to teach him how to cook and then you're going to get the fuck out of here."

Mr. Geraldo says to his doctor, "Doc, I had the worst dream of my life last night. I dreamed I was with twelve of the most beautiful chorus girls in the world. Blondes, brunettes, redheads, and they were all dancing in a row."

The psychiatrist says, "Now hold on, Mr. Geraldo. That doesn't sound so terrible."

Mr. Geraldo says, "Oh, yeah? I was the third girl from the end."

Q. Did you know they just discovered a new use for sheep in New Zealand?

A. Wool!

Jack is on his death bed, and he says to his wife, "Can you give me one last wish?"

She says, "Anything you want."

He says, "After I die, will you marry Larry?"

She says, "But I thought you hated Larry."

With his last breath, he says, "I do."

A flat-chested young lady went to Dr. Smith for advice about breast enlargements. He told her, "Every day when you get out of the shower, rub the top of your nipples and say, 'Scooby dooby dooby, I want bigger boobies.'"

She did this every day faithfully. After several months, it worked! She grew great boobs!

One morning she was running late, and in her rush to leave for work, she realized she had forgotten her morning ritual. At this point she loved her boobs and didn't want to lose them, so she got up in the middle of the bus and said, "Scooby dooby dooby, I want bigger boobies."

A guy sitting nearby asked her, "Do you go to Dr. Smith by any chance?"

"Why yes, I do. How did you know?"

The man stood up and cupped his balls and said, "Hickory dickory dock..."

Q. What do you call a nun with a sex change operation?

A. A tran-sister.

Bob says to Charlie, "You know, I think I'm about ready for a vacation, only this year I'm going to do it a little differently. The last few years I took your advice as to where to go. Two years ago you said to go to the Canaries. I went to the Canaries and Mary got pregnant. Then last year you told me to go to the Bahamas. I went to the Bahamas and Mary got pregnant again."

Charlie says, "So what are you going to do differently this year?"

Bob says, "This year I'm taking Mary with me."

A guy's eating in a restaurant and spots a gorgeous woman sitting all alone. He calls over his waiter and says, "Send that woman a bottle of your most expensive champagne, on me."

The waiter quickly brings the champagne over to the woman and says, "Ma'am, this is from the gentleman over there."

She says to the waiter, "Please tell him that for me to accept this champagne, he had better have a Mercedes in his garage, a million dollars in the bank, and eight inches in his pants."

The waiter delivers the message, and the guy says, "Please go back and tell her I have two Mercedes in my garage, three million dollars in the bank, but I haven't even met her, so why the fuck would I cut off four inches?"

Q. If you are having sex with two women and one more walks in, what do you have?

A. Divorce proceedings, most likely.

Two gay gentlemen were walking through a zoo. They came across the gorillas, and after a while, they noticed that the huge male gorilla had a massive erection. This fascinated the gay men so much they couldn't take their eyes off of it. One of the men just couldn't bear it any longer and he reached into the cage to touch it. The gorilla grabbed him, dragged him into the cage and screwed him for six hours non-stop.

When he was done, the gorilla threw the gay man back out of the cage. An ambulance was called and the man was taken away to the hospital. The next day his friend visited him in the hospital and asked, "Are you hurt?"

"AM I HURT?" he shouted. "Wouldn't you be? That big ape hasn't called, he hasn't written..."

There are two gay men who have anal sex every night. One night before sex one of the guys has to go to the bathroom. So the other guy says, "OK, but don't jerk off in there. Save it for later."

The first guy agrees. He's in the bathroom for a while, so the other gay guy decides to check on him. Once he opens the bathroom door, he sees lots of semen everywhere.

He gets angry and yells, "I thought I told you not to jerk off and to save it for later!"

The first gay guy replies, "I didn't jerk off. I just farted."

One night, an 87-year-old woman came home from Bingo to find her husband in bed with another woman. She became violent and ended up pushing him off the balcony of their 20th-floor apartment, killing him instantly. Brought before the court on the charge of murder, she was asked if she had anything to say in her defense. "Your Honor," she began coolly, "I figured that at 92 if he could screw, he could fly."

Charlie marries a virgin. On their wedding night, he's on fire, so he gets naked, jumps into bed, and immediately begins groping her.

"Charles, I expect you to be as mannerly in bed as you are at the dinner table," she says.

So Charlie folds his hands on his lap and says, "Is this better?"

"Much better!" she replies with a smile.

"Okay, then," he says, "now will you please pass the pussy?"

❖

Q. What do a blonde and a lottery ticket have in common?

A. All you have to do is scratch the box to win.

❖

A farmer was driving along the road with a load of fertilizer. A little boy, playing in front of his house, saw him and called, "What've you got in your truck?"

"Fertilizer," the farmer replied.

"What are you going to do with it?" asked the little boy.

"Put it on strawberries," answered the farmer.

"You ought to live here," the little boy advised him. "We put sugar and cream on ours."

❖

Q. What should you do if your girlfriend starts smoking?

A. Slow down and use a lubricant.

❖

"Honey," said a husband to his wife, "I invited a friend home for supper."

"What? Are you crazy? The house is a mess, I haven't been shopping, all the dishes are dirty and I don't feel like cooking a fancy meal!"

"I know all that."

"Then why did you invite a friend for supper?"

"Because the poor fool's thinking about getting married."

❖

A man goes to the doctor complaining of elbow pain. The doctor tells him he needs a urine sample to test. The man complies, and the doctor takes the cup to a very strange machine and pours it in. After a few seconds the machine prints out a sheet of paper. The doctor tells the man, "Well, it looks like you have tennis elbow."

The man argues, saying that there is no way. The doctor informs him that his new machine is 99% accurate. So the man, determined to fool the machine, goes home and has his daughter pee in a cup. Then he puts oil from his car in it and jacks off in it. He takes it to the doctor and tells him he's not feeling well and gives him the cup. The doctor puts it in the machine, and a few seconds later the paper prints out.

"Well, what does it say?" asks the man.

The doctor just looks at him and replies, "Well, your daughter is pregnant, your car needs an oil change, and if you don't stop jerking off you'll never get rid of that tennis elbow."

Bruce is driving over the Sydney Harbor Bridge one day when he sees his girlfriend, Sheila, about to throw herself off. Bruce slams on the brakes and yells, "Sheila, what the hell do you think you're doing?"

Sheila turns around with a tear in her eye and says, "G'day, Bruce. You got me pregnant and so now I'm going to kill myself."

Bruce gets a lump in his throat when he hears this. He says, "The truth is, Sheila, not only are you a great lay, but you're a real sport too," and drives off.

A little boy went up to his father and asked, "Dad, where did all of my intelligence come from?"

The father replied, "Well, son, you must have got it from your mother, 'cause I still have mine."

Paul was ambling through a crowded street fair when he decided to stop and sit at a palm reader's table. Said the mysterious old woman, "For $15, I can read your love line and tell your romantic future."

Paul readily agreed and the reader took one look at his open palm and said, "I can see that you have no girlfriend."

"That's true," said Paul.

"Oh my goodness, you are extremely lonely, aren't you?"

"Yes," Paul shamefully admitted. "That's amazing. Can you tell all of this from my love line?"

"Love line? No, from the calluses and blisters."

Two men were discussing popular family trends in sex, marriage and values. Stuart said, "I didn't sleep with my wife before we got married, did you?"

Steve replied, "I'm not sure, what was her maiden name?"

An old man goes to the wizard to ask him if he can remove a curse he has been living with for the last 40 years. The wizard says, "Maybe, but you will have to tell me the exact words that were used to put the curse on you."

The old man says without hesitation, "I now pronounce you man and wife."

Q. Which came first, the chicken or the egg?

A. Neither. The rooster came first.

A man goes to a shrink and says, "Doctor, my wife is unfaithful to me. Every evening she goes to Larry's bar and picks up men. In fact, she sleeps with anybody who asks her! I'm going crazy. What do you think I should do?"

"Relax," says the doctor, "take a deep breath and calm down. Now, tell me, exactly where is Larry's bar?"

Two men were sitting in the doctor's office and one asked the other, "What are you here for?"

The man replied, "I have a red ring around my pecker. What are you here for?"

The other man said, "I have a green ring around my pecker."

The doctor called the man with the red ring into his office first and examined him. As he was walking out he told the other guy it was no problem. The doctor called the man in with the green ring around his pecker and examined him. The doctor said, "Your pecker is going to fall off and you are going to die."

The mans said, "What?? You told the man with the red ring he was OK, but I'm going to die?"

The doctor said, "Yes, but there's a lot of difference between lipstick and gangrene!"

Three Italian nuns die and go to heaven. At the Pearly Gates, they are met by St. Peter. He says, "Sisters, you all led such wonderful lives that I'm granting you six months to go back to earth and be anyone you want to be."

The first nun says, "I want to be Sophia Loren." Poof! she's gone.

The second says, "I want to be Madonna." Poof! she's gone.

The third says, "I want to be Sara Pipalini."

St. Peter looks perplexed. "Who?" he asks.

"Sara Pipalini," replies the nun.

St. Peter shakes his head and says, "I'm sorry, but that name just doesn't ring a bell."

The nun then takes a newspaper out of her habit and hands it to St. Peter. He reads the paper and starts laughing. He hands it back to her and says, "No, Sister, the paper says it was the 'Sahara Pipeline' that was laid by 1,400 men in 6 months."

An Englishman, Irishman and a Scotsman were sitting in a bar drinking and discussing how stupid their wives were.

The Englishman says, "I tell you, my wife is so stupid. Last week she went to the supermarket and bought $100 worth of meat because it was on sale, and we don't even have a fridge to keep it in."

The Scotsman agrees that she sounds pretty thick, but says his wife is thicker. "Just last week she went out and spent $12,000 on a new car," he laments, "and she doesn't even know how to drive!"

The Irishman nods sagely and agrees that these two women sound stupid. However, he still thinks his wife is dumber. "Ah, it kills me every time I think of it," he chuckles. "My wife left to go on a trip to Greece. I watched her packing her bag, and she must have put about 100 condoms in there, and she doesn't even have a prick!"

There were these three farmers who wanted to win the state fair contest for having the largest hog. They decided that they should stick a cork in the pig's ass and feed him for a month before the fair. The only problem was that none of them wanted to be the one to stick the cork in. So they bought a monkey and trained him to stick corks in bottles.

After a week or two of this, they stuck the monkey in the pen with the pig and a cork, and after a minute, the monkey did what he was supposed to do. The farmers fed the pig for a month and, sure enough, they won first prize.

Once they got home, they realized they still had to take the cork out. So they trained this same monkey to take corks out of bottles. They stuck the monkey in the pen with the pig, and the farmers woke up three days later in the hospital with a reporter sitting next to them.

The reporter asked the first farmer, "What is the last thing you remember?"

"Shit flying everywhere," the farmer replied.

The reporter asked the second farmer the same question and got the same response. When she got to the third farmer and asked him what he could remember, he started crying. The reporter asked, "What's the matter?"

The farmer replied, "The last thing I remember is the look on the poor monkey's face as he tried to stick the cork back in."

One night after watching *Who Wants To Be A Millionaire?* a man and his wife went to bed and the man was getting very frisky. He asked his wife if she was in the mood. His wife answered, "Not tonight, dear, I have a headache."

The man replied, "Is that your final answer?"

She said, "Yes."

"OK, then I'd like to phone a friend."

There was a geriatric woman who thought she needed some toughening to cope with today's world and decided to join a gang. She rocked up to the Hell's Angels biker club and tapped on the door. "Excuse me, sirs, I'd like to join your club, if you please," she croaked in her feeble voice.

A grunt came from inside, "Ha! You got no chance, woman. We only take the toughest into our club. You can only join if you drink!"

"Oh boy, do I drink! I slam a few down every night after playing pool with the boys," she croaked back.

"Oh, umm, well... you can only join if you smoke," he lied, trying to brush her off.

"Does marijuana count? Because I don't mind a few joints after playing pool with the boys."

"Umm, I suppose it does count," the biker said, and thinking quickly on his feet, said, "Look, we're a gang only for the roughest, toughest men in town. Now, have you ever been picked up by the fuzz?"

"No," she replied, "but I've been swung around by the tits a few times."

A friend asked me the other day why I never got married. I replied, "Well, I guess I just never met the right woman. I guess I've been looking for the perfect girl."

"Oh, come on now," said my friend. "Surely you have met at least one girl that you wanted to marry."

"Yes, there was one girl—once. I guess she was the one perfect girl, the only perfect girl I really ever met. She was just the right everything. I really mean that she was the perfect girl for me."

"Well, why didn't you marry her?" asked my friend.

I shrugged my shoulders and replied, "She was looking for the perfect man."

A woman is picked up by a famous sportsman in a bar. They like each other and she goes back with him to his hotel room. He removes his shirt, revealing all his tattoos, and she sees that on his arm is one that reads, "Reebok." She thinks that's a bit odd and asks him about it.

He says, "When I play live on TV, the cameras pick up the tattoo and Reebok pays me for advertisement." A bit later, as he takes his pants off, she sees "Puma" tattooed on his leg. He gives the same explanation for the unusual tattoo. Finally, the underwear comes off and she sees the word "AIDS" tattooed on his penis.

She jumps back with shock. "I'm not going to do it with a guy who has AIDS!"

He says, "It's cool, baby, in a minute it's going to say 'ADIDAS.'"

Q. What do electric trains and women's breasts have in common?

A. They were originally intended for children but it's the men who play with them the most.

A cowboy gets captured by the Indians. They say they are going to put him to death, but before they do that, they will grant him three wishes. So, the cowboy thinks a moment and says,

"For my first wish, I want to talk to my horse."

So the Indians bring his horse over, and the cowboy whispers into the horse's ear. The horse goes trotting off, and comes back with a beautiful brunette on his back. The cowboy, upset, says to the Indians,

"For my second wish, I want to talk to my horse again."

So, although perplexed, the Indians bring over his horse, and, again, the cowboy whispers into the horse's ear. Again, the horse goes trotting off. The horse comes back about an hour later with a beautiful redhead on his back. At this, the cowboy is really mad. So the Indians ask what his final wish will be.

The cowboy again says, "Let me talk to my horse."

He again whispers into the horse's ear, and off trots the horse. He comes back an hour later with a BEAUTIFUL blonde on his back.

The cowboy—now furious—turns to the horse and shouts, "YOU STUPID ANIMAL... I SAID POSSE!"

Saturday morning I got up early, put on my long johns, dressed quietly, made my lunch, grabbed the dog, slipped quietly into the garage to hook the boat up to the truck and proceeded to back out into a torrential downpour.

There was snow mixed with the rain and the wind was blowing 50 mph. I pulled back into the garage, turned on the radio and discovered that the weather would be bad throughout the day.

I went back into the house, quietly undressed and slipped back into bed. There I cuddled up to my wife's back, now with a different anticipation, and whispered, "The weather out there is terrible."

She sleepily replied, "Can you believe my stupid husband is out fishing in that shit?"

Q. What's the difference between a gynecologist and a genealogist?

A. A genealogist looks up the family tree and a gynecologist looks up the family bush.

A couple had just driven in to the supermarket parking lot when their car broke down.

The man told his wife to carry on with the shopping while he fixed the car. The wife returned later to see a small group of people near the car. On closer inspection, she saw a pair of male legs protruding from under the chassis. Although the man was in shorts, his lack of underpants turned private parts into glaringly public ones.

Unable to stand the embarrassment, she dutifully stepped forward, quickly put her hand UP his shorts and tucked everything back into place. On regaining her feet, she looked across the hood and found herself staring at her husband who was idly standing by. The mechanic, however, had to have three stitches in his forehead and the smile wiped off his face!!

A guy walks into a bar with his midget wife and takes a stool, with his wife standing next to him. The bartender is busy at the other end and doesn't see them when they walk in. When he's done serving the customers there, he walks down the bar and asks the new customer what he would like. He asks for two glasses of beer, which the barman brings. After leaving him, the bartender goes about serving other patrons, when he notices the man has finished his beers. He asks if he would like a refill, and the man says, "Yes. I'll have a couple more."

The barman gets two more beers and sets them in front of the man. Never having seen anyone with the guy, his curiosity is piqued, and he asks him, "Why do you order two drinks at a time?"

The man replies, "Oh, one is for me, and the other for my wife."

Astounded, having not seen the midget wife, the bartender says, "Your wife? Where is she?"

"She's standing here next to me."

The bartender, standing on his toes, leaning forward and looking over the edge of the bar, utters, "Well, I'll be damned, she's no bigger than your fist!"

The man replies, "No, but she's a lot better!"

A man goes to a restaurant and orders a chicken dish. By the time the food is ready and he is about to eat, the waiter comes back and says, "Sir, I'm afraid there has been a mistake. You see, that police officer who is sitting at the next table is a regular customer of ours and he usually orders the chicken dish. The problem is, this is the last chicken in the house. I'm afraid I'll have to take this dish to him and arrange for another dish for you!"

The guy gets really upset and refuses to give up his food. The waiter walks over to the other table and explains the situation to the officer. A few minutes later the officer walks over to the man's table and says,

"Listen and listen good. That is MY chicken you are about to eat and I'll warn you, whatever you do to that chicken I'll do the same to you.

You pull out one of its legs, I'll pull out one of yours. You break one of its wings, I'll break one of your arms!"

The man calmly looks at the chicken, then sticks his middle finger in the bird's rectum, pulls it out and licks it. He then gets up, drops his pants, bends over and says, "Go ahead!"

Q. How do you know when your wife is really dead?
A. Your sex life is the same but your laundry pile gets bigger.

An old man in the nursing home got a bottle of wine for his birthday. He talked the old lady in the next room into sharing it with him.

After they were both totally bombed, he started groping the old lady and pulling at her clothes. He managed to get her blouse and bra off before she stopped him.

She said, "I can't do this! I have acute angina."

The old guy said, "God, I hope so, you've got the ugliest tits I've ever seen."

A big sister says to her little brother, "Johnny, do you know why mom and dad have been in their bedroom for the last three days?"

Laughing, Johnny replies, "Yeah!!! Dad asked for Vaseline and I gave him super glue instead!"

Q. Did you hear about the two homosexual judges?
A. They kept trying each other.

Q. What should you give a man who has everything?
A. A woman to show him how to use it.

A man from Texas buys a round of drinks for everyone in the bar as he announces that his wife has just produced a typical Texan baby boy weighing twenty pounds. Congratulations shower all around, and many exclamations of "wow!" are heard.

Two weeks later he returns to the bar. The bartender says, "Say, you're the father of the typical Texan baby that weighed twenty pounds at birth, aren't you? How much does the baby weigh now?"

The proud father answers, "Fifteen pounds."

The bartender is puzzled. "Why? What happened? He already weighed twenty pounds at birth."

The Texan father takes a slow sip from his beer, wipes his lips on his shirt sleeve, leans over to the bartender and proudly announces, "Had him circumcised."

One day a single mother was in the supermarket with her four children who were playing around. They were running around grabbing items off the shelves, crying and screaming all over the place. The mother cornered them and said, "I should have swallowed all of you!"

The wedding date was set and the groom's three pals—a carpenter, an electrician and a dentist—were deciding what pranks to play on the couple on their wedding night.

The carpenter figured sawing the slats of their bed would give them a chuckle or two. The electrician decided to wire the bed—with alternating current, of course. The dentist wouldn't commit himself, but wore a sly grin and promised it would be memorable.

The nuptials went as planned, and a few days later, each of the groom's buddies received the following note:

Dear friends,

We didn't mind the bed slats being sawed and the electric shock was only a minor setback, but Jesus, I'm going to kill the guy who put anesthetic in the Vaseline!

347

A Frenchman and an Italian were seated next to an Englishman on an overseas flight. After a few cocktails, the men began discussing their home lives. "Last night I made love to my wife four times," the Frenchman bragged, "and this morning she made me delicious crepes and she told me how much she adored me."

"Ah, last night I made love to my wife six times," the Italian responded, "and this morning she made me a wonderful omelette and told me she could never love another man."

When the Englishman remained silent, the Frenchman smugly asked, "And how many times did you make love to your wife last night?"

"Once," he replied.

"Only once?" the Italian arrogantly snorted. "And what did she say to you this morning?"

"Don't stop."

Q. What is the difference between a priest and a homosexual?
A. The way they say ahhhh-men.

Q. How many men does it take to open a beer?
A. None. It should be opened by the time she brings it in.

(Attention: This must be read with an Italian accent, preferably out loud.)

One day Ima gonna Malta to a bigga hotel. Ina morning I go to eat brekfast. I tella waitress I wanna two pissis toast. She brings me only one piss. I tella her I want two piss. She says go to the bathroom. I say you no understand. I wanna two piss onna my plate. She say you better not not piss on plate you sonna ma bitch. Later I go to eat at the bigga restaurant. The waitress brings me a spoon and knife but no fock. I tella her I wanna fock. She tell me everyone does. I tella her you no understand, I wanna fock on the table. She say better not fock on table, you sonna ma bitch. I don't even know the lady and she call me a sonna ma bitch. So I go to my room inna hotel, and there is no sheit. I call the manager and tella him I wanna a sheit. He tella me go to the bathroom. I say you no understand, I wanna sheit on my bed. He say you better not sheit on bed you sonna ma bitch. I don't even know the man and he call me a sonna ma bitch. I go to checkout and the man at the desk say, "Peace unto you." I say, "Piss unto you too ya, sonna ma bitch. I gonna back to Italy."

In Scotland, the most important time for a young lad is when he "comes of age" and is allowed to purchase and wear his first kilt.

A couple of weeks before his important birthday, a young lad went to a tailor shop and found the material he wanted for his first kilt. He took the material to the tailor and said, "I'd like ye to make me a kilt with this material here and, if ye don't mind, I'd like ye to make me a pair of matching underwear for it. I hear it gets a might drafty up them things!"

So the tailor took the material and promised to call the young lad when the order was completed.

A few days later, the tailor called the lad back to the shop. "Here's ye kilt, and here's ye matching underwear, and here's five yards of the material left over. Ye might want to take it home and keep it in case you want anything else made of it."

So the lad rushed home with his order, threw the material in his room, and donned his kilt. In his excitement, he decided to run to his girlfriend's house to show off his new purchase.

Unfortunately, in his excitement, he forgot to don his underwear.

When his girlfriend answered the door, he pointed to his kilt and said, "Well, what'd ye think?"

"Ah, but that's a fine looking kilt," she exclaimed.

"Aye, and if ye like it, you'll really like what's underneath," he stated as he lifted his kilt to show her.

"Oh, that's just dandy," his girlfriend shouted admiringly.

Still not realizing that he didn't have his underwear on he exclaimed quite proudly, "Aye, and if ye like it, I've got five more yards of it at home!"

All the organs of the body were having a meeting, trying to decide who was in charge.

The brain said, "I should be in charge, because I run all the body's systems. So without me nothing would happen."

"I should be in charge," said the heart, "because I pump the blood and circulate oxygen all over the body. Without me you'd all waste away."

"I should be in charge," said the stomach, "because I process food and give all of you energy."

"I should be in charge," said the rectum, "because I'm responsible for waste removal."

All the other body parts laughed at the rectum and insulted him, so in a huff, he shut down tight. Within a few days, the brain had a terrible headache, the stomach was bloated and the blood was toxic. Eventually the other organs gave in. They all agreed that the rectum should be the boss.

The moral of the story?

You don't have to be smart or important to be in charge—just an asshole.

A captain in the Foreign Legion was transferred to a desert outpost. On his orientation tour he noticed a very old, seedy-looking camel tied out in back of the enlisted men's barracks. He asked the sergeant leading the tour, "What's the camel for?"

The sergeant replied, "Well, sir, we're a long way from anywhere, and the men have natural sexual urges, so when they do we have the camel."

The captain said, "Well, if it's good for morale, then I guess it's all right with me."

After he had been at the fort for about six months, the captain could not stand it anymore, so he told his sergeant, "BRING IN THE CAMEL!!!"

The sergeant shrugged his shoulders and led the camel into the captain's quarters. The captain got a foot stool and proceeded to have vigorous sex with the camel. As he stepped down, satisfied, from the stool and was buttoning his pants he asked the sergeant, "Is that how the enlisted men do it?"

The sergeant replied, "Well, sir, they usually just use it to ride into town."

There is a boy and a girl in a religious education class. The girl falls asleep.

The teacher asks a question. "Who created Earth?"

The boy pokes her with a pen and she yells, "God." She falls back to sleep.

The teacher asks another question. "Who were the Holy family?"

The boy pokes her with a pen and she says, "Jesus, Mary, and Joseph." She falls back to sleep.

The teacher asks another question. "What did Mary say to Joseph after their 23rd baby?"

The boy pokes her with a pen and she says, "If you stick that thing in me one more time I swear I will snap it in half!!!"

A little girl is in line to see Santa. When it's her turn, she climbs up on Santa's lap. Santa asks, "What would you like Santa to bring you for Christmas?"

The little girl replies, "I want a Barbie and a G.I. Joe."

Santa looks at the little girl for a moment and says, "I thought Barbie comes with Ken."

"No," says the little girl. "She comes with G.I. Joe. She fakes it with Ken."

A 40-year-old woman wants to get married, but she is only willing to marry a man if he is still a virgin. After several unsuccessful years of searching, she decides to take out a personal ad. She ends up corresponding with a man who has lived his entire life in the Australian Outback.

They end up getting married. On their wedding night, she goes into the bathroom to prepare for the festivities. When she returns to the bedroom, she finds her new husband standing in the middle of the room naked and all the furniture from the room piled in one corner.

"What happened?" she asks.

"I've never been with a woman," he says, "but if it's anything like a kangaroo, I'm going to need all the room I can get."

A teenage boy and his grandfather go fishing one day. While fishing, the old man starts talking about how times have changed. The young man picks up on this and starts talking about the various problems and diseases going around.

The teen says, "Grandpa, they didn't have a whole lot of problems with all these diseases when you were young did they?"

Grandpa replies, "Nope."

The teen says, "Well, what did you guys use for safe sex?"

Grandpa replies, "A wedding ring."

Q. What is the difference between a battery and a woman?

A. A battery has a positive side.

When the gynecologist confirmed her suspicion that she was pregnant, Celeste got a little scared. "It'll be my first baby," she confessed with a blush, "and actually, I don't know the first thing about how babies are delivered."

"Don't worry about a thing," reassured the doctor. "It's really not all that different from how the baby got started in the first place."

Startled, Celeste exclaimed, "You mean twice around the park with my legs hanging out of the cab?"

A modern Islamic couple preparing for a religious wedding meet with their Mullah for counseling. The Mullah asks if they have any last questions before they leave. The man says, "We realize it's tradition in Islam for men to dance with men, and women to dance with women. But, at our wedding reception, we'd like your permission to dance together."

"Absolutely not," says the Mullah. "It's immoral. Men and women always dance separately."

"So, after the ceremony I can't even dance with my own wife?"

"No," answers the Mullah. "It's forbidden in Islam."

"Well, OK," says the man. "What about sex? Can we finally have sex?"

"Of course!" replies the Mullah. "Alla ho Akber! Sex is OK within a marriage to have children!"

"What about different positions?" asks the man.

"Alla ho Akber! No problem," says the Mullah.

"Woman on top?" the man asks.

"Sure," says the Mullah. "Alla ho Akber. Go for it!"

"Doggy style?"

"Sure! Alla ho Akber!"

"On the kitchen table?"

"Yes, yes! Alla ho Akber!"

"Can I do it with all my four wives together on rubber sheets with a bottle of hot oil, a couple of vibrators, leather harnesses, a bucket of honey and a porno video?"

"You may, indeed. Alla ho Akber!"

"Can we do it standing up?"

"No," says the Mullah.

"Why not?" asks the man.

"Because that could lead to dancing."

The wives of four presidents and prime ministers are talking together about how to say "penis" in their languages.

The wife of Tony Blair says that in England people call it a gentleman, because it stands up when women are entering.

The wife of Boris Yeltsin says that in Russia you call it a patriot, because you never know if it will hit you on the front or on the back side.

The wife of Chirac says that in France you call it a curtain, because it goes down after the act.

The wife of Clinton says that in the United States you call it a rumor, because it goes from mouth to mouth.

Every Sunday, the town preacher rode his bike to church. This particular day, a member of the church noticed that the preacher was walking.

He asked, "Where's your bike?"

The preacher said, "Someone stole it. It may have been one of the members."

"Well," the member proceeded to tell him, "for next Sunday's sermon, preach on the Ten Commandments. When you get to Thou Shalt Not Steal, really stress it and you'll get your bike back."

The next week the same member of the church had seen the preacher riding his bike.

"I see you have your bike back? Did you do what I told you about preaching about the Ten Commandments?"

"Yes," replied the preacher.

"Did you stress Thou Shalt Not Steal?" he asked.

"No," the preacher answered.

"What happened?" asked the member.

"Well," said the preacher, "when I got to Thou Shalt Not Commit Adultery, I remembered where I left it."

A vet is making love to his wife when the phone rings. Being on duty he answers it and the client says, "I've got a dog and a bitch humping on my doorstep How can I stop them?"

The vet says, "Put a cell phone next to them and call it."

The client says, "And will that work?"

The vet says, "It just stopped me!"

Two male flies are buzzing around, cruising for good-looking females. One spots a real cutie sitting on a pile of cow manure and dives down toward her.

"Pardon me," he asks, turning on his best charm, "but is this stool taken?"

A ninety-year-old lady is on her way to the gynecologist due to an itchy rash in her vagina. When she gets there, the doctor checks her out and asks, "When was the last time you had sex?"

The old lady tells the doctor that she is still a virgin. He checks her out again and the doctor tells the lady, "I don't really have a medical term for this, so I will be blunt: Your cherry has rotted."

Q. Why do women fake orgasms?
A. Because they think men care.

A man was driving down a quiet country lane when out into the road strayed a rooster. Whack! The rooster disappeared under the car in a cloud of feathers. Shaken, the man pulled over at the farmhouse and rang the doorbell. A farmer appeared. The man somewhat nervously said, "I think I killed your rooster. Please allow me to replace him."

"Suit yourself," the farmer replied, "the hens are around the back."

A group of prisoners are in their rehabilitation meeting. Their task for today is to each stand up in turn, speak their name and admit to their fellow inmates what crime they committed. The first prisoner stands and says, "My name is Daniel and I'm in for murder."

Everyone gives him approving looks and pats on the back for admitting his wrongdoing. The next guy stands up and says, "My name is Mike and I'm in for armed robbery."

Again, there is a round of approving looks. This goes around the circle until it gets to the last guy. He stands up and says, "My name is Luke, but I'm not telling you what I'm in for."

The group leader says, "Now, come on, Luke, you have to admit it to us to make any progress. Tell us what you did."

"OK, then. I'm in for fucking dogs."

Everyone is disgusted! They all shout, "What??!! How LOW can you get!"

"Well, I did manage to fuck a dachshund one time, but I had to lift her back legs up a little," Luke replies.

One day at a bus stop there was a girl who was wearing a skin-tight miniskirt. When the bus arrived and it was her turn to get on, she realized that her skirt was so tight that she couldn't get her foot high enough to reach the step.

Thinking it would give her enough slack to raise her leg, she reached back and unzipped her skirt a little. She still could not reach the step. Embarrassed, she reached back once again to unzip it a little more.

Still, she couldn't reach the step. So, with her skirt zipper halfway down, she reached back and unzipped her skirt all the way. Thinking that she could get on the step now, she lifted up her leg only to realize that she still couldn't reach the step.

So, seeing how embarrassed the girl was, the man standing behind her put his hands around her waist and lifted her up on to the first step of the bus. The girl turned around furiously and said, "How dare you touch my body that way; I don't even know you!"

Shocked, the man says, "Well, ma'am, after you reached around and unzipped my fly three times, I kind of figured that we were friends."

There was a loser who couldn't get a date. He went to a bar and asked another man how to get a date.

The man said, "It's simple. I just say I'm a lawyer."

So the loser went up to a pretty woman and asked her out. After she said "No," he told her that it was probably a good thing because he had a case early in the morning.

She said, "Oh, you're a lawyer?"

He said, "Why, yes I am!"

So they went to his place and when they were in bed screwing, he started to laugh to himself. When she asked what was so funny he answered, "Well, I've only been a lawyer for an hour, and I'm already screwing someone!"

A father and son went hunting together for the first time. The father said, "Stay here and be very QUIET. I'll be across the field."

A little while later, the father heard a bloodcurdling scream and ran back to his son. "What's wrong?" the father asked. "I told you to be quiet."

The boy answered, "Look, I was quiet when the snake slithered across my feet. I was quiet when the bear breathed down my neck. I didn't move a muscle when the skunk climbed over my shoulder. I closed my eyes and held my breath when the wasp stung me. I didn't cough when I swallowed the gnat. I didn't swear or scratch when the poison oak started itching. But when the two squirrels crawled up my trouser leg and one of them said, 'Should we eat them here or take them with us?' well, I guess I just panicked."

A jealous husband hired a private detective to check on the movements of his wife. The husband wanted more than a written report—he wanted a video of his wife's activities.

A week later, the detective returned with a video. They sat down together to watch it. Although the quality was less than professional, the man saw his wife meeting another man! He saw the two of them laughing in the park. He saw them enjoying themselves at an outdoor cafe. He saw them dancing in a dimly lit nightclub. He saw the man and his wife participate in a dozen activities with utter glee.

"I just can't believe this," the distraught husband said.

The detective said, "What's not to believe? It's right up there on the screen!"

The husband replied, "I can't believe that my wife could be so much fun!"

Q. What's the definition of trust?
A. Two cannibals giving each other a blow job.

The judge says, "Please tell me why you're seeking a divorce."

John says, "Because I live in a two-story house."

The judge says, "What kind of a reason is that? What's the matter with a two-story house?"

John says, "I'll tell you what the matter is. One story is 'I have a headache' and the other story is 'It's that time of the month.'"

A little boy goes to his father and asks, "Daddy, how was I born?"

The father answers, "Well, son, I guess one day you were going to find out anyway. Your mom and I first got together in an internet chat room. Then I set up a date via e-mail and we met at a cybercafe. We sneaked into a secluded room, where your mother agreed to a download from my hard drive. As soon as I was ready to upload, we discovered that neither one of us had used a firewall. Since it was too late to hit the delete button, a little Pop-up window appeared nine months later that said, 'You got Male.'"

The science teacher stood in the front of the class and said, "Children, if you could have one raw material in the world, what would it be?"

Little Stevie raised his hand and said, "I would want gold, because gold is worth a lot of money and I could buy a BMW convertible."

The teacher nodded, and then she called on little Susie.

Little Susie said, "I would want platinum because platinum is worth more than gold and I could buy a Porsche."

The teacher smiled, and then she called on Little Johnny.

Little Johnny stood up and said, "I would want silicone."

The teacher said, "Silicone? Why silicone, Little Johnny?"

"Because my mom has two bags of the stuff, and you should see all the sports cars outside our house!"

A little boy and his dad are walking down the street when they see two dogs having sex. The little boy asks his father, "Daddy, what are they doing?"

The father says, "Making a puppy."

So they walk on and go home.

A few days later, the little boy walks in on his parents having sex. The little boy says, "Daddy, what are you doing?"

The father replies, "Making a baby."

The little boy says, "Well, flip her around! I'd rather have a puppy instead!"

Two young guys were picked up by the cops for smoking dope and appeared in court on Friday before the judge. The judge said, "You seem like nice young men, and I'd like to give you a second chance rather than jail time. I want you to go out this weekend and try to show others the evils of drug use and get them to give up drugs forever. I'll see you back in court Monday."

Monday, the two guys were in court, and the judge said to the first one, "How did you do over the weekend?"

"Well, Your Honor, I persuaded seventeen people to give up drugs forever."

"Seventeen people? That's wonderful. What did you tell them?"

"I used a diagram, Your Honor. I drew two circles and told them that the big circle is your brain before drugs and the small circle is your brain after drugs."

"That's admirable," said the judge.

"And you, how did you do?" he asked the second boy.

"Well, Your Honor, I persuaded 156 people to give up drugs forever."

"156 people! That's amazing! How did you manage to do that?!?"

"Well, I used a similar approach. I drew two circles and I said, pointing to the small circle, 'this is your asshole before prison.'"

A husband and wife are traveling by car from Atlanta to New York. After almost twenty-four hours on the road, they decide to stop at a nice hotel and take a room. They only plan to sleep for four hours and then get back on the road.

When they check out four hours later, the desk clerk hands them a bill for $350. The man explodes and demands to know why the charge is so high. He tells the clerk that although it's a nice hotel, the rooms certainly aren't worth $350. When the clerk explains that $350 is the standard rate, the man insists on speaking to the manager.

The manager enters the conversation and explains that the hotel has an Olympic-sized pool and a huge conference center which were available for the husband and wife to use. He also explains that they could have taken in one of the shows which the hotel is famous for. "The best entertainers from New York, Hollywood and Las Vegas perform here," explains the manager.

"No matter what facilities you have," the man replies, "we didn't use them!"

The manager is unmoved. Eventually, the man gives up and agrees to pay. He writes a check and hands it to the manager. "But, sir," the manager says, "this check is only made out for $100."

"That's right," replies the man. "I charged you $250 for sleeping with my wife."

"What! I didn't sleep with your wife!" exclaims the manager.

"Well," the man replies, "she was here, and you could have."

A man is dating three women and wants to decide which one to marry. He decides to give them a test. He gives each woman a present of $5,000 and watches to see what she does with the money.

The first does a total makeover. She goes to a fancy beauty salon, gets her hair done, purchases new makeup and buys several new outfits and dresses up very nicely for the man. She tells him that she has done this to be more attractive for him because she loves him so much.

The man was impressed.

The second goes shopping to buy the man gifts. She gets him a new set of golf clubs, some new gizmos for his computer, and some expensive clothes. As she presents these gifts, she tells him that she has spent all the money on him because she loves him so much.

Again, the man is impressed.

The third invests the money in the stock market. She earns several times the $5,000. She gives him back his $5,000 and reinvests the remainder in a joint account. She tells him that she wants to save for their future because she loves him so much.

Obviously, the man was impressed.

The man thought for a long time about what each woman had done with the money, and then he married the one with the biggest boobs.

A woman walks into a drugstore and asks the pharmacist if he sells size extra-large condoms.

He replies, "Yes, we do. Would you like to buy some?"

She responds, "No, but do you mind if I wait around here until someone does?